MOVING ABROAD

MOVING ABROAD

A Guide

to

International Living

Virginia L. McKay

VLM Enterprises, Wilmington, DE

© 1982 Virginia L. McKay
© 1989 Virginia L. McKay. Revised edition.
Second printing 1990.

Library of Congress Catalogue Number: 89-090449
ISBN 962-7060-01-1

All rights reserved. No part of this book may be reproduced in any form without written permission of the author.

Published and distributed by VLM Enterprises, P.O. Box 7236, Wilmington, DE 19803

Typography by Publishers Ink
Printed by Farley Printing Company

Printed in the United States of America

ACKNOWLEDGEMENTS

Countless individuals have contributed unknowingly to *Moving Abroad.* Through conversations, initiated and overheard, while living in Europe and Hong Kong and during travels to many parts of the world, the joys and difficulties of overseas experiences have been shared. Corporate human resource executives have offered valuable insights.

Most greatly appreciated is the assistance of all the special individuals who have shared their talents and expertise for this completely revised edition -- Jean des Jardins, Helen Giammattei and Katherine Slaughter, Douglas Drayton, Terry Schaberg, Betty Robbins, Marcia Andrews, Phil Winkler, Lynn Kelleher and Barbara Fleischman.

To Alison Lanier, *la grande dame* of international relocation, my sincerest gratitude for warm friendship over many years. Her sharing personality, genuine interest and thoughtful suggestions for this book are highly valued. Articles from *The International Assignment*, of which she was founder and editor, gave thoughts and concerns from many individuals and families living overseas.

CONTENTS

HERE

DECIDING TO GO 1
Personal considerations. Essential considerations: health, education, dual-career families, personal aspects. A pre-move visit.

TELLING THE CHILDREN 7
Infants. Toddlers. Pre-school children. School age children. Teenagers. College students. Timing. Books for moving children.

SELLING OR RENTING 13
When and how to sell by owner. Listing with a realtor. Getting your house ready. The offer and counter-offer. Settlement and possession dates. After the sale. Renting your house. After the lease is signed.

TAXES 24
Federal income taxes. Professional advice. Tax equalization. Moving expenses. Tax concerns of selling a house. Tax concerns of renting a house. Social security taxes. State and local taxes. Foreign country tax obligations.

TRAVELING PAPERS 29
Passports. Visas. Permits. Social security numbers for children. International certificate of vaccination. Inoculations and immunizations. Health insurance policies.

LEARNING THE LANGUAGE 39
Learning the money, too.

ORGANIZING THE DETAILS 42
Change of address. Inventories. Banking. Insurance. Medical information. Dental records. School information. Accountant. Tax records. Attorney, power of attorney. Wills. Driver's license. Passport pictures. Pets. Flight and hotel reservations. Register with customs. Things-to-do checklist. Personal inventory checklist.

PACKING AND MOVING 65
The company move. Prohibited items and special regulations. The movers. Before the packers come. Packing and moving days. Exporting a car. Papers to take with you checklist.

ORIENTATION: Pre-move and after arrival 89

AND

AND 92
The flight. On arrival. Hotel days. Things to do.

THERE

COPING WITH CULTURE: Adapting to change   99
"Culture shock" -- it's a normal part of moving, anywhere. Phases in the adjustment process. Expectations. Anticipate adjustments. Importance of language. Don'ts and do's. Especially for her. Especially for him.

HOUSING   109
How to find housing. Housing considerations and questions for realtors. When you think you've found housing. A "leave house." The lease. Before you move in. Unpacking. Settling in. Housing miscellany.

CHILDREN   121
Young children. School age children. Teenagers. Getting ready for college from abroad. Rewards.

LEARNING MORE LANGUAGE   127
Body language.

THE EXECUTIVE ABROAD   130
Cultural understanding. Communicating effectively -- verbal language, body language. Introductions, business cards and titles of address. Time and timing. Entertaining. Business etiquette and customs. Before you travel. Books for the international business person.

GETTING AROUND: Transportation   138
Public transportation abroad. Driving abroad: getting a license, registering a car, insurance. You need to know. In case of an accident. Helpful hints. Safety aspects.

HOUSEHOLD HELP   148
General information. Au pair. Part-time help. Live-in help.
Employing a driver.

MEETING MEDICAL NEEDS   158
Investigate medical facilities. Potential medical problems.

TROPICAL AREAS, TYPHOONS AND TREMORS   166

TRAVELING ABROAD   174
Traveling necessities. Getting there. Travel by bus, train and car.
Accommodations. Ways to travel economically. Packing.
Baggage. At the airport. Health. Sightseeing. Shopping.
Bargaining.

POTPOURRI   188
Alien registration. Banking. Birth of a child abroad. Change of
address in host country. Emergencies. Exit visas. Insurance.
Laundry and dry cleaning. Legal status. Manners. Receipts.
Repairs. Shopping. Telephones. Time. Tipping. U.S. embassy
services. Wallet card.

RETURN MOVE   199
Departure details. Packing and moving. U.S. customs regulations. You and the family.

APPENDIX   208

INDEX   227

INTRODUCTION

Moving Abroad is a practical guide for moving anywhere in the world. Its aim is to ease the process of changing from your familiar culture to a new one where there will be expected and unexpected aspects.

Universally you can find Kodak, Coca Cola, Exxon, Sunkist and Dr. Scholl's. American music has reached the far corners of the world -- from the airport in Taipei to a department store in Amsterdam, a coffee shop in Nairobi and in discos everywhere. Friendliness, courtesy and a smile are parts of a common world language. And there is an international vocabulary which includes "please," "thank you," "bye-bye," "out of stock," "tomorrow," "not to worry," "can do," "no problem" and "don't understand!"

Along with the familiar there will be new sights, new experiences and unknowns. Each city and each country has its unique characteristics, curios, culture and charm. The vendor selling soft pretzels with mustard on a Philadelphia street corner has his counterpart in Tokyo selling charcoal-cooked sweet potato pieces and the hourly bells of St. Patrick's Cathedral in New York become the call of the muezzin in the Moslem world.

Any move is easier with prior knowledge and preparation. They help allay misapprehensions and provide guidance for the many aspects involved whether they are about business courtesies, climate, clothes, housing or a teenager's adjustments.

MOVING ABROAD

The family encyclopedia and community library books will give geographical, historical and general information. The embassy of the host country has additional information and you can ask them about permits, visas, import regulations and the like. Publications from an American club or chamber of commerce for the assigned country will give background information as well as helpful hints for someone moving there. Best of all, try to find someone from the country (perhaps through your company, at a nearby college or university or on the local hospital staff) or someone who has lived in the country within the past year. Their information can give your move realism with practical, up-to-date information -- how basic needs may be met differently, suggestions of what to take, timing of international news or mail, community resources, social and business customs.

Undoubtedly you will receive advice: from individuals who know a great deal about international living -- from tourists whose travel experiences are very different from the daily encounters you will have -- from people who have never been outside the U.S.! Tuck all the information away and when you're in your new community, talk with the people who can confirm what you have heard, remove exaggerations and tell you how things *really* are -- available services, where you can find needed items (and what to do if they are not available) and local customs.

In any international move there will be aspects that are different -- yes, even difficult. In a move to one of the European countries you will find many similarities. Still there will be differences. You should expect greater differences when moving to South America, Asia and developing countries -- from living comforts to cultural values and religious customs. The basic beliefs and attitudes of the people, their ways of communicating, from silence to smiles to verbal meanings, will need interpretation and understanding. The role of women in modern society varies worldwide. Learn as much as you can beforehand, making the daily surprises after arrival fewer and easier to handle.

Moving anywhere is awesome. The physical process is exhausting and seems endless with all its details. The challenging work opportunity is exciting for the employee but will mean a new routine and, usually, a variety of pressures. A wife often will have mixed feelings about pulling up family roots, resettling and making new friends, perhaps even leaving a career. Both should recognize the many changes for each and be understanding. Parents need to foresee the reactions of children.

The many adjustments when moving abroad are real and varied -- as will be the rewards for the opportunity you have. There is a definite personal enrichment for all the family. To best prepare for your international adventure, you need to do certain things

HERE --- AND --- THERE.

Pre-departure checklists in the book will help organize the many details of moving. The *Appendix* has valuable information for before you move and after you arrive overseas. *Moving Abroad* will be most useful, however, if you highlight the special areas of information helpful to you and make your own notes in the margins and extra pages.

Bon Route!

MOVING ABROAD

HERE

DECIDING TO GO

You've been offered an overseas assignment, a chance to move abroad -- fantastic! An opportunity to travel to far-away places and see new parts of the world -- Bogota, Brussels, Sydney, Seoul!

Most people view an overseas move enthusiastically and are eager to accept the transfer. It offers career and personal opportunities; it also will challenge you -- to learn and adapt in a foreign culture.

The decision to go should not be based on the glamorous idea of living abroad. The international experience is much more than a world tour of historical sites and gourmet restaurants. Certainly learning more about ancient and current history, discovering how other people live, trying new foods and generally broadening horizons are bonuses of a successful assignment abroad.

For the business person, think first of your motivations and expectations for the assignment. When family will accompany you, their daily life and needs are of prime importance for a successful overseas experience. Just as your employer gives careful deliberation to choosing the right person to send abroad, you must carefully consider the move -- *from all aspects*. The move has to be right for the individual, for the accompanying family, as well as the corporation.

PERSONAL CONSIDERATIONS

Moving anywhere involves adjustments. In a move from Pittsburgh to Seattle many things remain the same: you still drive on the right side of the road, you can shop at Sears Roebuck and iceberg lettuce is available in the supermarket. Some things change: you will have to adjust to new neighbors, newspapers and community resources. Moving from Pittsburgh to Bangkok necessitates additional changes and challenges: language, food, driving rules, customs and culture. The international move requires the ultimate in patience and adaptability -- and, a sense of humor.

Flexibility will be a key to your success as you leave certain ways behind and learn new ones. Differences you may have to allow for can range from business manners and social mores to driving mannerisms and cleanliness standards. Learning and accepting cultural differences and attitudes will require great understanding. For example, in Asia the concept of "face" means courtesy is more important than accuracy. It is acceptable for a person to "bend the truth" to avoid disappointment to you or embarassment to the responder. To "lose face" by giving a negative response is worse than bending the truth. Therefore, the "yes" reply may be a "no" answer -- but the acceptable response in that culture.

Your patience will be tested many times -- and in many ways. Americans are recognized as impatient. When this is the case, you may become frustrated in places where there is a general disregard for time, be it a business appointment or a repairman's visit. The *mañana* of Spain has its counterpart in Italy, Greece, India, Argentina, etc. etc. Another instance is the Japanese manner of making business decisions based on consensus which means long, drawn-out, time-consuming negotiations.

The newcomer must accept and adapt -- not expect to alter. This can encompass political viewpoints, cultural attitudes, inconveniences, sanitation conditions and other unforeseen aspects. The initial period of learning the "where" and "how to" will have moments of discouragement and frustration. But just as you can adjust and cope with daily situations in Pittsburgh or Seattle, you can do it anywhere in the world by approaching it in the right way.

A sense of humor will help more than you can imagine! Warm beer, hot tea in a glass, rice without butter -- or a fork, etc., etc., etc. Recalling such incidents in years to come will bring laughter but at the time your surprise or frustration undoubtedly evoked another reaction!

For the business person, an international assignment involves working with -- and within -- different cultural values. Your professional expertise and managerial talents must be balanced with people skills. Do you have the tolerance and patience to respect new business attitudes? Can you accept alien cultural values? Can you be an international team person -- not one who would "rather do it myself?" It is important, also, to analyze your expectations for the international experience and how it fits into career objectives and the company plans for your future.

The woman, wife and mother has to make adjustments in the home, family life and for herself. Travel demands on a husband may mean she will have responsibilities previously always shared. She undoubtedly will find, at least initially, husband and children depend on her more than before. Being a supportive wife, efficient housekeeper and understanding mother is more difficult when many things are unfamiliar. How are you at adjusting to new situations? How willing are you to adapt? Most early returns from a foreign assignment are due to an unhappy wife and her inability to make the necessary adjustments. A decision to go abroad based only on furthering a spouse's career development is not rational. It must be the right move for the spouse as well.

A move affects all family members and all need to understand the challenges involved. What is the reaction of your children to the move? A positive response from them is needed.

ESSENTIAL CONSIDERATIONS

The financial investment a company makes to send an employee and family overseas is enormous. It includes house sale reimbursement, storage or shipment of furniture, cultural training and orientation, transportation, in-transit housing, language instruction, foreign housing and transportation, schooling, home leaves, foreign service premiums, cost-of-living and other allowances, tax equalization, benefits and 'perks' -- and more. Choosing you and your family to represent the corporation and to do the job is a thoughtful process. Your decision to accept the move deserves the same thorough consideration.

Many personal factors are involved. Some to be aware of include:
- separation from loved ones
- obligations to elderly parents and other family members
- adjustments at home, work, school
- language compatibility (or incompatibility!)

- medical requirements
- educational facilities
- security -- political stability, crime, terrorism
- cultural differences
- climate
- recreational opportunities

The special needs of each family member need consideration. Don't lightly dismiss potentially important aspects. A move could aggravate some situations and cause others. Look realistically at the following.

Health

Do you or anyone in the family have special health needs? Are needed treatments, doctors, medications available in the destination city? Could a decision to go abroad cause complications in the future? In-depth information on the health facilities in your proposed location site will help answer these and related questions.

Education

How will your children's education be affected? If a child is gifted, has a learning disability or other special education needs, the available facilities and capability to provide adequately for the child need to be determined. Future difficulties can be avoided with accurate information. Direct contact with the available schools is the only way to get precise information on their programs. Telephone the school registrar or principal of the child's age group, discuss needs and get your questions answered. (Direct dialing almost anywhere in the world is as simple as dialing another state.)

Dual-Career Families

The majority of American women are employed today. The dual-career family is the norm. The role of women in foreign societies differs greatly from the U.S. Opportunities for a spouse to find suitable, satisfying employment abroad are good in some countries, limited, restricted or impossible in others. Could this cause unacceptable frustration? How will your present career be affected?

The law may not allow a dependent spouse to work at all. Sometimes employment may be possible with a work permit, but it can be difficult to obtain. To work illegally can jeopardize the transferee's work permit. Before you go, inquire about the possibility to work and potential opportunities in your field. Perhaps part-time work in a related field is possible. Many transportable jobs, such as bilingual secretary (as long as the "bi" is in the right language!), computer programmer and banking are easily transferred. Professions such as law and nursing may have special examinations; teachers may have to meet special educational requirements. Expect salaries to vary greatly from the U.S.

Volunteer opportunities of many kinds are a possibility. The American woman is known worldwide for her community services. Usually there are meaningful ways anywhere you will be to spend your time even if not for pay or in your profession. Could this take the place of the career you might be asked to forfeit?

Personal Aspects

This is a most delicate topic, a very important aspect. Companies try to respect individual privacy by not prying into personal matters. If an overseas move would neither cause nor aggravate an individual or family problem, there would be no need to mention this. Such is not the case. Therefore responsible, honest self-questioning is absolutely essential for yourself, your marriage, your family.

The idea of "starting fresh" often is mentioned as a solution to all kinds of problems: marital, alcohol, emotional, scholastic, disciplinary and drug. It's a normal instinct to hope for the best. But there are no guarantees that a change of scenery will make the problem disappear, much less solve it. More likely than not, there is a greater chance relocation will intensify a problem situation especially with the already mentioned need to adapt, find new friends and adjust to new circumstances in the foreign environment. In international situations strong marriages become stronger, weak ones become weaker. A foreign assignment is not a viable solution to a personal or family problem. One person is almost always happier than the other overseas. Is your marriage stable or quivering? How supportive are you to each other?

A PRE-MOVE TRIP

Many corporations provide a pre-move trip to the proposed assignment area to assess the job, find out about housing, schools and lifestyle. There are many benefits to including a spouse on an advance trip. Things to do include:

- Explore the way you will live once you will be unpacked.
- Find other Americans to answer questions about what daily living is actually like.
- Get guidance on what to bring (and not to bring!) and how to avoid mistakes others have made.
- Visit doctors, a drugstore, schools, markets and supermarkets (if any!)

Keep an open mind. Evaluate all you see and hear and recognize there will be adjustments and tradeoffs. Are you willing to give up your large suburban house for a 2,000 sq. ft. apartment on the 32nd floor with a balcony? (And how big is 2,000 sq. ft?) What do you mean I can't drive? Live-in household help sounds wonderful, but you now become an employer and people-manager, often a new 'position' for the homemaker and one not without demands and difficulties.

Take a camera along, especially when there are children in the family. They will appreciate pictures of the schools they might attend and aspects relating to them. Pictures of any housing found will be helpful in your planning and appreciated by others in the family. Also, tuck a tape measure and small notebook in your suitcase. If you find housing you can measure rooms and wall space helping you decide whether the sectional sofa, buffet or refrigerator will fit.

TELLING THE CHILDREN

Share the news as soon as possible. And don't expect it to be kept a secret -- a move from Omaha to Singapore is BIG news, and everyone wants to spill it!

Moving means change and everyone is affected. How you tell your children is so important. Be enthusiastic and positive! How easy or how difficult the move will be is greatly influenced by attitude.

Moving is an emotional time. Each family member will have a different reaction -- enthusiasm, sadness and anger are all possible -- and each should express his or her feelings. Parents especially need to share their emotions and concerns with children letting them know they are not alone in their feelings.

Regardless of age, children need to understand why they are moving, what is involved and what new experiences there will be. Together, the family should discuss individual expectations. Accentuate the advantages but accept any disadvantages and try to deal with them.

If your children have moved previously, they may remember many of the feelings experienced during those moves. They often adjust more readily than children who have never relocated. This certainly makes it easier; however, variables such as age, destination country, place in school, involvements, etc. will influence their feelings. For children who have not moved before, this may be their first experience of giving up the known for the unknown. Parents should anticipate reactions and understand feelings about the uncertainties involved.

8 MOVING ABROAD

Each child will be affected differently. As well as the family communicating as a unit, talk to each one, separately at his level of understanding, about the many aspects of moving. Listen, be supportive and reassuring. Attitude will have a significant impact on the transition process.

The *esprit de corps* of the family is the essential element in a happy move. By all means, get your children involved in the move. Let them share all aspects, ask questions and assist in whatever way they can.

Infants

An infant will be the least disrupted by the change. Keep to the normal routine as much as possible. The time difference between continents and the resulting disruption of the sleeping schedule may be the biggest problem for the little tyke. This turning night-into-day, regrettably, will not aid anyone's adjustment to time zone changes.

Toddlers

For the child who is still "at home" with mother, the adjustment is not too great. Proximity of parents is more important than physical surroundings but toddlers still need an explanation of moving in terms of living in another house in another area. Other children will be there, pets, playschools -- lots of familiar aspects but also new ones. Because very young children cannot truly understand what such changes are, they need reassuring when you first tell them and when they arrive and see and sense the differences.

Toddlers may react to the changes and the new location by becoming clingy, reverting to babyish actions, tantrums and other unusual behavior. Any misbehavior may be a way of showing distress. Recognize the child is having difficulty adjusting -- an adjustment he does not understand. Patience! Time will bring normalcy.

Pre-school Children

Pre-school children depend on parents for continuity and stability. Without that support they may develop problems in eating, sleeping or temperament. They especially need an explanation of what will occur during the uprooting period. Having familiar belongings packed in cartons, seeing rooms dismantled and knowing from everyone scurrying about that usual routines are changed can be most upsetting.

Anticipate these changes. Explain about everything being put in boxes, the van coming, the airplane flight, opening the boxes in a new place. Game-playing with a wagon as a moving van, boxes, old suitcases and a toy airplane can show how things will happen. When you see a moving van on the street, stop and talk about it. Coloring books can help explain the process. Picture books on moving and on the new country will be reassuring.

Include children in the planning and doing. Let them help in any way you can think of -- from cleaning out the toy box to packing favorite things to carry on the trip. Let them make the decisions about the things to take, the things to keep.

If your furniture is to be shipped, reassure the child he will see his possessions again in a few weeks but in a different place. When you are moving without most household items, if at all possible, include some furnishings from the child's room. (This is *not* the place to do the ruthless housecleaning suggested in a later chapter!) Take as many familiar objects as possible; you can sell, trade or give them away later. For the usual three- to five-year assignment of overseas transfers, the child will have outgrown many of the items you leave behind.

School Age Children

School age children can understand about the move but your enthusiasm and reassurances are still important and necessary. Tell them what to expect and make them part of the entire move. Encourage expression of whatever feelings they have. This 6- to 12-year age group seems to experience less stress than adolescents, perhaps because they are not as influenced or pressured by peer relations. However, it is possible they could go into a slump at school, become moody or depressed or have behavior problems until re-established.

Since the new country is an unknown, expect lots of questions. Books will be helpful to all the family. Visit community and school libraries. Read *with* your children about the destination country and its people. A world map in the family eating area will spark conversation and more questions -- some that may require research by you. Try to find the answers. It's important to avoid "I don't have time" replies. Make a game out of learning some language phrases (as a starter those universal ones good morning, please and thank you), the money and the customs of the host country (hand shaking, respect for elders).

As with any younger brothers and sisters, give children as many responsibilities as possible to help. Let them clean the aquarium, the car interior, and sort through the shoe boxes of football cards, rock and shell collections!

Teenagers

Hopefully you will find your high schoolers eager for the experience of living abroad. They will gain an unequaled perspective of the world and its cultures as well as strengthen their own cultural values. Parents need to be sensitive, however, to the problems associated with a move involving teenagers and prepared for possible opposition. They usually have the most difficulty adjusting to the move. Social activities and friends are their main sources of identity and changes in these areas pose important emotional adjustments. At best, the adolescent years involve problem periods as teenagers establish peer ties and strive for peer recognition at the same time they are seeking independence from parents. The "weaning" period during the teen years can be a time of poor family communication and relationships.

Negative aspects usually come to mind more readily than positive ones. For example, can you imagine being captain-elect of the football team and move to a school where "football" is soccer or rugby? Talk openly together of their concerns. Be patient with their moods and understanding -- hearing from you "It's okay to feel that way," can help them immensely.

Find out all you can about the schools your children will attend. Curriculum, sports and extra-curricular activities are important to this age group. Try to get school newspapers, yearbooks, student handbooks and course outlines. Find out how kids dress at school. Understandably, they want to know what to expect.

In some instances you may decide your high schooler will remain in his present home area, living with a close friend or relative, to finish a school year or a senior year in high school. Occasionally a boarding school has to be considered if the new school's curriculum is not adequate for your child's needs.

College Students

Outside the U.S. and United Kingdom, few universities teach classes in English. It is impossible to contemplate entering a foreign school without extensive language skills.

During summer visits with the family, an interesting volunteer or paying job may or may not be possible. However, these visits offer wonderful opportunities to travel together in your new area or vacation to other countries.

Timing

Many families with children feel summer is the only time to move. This is not always feasible nor is it always best. Since school is the primary source of friends and activities, a move during the school year allows children to go directly into a familiar routine and from one social setting to another. International schools are accustomed to midyear and midterm transfers. Teachers are aware of the need to give special attention to new students so they integrate quickly and satisfactorily into course work and the classroom. High school students should know, nonetheless, wherever they go, course studies will be different whether they enter at midyear or beginning of the fall term.

A summer move means arriving in new surroundings, often with long hotel stays while housing is found or furnishings arrive. Since this is the most popular time for vacation and home leave, there is a huge exodus of families from international communities and limited opportunities to meet other children. It can be difficult, therefore, to make acquaintances and find activities. If lucky, you'll find other hotel guests also in the resettling process with children who can offer companionship. Call or visit schools to see if they have summer programs allowing a chance to meet other students.

You may not have a choice of when you move. Recognize the advantages and possible problems of different arrival times and you will do the best you can under your circumstances.

BOOKS FOR MOVING CHILDREN

General
Children Abroad. Deneau Publishers, Toronto, Ontario. 1986. By four medical specialists, this practical guide is full of tips you'd never think of for families with children moving to developing countries. Health aspects are thoroughly covered as well as how to help children deal with different values (e.g., poverty).

Kids on the Move, A Parental Guide to Help Your Child Relocate, Nancy Ervin. For this informative booklet send $5 check to Conquest Corporation, P.O.Box 1090, Birmingham, MI 48012.

For Young Children
Goodbye House: A Kids' Guide to Moving, Ann Banks and Nancy Evans. Harmony Books (Crown Publishers). 1980. An excellent workbook for children to document their moving process.

Moving is an Adventure. A delightful activity booklet designed to involve children ages 5 to 10 in the family move. Individual copies are $2.50 from Professional Publishing Associates, 2655 Villa Creek Drive, Suite 224, Dallas, TX 75234.

Berenstain Bears: Moving Day, J. and S. Berenstain. Random House. 1981.

It's Your Move -- Picking Up, Packing Up and Settling In, Linda Bourke. Addison Wesley Publishing Co. 1981.

Mitchell is Moving, Marjorie Shalrmat. Scholastic Book Services, N.Y. 1978. Mitchell, a make-believe animal, misses his friend when he moves to "two weeks away."

For Teenagers
The Teenager's Survival Guide to Moving, Patricia Nida and Wendy Heller. Atheneum, N.Y. 1987. Helpful insights addressing the emotional issues of disconnecting, changing and reconnecting.

SELLING OR RENTING

Many unknown factors are involved in the decision to sell or rent your house. Will you return to the same area? Will the house and area retain their value? Will the house fit your future needs? Is renting feasible? Whatever the answers, prompt action toward either decision is needed.

SELLING YOUR HOUSE

A realtor's appraisal is needed to determine a market price for your house. Ask two well-recommended real estate agents to see your house separately. After a brief tour a verbal estimate of its value is possible. Usually no cost is involved, and you don't have to commit yourself to selling your house through them to get the estimate. If you are considering selling your house yourself, explain this when you ask the realtor for the estimate.

Obtain an accurate idea of a fair asking price as well as an expected selling price from each realtor. Instead of listing with the realtor who quotes the highest market value, choose the one you consider the best salesperson. If they sell you on theirself they're likely to be successful in selling someone else your house!

The Federal Housing Authority (FHA) will appraise a house when the buyer asks for a loan insured by them. A seller also can request their appraisal to help determine an asking price. The fee, currently $175, is paid by the person requesting the appraisal.

Professional real estate appraisers are available also. Check the Yellow Pages of the telephone directory for real estate companies who belong to the Society of Real Estate Appraisers (SRA) or are a Member of Appraiser's Institute (MAI). The fee is $200 to $250 for an average house.

Most corporations have a policy for the sale or rental of homes of their transferred employees and many offer assistance. They may take over your property if you are unsuccessful in selling it. Know their policy on broker commission and, if appropriate, add the following clause to any sales agreement with realtors: No commission shall be payable hereunder should seller decide to convey the subject property to his employer.

When and How to Sell by Owner

The decision to place your house with a realtor may be simple if you already know a well-qualified salesman and you want him to sell your house. The decision may not be so easy if several people in your area have successfully sold a house "by owner," tempting you to try selling your house directly. In either case, you will need the services of a lawyer. His assistance is essential and more extensive when you sell directly. The decision depends on whether you can cope with the selling responsibility or whether you prefer to pay a professional salesperson a percentage of the selling price to take that responsibility. Don't make the decision to sell directly because you want to save money unless the conditions and your situation are favorable. Try selling directly:

- if you are not in a hurry
- if houses in your area are in demand
- if mortgage money is generally obtainable
- if your house is appealing and standard in its offerings
- if it is springtime or early fall -- the most likely time for buyers
- if the local school district is good
- if the surrounding neighborhood is good

- if your house is where a *For Sale* sign can be seen by Sunday drivers
- if your price is right and selling by owner is successful in your area

The advantage of selling by owner is you save the commission that would otherwise go to a realtor. There is no assurance, however, you will get the price a realtor may get. Prospective buyers purposely make a lower bid when a house is being offered by owner because they know you are saving the commission.

In exchange for the money you might save, the entire marketing responsibility is yours. You have to write the ads, place them, pay for them, answer the inquiring calls, receive the Sunday "lookers," stay home to answer the telephone, conduct tours for all interested and negotiate the sale contract with your lawyer's help. All this is demanding and time-consuming.

Waiting for a buyer is much more discouraging when you are selling directly rather than having a professional do it. The following suggestions should be helpful:

- Set a fair, realistic price. Don't try, or expect, to "make a killing."
- Set a time limit of two to four weeks -- you will have exhausted the local potential buyers as well as your own enthusiasm.
- Select the salesperson who impressed you most favorably and tell him you plan to list your house with him if you are not successful in the two to four weeks.
- Tell other realtors who want to list or show your house you have already made definite plans to list.
- Write newspaper ads stating the basic assets of your house. Include the asking price and address if you want to save yourself unnecessary telephone calls or visits.
- Know the following: taxes, cost of heating and cooling, room sizes, square footage, age of house and size of lot.
- Tell your company personnel office your house is for sale and provide them information to give incoming transferees.
- Consider whether the buyer can assume your mortgage. Stipulate that mortgage assumption is possible *only if you can be released from responsibility by the mortgage company.*

- Prepare a *For Sale by Owner* sign that doesn't look homemade. Include a telephone number. Add *By Appointment Only* if you want time to prepare. Strangers will have access to your home; keep your own protection in mind and also your valuables.
- Don't let visitors wander on their own. Take them around, making minimum explanations. Most people know what they're looking for.
- Realize that the worst drawback in selling by owner is you have no follow-up once the potential buyer walks out the door.
- Obtain several copies of the local real estate sales contract form. Make decisions concerning terms before an offer is made and be familiar with:
  - amount you want from the buyer
  - date of closing and possession you prefer
  - items you plan to sell with the house
- Contact a lawyer familiar with real estate transactions when an offer is made. In a sale involving thousands of dollars, you need legal protection. (Discuss the lawyer's fee with him before you engage him.)
- If an offer doesn't come and you decide to list with a realtor, give the realtor the names of any potential buyers to whom you have shown the house and ask for commission exemption rights in case your house is sold to any of these parties. Realtors will usually agree to this but may want a maximum time limit of 15 to 30 days.

When you are selling directly, discuss with the buyer the most important terms -- the price, your mutual timing needs and his plans for financing. If the offer is contingent upon the buyer's selling his present house or financing yours, specify a deadline in your agreement. When these terms are satisfactory to both parties, the buyer and his lawyer should draw up a contract. You will need to supply a legal description of the property from your deed or former purchase contract. The buyer should give you five to ten percent of purchase price as a deposit at the time the contract is presented. Have your lawyer check any contract before you sign it.

Listing with a Realtor

It is wise to sell with a realtor:
- when there are many houses for sale in your area
- when you are in a hurry to move or to sell your house
- when mortgage money is hard to get
- when it's mid-winter and fewer people are house-hunting
- when your house is on a dead-end street, far out of town or in a rural area
- when your house appeals in a limited way to the average buyer (e.g., it may lack a downstairs lavatory, center hall or garage)

Listing your house with a realtor saves you work and often brings quicker results than a sale by owner. In addition, a professional will bring a higher price for a house because he can bargain objectively and from experience.

"Listing" a house means signing an agreement to pay a salesperson or broker part of your selling price to find a buyer for you. Real estate listing procedures differ widely. In some areas, each agency maintains exclusive listings; a salesperson can only show and sell houses listed by his agency. The local real estate board dictates whether you can list with more than one agency. You may not even have to sign a contract when you list with several agencies; thus, if you find your own buyer, you do not have to pay a real estate commission.

In most areas, real estate companies have a co-operative service called "multiple listing." If the agency which lists a house also finds a buyer, they retain the full commission (six or seven percent in most areas). If one agency has listed the house and another one finds the buyer, the commission is divided by the two agencies. The real estate commission is paid by the owner of the house to the agency who has listed the house. Selling through a realtor eliminates the seller's expense in advertising and may decrease lawyer fees, but closing costs are not affected.

Listing with a realtor is advantageous because your realtor will:
- arrange for other realtors to tour your house
- make appointments with you for potential buyers, giving you time to get ready

- expose your house to out-of-town buyers who *must* find a house instead of to those who are only casually house-hunting
- keep in touch with potential buyers
- coordinate all aspects of presenting and discussing offers with you
- arrange the closing between you, the buyer and the mortgage lender

Your real estate salesperson has the main responsibility of selling your house but you can help in these ways:

- Give your salesperson accurate information about your house, from taxes to heating bill.
- Tell your salesperson whether drapes, carpeting, light fixtures, appliances and other movables are included in the asking price. Sometimes you can use these for negotiating when a bid is received.
- Let the salesperson show the house. Don't volunteer information unless you are asked. The selling job belongs to the realtor. Your children also should know this!
- When potential buyers are coming,
    - open drapes, raise shades and turn on advantageous lights, especially on cloudy or rainy days
    - close the garage door
    - put your dog in the yard or garage
    - put the house in good order throughout

Getting Your House Ready

What will make your house appealing to potential buyers or renters? Take a tour of your house and, with pad and pencil in hand, list all the things needed to get the house -- from curbside to attic corners -- ready for presentation.

The first impression of your house is its external appearance. Prune shrubs, shape up the lawn, edge borders, cultivate flower areas and mulch under trees, tidy up the entranceway and paint the front door, if needed.

An uncrowded house, an appearance of orderliness and cleanliness make favorable impressions. Give the children first chance at their rooms!

- Any prospective buyer will want to open every door. Attack closets ruthlessly! Clean the clutter, organize shelves and shoes, get rid of unused and unwanted items.
- Call your favorite charity or thrift shop to take away unwanted furniture, out-of-date clothing and outgrown toys. Get a receipt for donated items; their value is a charitable deduction on your federal income tax return.
- Consider a garage or turnkey sale for items you don't want to give away.
- Don't neglect the attic, basement and garage. When was the last time you stacked the suitcases together in one area of the attic, organized the laundry room, washed off the hot water heater and put the garden tools on their storage hooks?
- Repair broken windows, damaged screens, dripping faucets.
- Spot clean carpets, at night when children and pets won't be walking on them!
- Clean water marks and streaks off shower walls and other tiled areas.
- Wash fingerprints from light switch plates and door jambs.
- Wash conspicuously dirty windows.
- The cost of some painting or redecorating can enhance sale possibilities.

Hire an energetic high school student to help with outside projects, indoor repair and cleaning jobs. Consider a sitter to get the children from underfoot allowing you to get at closets and organizing jobs.

The Offer and Counter-offer

An offer from an interested buyer is usually presented in written form by your salesperson. You have three alternatives.

- If the price and terms satisfy you, have your lawyer approve it, then sign and return the offer, completing a legal contract.
- If the terms of the offer are partly acceptable, change the contract and initial the change thus making a counter-offer.

If the prospective buyer agrees to your terms, he will sign or initial each change of the counter-offer. This process can continue back and forth until an agreement is reached or until the buyer or seller decides not to sign and returns the contract.

- If the offer is not satisfactory, return it unsigned and indicate you are not interested.

The decision to make a counter-offer depends on many variables. If your house has been on the market a short time and other people seem interested, you can justify making a counter-offer. Your realtor's advice will be helpful to decide the amount. Any serious offer should be accompanied by a deposit (earnest money). Depending on the terms, if the buyer reneges on the contract you've lost time in selling the house, but the earnest money will be yours.

The mortgage clause in the offer should contain a cut-off date, such as: This contact is contingent upon Buyer's obtaining a mortgage of $_____ at __(prevailing)__ percent rate for __(15-30)__ years by __(4 to 6 weeks)__. If this mortgage is not obtained the Buyer may void this contract and all deposit monies are to be returned and his contract will be null and void.

Settlement and Possession Dates

When you accept an offer, the closing date and date of possession are included in the contract. The closing or settlement date you and the buyer agree on is the day the financial transaction takes place. At that time your buyer becomes the legal owner of your house. As the owner, he must have access to it.

Before the agreed-upon settlement date, learn the closing costs you must make when you meet with the buyer. They will include realtor's commission, lawyer's fee, certification of title, federal revenue stamps, prepayment mortgage penalty (if applicable), state real estate transfer tax (if applicable) and a possible return of escrow funds for insurance and prepaid taxes.

You will be responsible for turning over the title and the keys to the house in return for a certified check from the new owner.

Insurance coverage on the house will need to be canceled.

After the Sale

Whether you sell or rent your house, a nice gesture toward the new occupant is a page of information about the neighborhood, including:
- names of neighbors, local newsboy, babysitters in the area
- neighbors' attitude toward pets
- emergency telephone numbers for fire, police and ambulance
- trash day, neighborhood snow removal policy, if any
- shopping areas and restaurants

If the new owner is not from the local area he also might appreciate a list of service people: trash collector; handyman; hardware store; electrician, plumber, painter; supplier of gas or oil; furnace maintenance service; pest control service (other than the SPCA!); dry cleaner; yard care people.

RENTING YOUR HOUSE

Sales agreements and rental contracts are fairly standard throughout the U.S. Ask a real estate agent for a copy of a standard lease. Most rental leases contain a damage clause to cover refurbishing and damage costs at time of lease termination. Leases also can require a security deposit, usually one month's rent. A deposit for pets, which can be from $250 to a month's rent, is usual. Check to see if such clauses are in the lease agreement you expect to sign.

You may want a clause stating you have the right, with notice, to enter the house. On trips you make to the U.S. plan to visit your agent and the rental property. You'll get better attention from the agent this way. An annual inspection trip to owned real estate is an acceptable expense on your tax form.

Renting through a realtor may involve a charge to find a tenant and certainly will involve paying a commission, usually a percentage of each month's rent. Know exactly what commission rates include (e.g., gross or net rent).

Although you may be able to find a tenant and avoid the commission, it is difficult to manage from abroad any problems that arise. A lot of situations that can develop may be eliminated if the agent does the proper job to earn his commission. Good luck in finding one who will follow through and do all that he says. In too many cases, it is "out of sight, out of mind" so do ask friends for names of real estate companies they know who have successfully managed rental properties and ask any agents for references.

Corporations often have an individual in their employee relations section to assist company personnel moving into a community. Ask about arriving transferees as possibilities for renting your house during their stay in your area.

After the Lease is Signed

Label the keys you give the agent and the renter.

Add more information to the earlier list for a new owner. You know it will be useful -- let's hope it will be heeded. As previously mentioned, a damage clause and security deposit are recommended in rental agreements. Perhaps your effort to show how you care for items in your house will inspire the renter to do the same. An ounce of prevention may eliminate future frustration and elbow exercise!

Additions to the list include:

- instruction brochures and names of service contacts for appliances in the house -- dishwasher, disposal, stove
- special products you use -- for kitchen cabinets and care of stone, wood, tile or other floors
- instructions for dehumidifier, heater, humidifier and hot water heater
- location of well, if you have one, and the maintenance company -- be sure location of water pump is known by renter
- specific instructions for septic systems, if you have one, and location of external system box or drain field
- special treatment you have for lawn, trees, shrubs
- emergency telephone number of nearby relative, friend or property manager of real estate agency

For your own protection:

- Continue your pest control contract.
- It is worthwhile to have a furnace maintenance plan.
- Have the furnace oil tank filled and agree with tenant that he will fill it when the lease is terminated.

- Get the insurance coverage you need as a lessee.
- Be sure renter knows when and where to deposit the rental checks -- and the penalty (stated in the lease) for late payment. You may wish to have a separate bank account for rent deposits and expenses.
- Arrange for yard maintenance (fertilizing of lawn, trees and plants, pruning of shrubs) and cleaning trash from roof gutters.

TAXES

Moving overseas has significant tax implications and careful tax planning is needed before the move takes place.

FEDERAL INCOME TAXES

Informative, free booklets from the Internal Revenue Service (IRS) will be helpful. These can be obtained from a local federal tax office, by phoning 1-(800)-424-3676 or by writing the IRS Distribution Center, P. O. Box 25866, Richmond, VA 23260.

No. 54 - *Tax Guide for U.S. Citizens and Resident Aliens Abroad*
No. 521 - *Moving Expenses*
No. 523 - *Tax Information on Selling Your Home*
No. 527 - *Rental Property*
No. 530 - *Tax Information for Owners of Homes, Condominiums and Cooperative Apartments*
No. 593 - *Income Tax Benefits for U.S. Citizens Who Go Overseas*

Every U.S. citizen, regardless of place of residence, is required to pay U.S. federal taxes on worldwide income. U.S. embassies in many locations have IRS representatives to give filing assistance:

| Bonn | Manila | Rome |
| Caracas | Mexico City | Sao Paulo |

Jidda   Nassau   Singapore
Johannesburg   Ottawa   Sydney
London   Paris   Tokyo

Embassies and consulates elsewhere have annual visits from IRS personnel who assist with information for filing federal returns. An automatic two-month extension is granted all U.S. taxpayers who are legal residents abroad. However, though the filing date may be extended until June 15, interest for any outstanding balance of taxes due accrues at a rate of 12% (1989) compounded daily from April 15. A 1980 revenue ruling provides that if a federal tax return mailed by a taxpayer in a foreign country bears an official postmark dated on or before the last filing date, such return will be considered as timely filed.

Professional Advice

The assistance of a tax professional is imperative when moving abroad. Each individual has different facts and circumstances affecting him -- from selling or renting a house to estate planning -- necessitating this expertise.

Most corporations retain the services of accounting firms for pre-departure briefing as well as assistance with tax returns while the transferee is overseas. Several U.S. accounting firms (Arthur Andersen, Deloitte Haskins & Sells, Ernst & Young, Peat Marwick Mitchell and Price Waterhouse) have worldwide offices to assist filing U.S. as well as host country taxes. Most publish tax guides on individual countries.

As tax laws, federal and state, can be changed at any time, it is important to inquire regularly about them from your personal tax consultant as well as any corporate financial advisors provided.

Tax Equalization

The employee needs a thorough understanding of all financial aspects so potential problem issues are resolved ahead of time allowing the move, and the return move, to go smoothly. Employers are familiar with the many tax problems that arise with international transfers and most have tax equalization policies. Ask specific questions about aspects important to you. For example, how are investment tax liabilities, state tax liabilities and possibly extra taxes on stock options handled? The subjects discussed under the next headings have related equalization issues.

Moving Expenses

For purposes of determining the allowable moving expense deduction, a foreign move is defined as a move from the U.S. to a foreign country or between foreign countries. A move from a foreign country to the U.S. does not qualify as a foreign move but is treated as a U.S. move.

A record of all expenses and substantiating receipts related to the move will be needed for filing U.S. tax returns and also for reimbursement from your employer. Deductible moving expenses include:

- travel expenses to new location
- moving costs of household goods and personal effects, including storage costs for the entire length of the assignment
- house-hunting trip
- temporary living expenses at new location (possibly time-limited)
- sale and lease expenses relating to old and new residences

Complete details of deductible and non-deductible items are discussed in IRS publications 521, 523 and 530.

All moving reimbursements and allowances must be included in the taxpayer's gross income. Reimbursements for moving expenses received after the move are included as income in the year reimbursements are received. The allowable moving expense deduction is subject to dollar limitations. All too often the reimbursement will exceed the allowable deduction and this means additional tax arises even though none was intended or foreseen. This extra tax usually is covered in a tax equalization or allowance policy so it becomes the liability of the employer rather than the employee.

Tax Concerns of Selling a House

When a move is made, expenses are incurred selling your residence, searching for and purchasing a new one, moving household goods and family. These expenses can be substantial. Federal tax laws recognize this and allow certain expenses as deductions from income within specified dollar limitations. When a house is sold for more than its original cost, a taxable gain arises. If the funds are reinvested in a replacement home of equal or greater value, there may be no money left with which to pay the tax. Mindful of this fact, U.S. tax laws have been designed to encourage the taxpayer to reinvest in another principal residence without penalizing him by taxing the gain from the original sale. If the cost of a new residence is less than the sales proceeds of the old residence, pro rata allocation of the gain is required and part will be taxable.

Federal tax law recognizes it is not usual for a taxpayer who has sold his principal residence in the U.S. to purchase a replacement home in a foreign country. To help the taxpayer moving to a foreign country, if you decide to sell your house, the 24 month time limit to re-purchase a residence for deferral of the gain on the sale of the former residence is extended while you reside abroad, to a maximum of two additional years. The total replacement period shall not extend beyond four years after the date of sale of the old residence while residing abroad.

Many things need consideration and planning when tax equalization policies are involved, such as:

- If a house is sold and the gain cannot be deferred, who pays the additional tax when overseas allowances and premiums have placed the employee in a higher tax bracket?
- When it is not possible to sell your house because of a depressed housing market or high interest rates, who bears the cost of carrying the property if it cannot be rented or is rented at a substantial loss?
- If the house is sold at a loss, should the employer cover part of the loss?
- What happens when the employee returns to the U.S. after his foreign assignment and finds he cannot replace his house with an equivalent one because of increased housing costs or interest rates? Does the employer assist?

Tax Concerns of Renting a House

Rental income and expenses are reportable items on federal tax returns. If a taxpayer rents his residence while he is overseas and sells the house on his return, he may not be able to defer the gain on the sale of the property because at the date of sale it may not be considered his principal residence. However, if the taxpayer intends to return to his former place of residence but is prevented from doing so because of a change in circumstances (e.g., transfer to a different city or the house no longer is adequate due to family size), the gain may still be deferred.

SOCIAL SECURITY TAXES

The U.S. citizen employed abroad for a U.S. employer remains subject to social security payments. FICA contributions will continue to be withheld from your salary even if some or all of the remuneration is exempt from U.S. income tax. U.S. citizens employed by foreign employers are not liable for FICA payments. If your compensation is subject to both U.S. and foreign social security taxes, certain countries have totalization agreements with the U.S. to resolve the double taxation.

All tax returns require Social Security numbers for dependents age 5 and over. (The *Traveling Papers* chapter has details for obtaining these numbers for children born in the U.S., the *Potpourri* chapter for children born abroad.)

STATE AND LOCAL TAXES

Most states define residents under the concept of domicile. An individual can be considered domiciled (resident) if he intends to return to a state after the foreign assignment. Domicile also may be the state where you own property or investments, where you have a bank account or where you have been paying state income taxes. Know your state and local tax responsibilities, if any, during the overseas assignment. Pay attention to possible continuing tax liability. This may be imposed upon you in certain states particularly if you maintain a residence. (Florida, Nevada, South Dakota, Texas, Washington and Wyoming do not have state income taxes.)

As a non-U.S. resident, you may be permitted only a limited number of tax-free U.S. workdays by some states.

FOREIGN COUNTRY TAXES

A tax responsibility in your host country is common. The U.S. and many countries have agreements regarding double taxation, a matter for you to investigate. Contact the tax office of the country and your nearest U.S. embassy or consulate so you understand requirements and time schedule. Again, help from an accounting firm may be needed to understand all aspects of foreign tax forms.

Most countries require pre-payment of current year taxes before you are permitted to depart the country permanently.

TRAVELING PAPERS

PASSPORTS

Individual countries issue passports to their residents allowing permission to travel outside that country. A passport establishes your national identity. Most countries require presentation of this document before entry. Exceptions for U.S. citizens generally relate to travel between the U.S., Mexico and Canada, some countries in South and Central America and the Caribbean islands. However, it is essential to have a passport if you are going to live anywhere outside the U.S. Passports are issued by regional U.S. passport offices (see list in *Appendix*), at specific post offices and clerks of court. A U.S. passport issued to an adult is valid for ten years, five years for a minor (under 18 years of age).

A permanent resident alien, commonly known as a green card holder, must get a re-entry permit from the Department of Immigration from the state in which he or she resides before leaving the U.S. for more than one year. An extension to the permit can be applied for.

You must apply in person for your passport if this is your first passport and you are over 13 years of age. Parents may apply for children under the age of 13.

You will need (1) proof you are a U.S. citizen and (2) proof of your identity, such as a driver's license or another card with an identifying photograph. (Credit cards, temporary driver's license or Social Security cards are not acceptable.) Proof of citizenship could be your *certified* birth certificate or, if that is not available, a document of secondary evidence of U.S. birth. This would be a notice from a state registrar stating no birth record exists and accompanied by the best combination of secondary evidence possible: baptismal certificate, hospital birth record, affidavits of individual having personal knowledge of the facts of your birth, or other documentary evidence such as early census, school or family Bible records, newspaper files and insurance papers.

If you were born abroad you can use:

- a Certificate of Naturalization
- a Certificate of Citizenship
- a Report of Birth Abroad of a Citizen of the U.S.A. (Form FS-240)
- a Certification of Birth (Form FS-545 or DS 1350)

Two identical full-face photographs taken within the previous six months, either black and white or color, 2"x 2", must accompany a Passport Application (Form DSP-11). Vending machine prints are not acceptable. The fee for adults is $42 and for minors (under 18 years) $20, each plus a $7 acceptance fee. It is payable by cash, money order, personal or travelers check. Allow two weeks minimum to obtain a passport.

Each individual must have his or her own passport, including newborn babies.

You may apply for a passport by mail if:

- you have been issued a passport within 12 years prior to the date of a new application, and
- you are able to submit your most recent U.S. passport with your new application, and
- your previous passport was not issued before your 16th birthday.

Obtain *Application for Passport by Mail* (Form DSP-82) from a post office that accepts applications. You will need to enclose your previous passport, two identical photographs (taken within six months of the date of application) signed both on the front left-hand side and in the center on the reverse of the pictures and a $35 passport fee.

If you know you will travel extensively, ask for a 48-page passport rather than the standard one. Additional pages can be inserted in either during the period of validity.

When received, sign your passport in place indicated and complete the information on personal notification. Make a note of the passport number, issue place and date and expiration date and keep this information at your home or office. Also, **photocopy the double page with your picture and issue information. Carry this in your wallet, purse or suitcase, separate from your passport, when you travel.** This can assist in obtaining a replacement in case of loss or theft. (It is wise also before traveling to photocopy the many cards in your wallet. Pack the copy in your suitcase or briefcase. If your wallet is lost or stolen you'll have quick knowledge of credit card numbers for notifying the issuing companies.)

If you are traveling or living abroad when your passport needs renewing, contact the nearest U.S. embassy or consulate. A lost passport should be reported **immediately** to the nearest U.S. embassy or consulate **and** police authorities in the place where the loss occurs.

Travelers should be aware that there are a number of countries which will not permit visitors to enter (and will not issue visas) with passports which have a remaining validity of less than six months.

Your passport is the most valuable document you will carry abroad. It is universally accepted as an identification document not only for traveling but also when you check into a hotel, cash a check or pick up mail. Losing a passport or having it stolen is usually through carelessness. Guard it like a $10,000 bill!

VISAS

A visa is permission to visit a country for a specified purpose and limited period of time, for example, a resident visa, a three-month business visa, a tourist or diplomatic visa. Visas are issued by the government of the country to be visited; they are obtained from an embassy or consulate. Although few Western countries require visas, most Middle East and Eastern European countries, Russia, Australia, African, Asian and South American countries do.

Required visas must be obtained before you go to the country. Entering a country on a tourist visa while awaiting final approval of a required work visa, for example, could prevent customs clearance of your household shipment -- even when your work visa is received. In an extreme instance, the customs clearance could take a year with great inconvenience, frustration and cost.

A visa most commonly is stamped on a page in your passport. The visa occasionally must be legalized by the country's embassy or consulate. When traveling as a family, a visa is required for each individual.

Each country has specific requirements when applying for a visa. An application form, photograph(s), valid passport and sometimes a fee are usually needed. Ask very specific information regarding photographs before you apply: size and number required, black and white or color acceptable, full face, machine-type permitted? You may need to have your passport information translated to the language of the country you will visit. Sometimes a health certificate or statement regarding absence of a police record is required. (See sample letters in the *Appendix*.) The time needed to obtain a visa varies (it can be ten weeks) so when you know your travel plans inquire about visa requirements. Let your travel agent take care of the application whenever possible -- you have many other details to attend to. If this is not possible, it will be necessary to apply to the appropriate embassy or consulate through your employer or personally.

Denials are mostly on the basis of prior travel to countries felt to be unfriendly to the host country, political or religious incompatibility. Israel, the Arab countries, South America and many African countries are especially sensitive in this regard.

The period of validity varies from a few weeks to several years. Some visas are valid from date of issue, others from date of entry. Read the fine print! It may be a single-entry or multiple-entry visa. It may have to be used within a specified period. If possible, apply for an extended stay visa. When this is not feasible, apply for a multiple re-entry visa after arrival. Renewal reminders are not sent. **Do not let a resident or work visa expire while you are in the country.** You, your family or your belongings may have quite an ordeal if an expiration date slips by without renewal.

In some instances before a visa is granted, you can be required to have proof of outward transportation from the country (such as a prepaid ticket) and adequate means to support oneself while in the country. If traveling on business, a letter from your employer stating he will assume this responsibility is acceptable. Ask your travel agent or the appropriate government office about this so you are not caught unprepared.

In some countries **exit visas** or permits are required to leave a country. These can take several weeks to obtain. Where required, and where possible, you must always have a valid one. Imagine the dilemma you would be in if you need to leave for an emergency health, family or business purpose and did not have one. In a few places a mother cannot take a child out of the country unless accompanied by her husband or a letter from him granting her this permission. Know the regulations.

> Regulations change.
> Always check latest visa requirements before you travel.

PERMITS

Permits of various types are required in most countries:
- diplomatic, government officials, business
- transit, tourist, student, commercial
- residence
- employment

It is essential to know and comply with permit requirements before you depart. All family members accompanying you should be mentioned in any application. Employment and residence permits can be complex. A health certificate, chest x-ray, character references or certified copies of diplomas may be needed. In some countries when a husband is given an employment permit the wife also can have a job. However, the reverse is seldom the case. Work permits may be required before a resident permit is possible. In Sweden, in addition to the permit, housing must be arranged before you arrive. A permit may be required before admission to school is allowed.

Apply as far in advance as possible. There always seem to be red-tape delays for these permits and they can require weeks to obtain. **Do not move without your proper work permit in hand.** In addition to the worrisome knowledge that you are in a country illegally and the resulting fear of unknown consequences, lack of a required permit can involve having to leave the country to obtain the permit or until it is issued, fines or surrendering of your passport until the proper papers are issued. Worse yet, you may not get in. There are few exceptions to this. Singapore is one; they permit a person to enter with a visitor pass and conclude employment formalities after arrival. But don't go anywhere until you know you are proceeding legally as required by specified regulations. This also can avoid possible under-the-table requests for "expediting" help.

Telephone the embassy or consulate of the country where you will reside. Many countries have representative offices in the larger U.S. cities. Ask them their specific requirements for residence and employment permits. If you don't ask specific questions people assume you have information and they do not volunteer it. While you have the immigration person on the line, ask other questions.

- Do permits need to be approved or legalized by the embassy before departure for the new country?

- Would birth or marriage certificates, divorce papers ever be required during residency in that country? Is a copy of these items (rather than the original) acceptable?

- Is personal financial guarantee required for residency?

- Is translation of passport information, driver's license or household inventory required? Can the embassy do this for you? How long will it take?

- Are there any health problems in the country requiring special immunizations (cholera, typhoid or malaria)?

- What import restrictions does the country have on household goods? What taxes are made on specific imported items, new or used? What items are prohibited? What items require a license or permit? (More details on this subject are in the *Moving and Packing* chapter.)

- What restrictions are there for taking pets into the country? Are permits required?

SOCIAL SECURITY NUMBERS FOR CHILDREN

A Social Security number for dependents age 5 and over is required on federal tax returns. This number can be obtained by completing Form SS-5 obtainable from your local Social Security office. Evidence of the child's age, citizenship and identity are required. The person applying on behalf of the child must present proof of his/her identity.

For a child born in the U.S., you need a document establishing age and citizenship and another proving the child's identity. The former could be a public birth certificate or hospital record of the birth. The document establishing identity must show the child's name, age, date and place of birth and should be at least one year old. Only original or certified documents are accepted (no photocopies).

OTHER PAPERS

Other papers may be required by your destination country: medical, police and business. Sample letters are in the *Appendix*. All letters should be on letterhead stationery of the sender.

The **medical** letter should state you are in good health.

A **police** certification of good character standing can be required before a residence or work permit is issued.

Any required **business letter of recommendation** is addressed to the Consul General of the country where you are applying for a visa. It must come from your business organization, a bank, trade association, chamber of commerce or public official. The letter should state your occupation, title, business connections and that you are a person of good standing and financially responsible.

INTERNATIONAL CERTIFICATE OF VACCINATION

Under the international health regulations adopted by the World Health Organization (WHO), a country may require an international certificate of vaccination against cholera and yellow fever. Because smallpox has been virtually eradicated, vaccinations for that disease are rarely required.

The embassy or consulate of the country where you will reside can advise you on inoculations and immunizations. Before allowing entry **or** re-entry, countries can require inoculation if you have traveled in an area where there is a problem disease. Specific information regarding diseases can be obtained from local health authorities abroad or private or public agencies who advise international travelers (see *Appendix*).

Inoculations

Cholera. This is an acute, infectious epidemic disease usually only found in developing countries where sanitation is inadequate.

Generally it is spread by contaminated water or milk, uncooked food and by flies. It is characterized by diarrhea, high temperature, abdominal pains and vomiting. Immunization becomes effective six days after the injection and lasts for six months only. Two doses from 7 to 30 days apart are recommended.

Yellow fever. This is a viral infection spread by certain species of mosquitoes. Immunization is required for travelers to Central America and Central Africa. Yellow fever requires specific scheduling before or after other vaccinations (e.g., poliomyelitis). In the U.S. and some other countries, this injection is given only by special health offices. The vaccination is valid after ten days and is effective for ten years.

Immunizations

If you need immunizations, consult a physician as soon as you know about your international travels. If pregnancy is known or suspected, be sure the doctor knows this before scheduling inoculations.

Specific time intervals are necessary between certain shots. Plan to have them a month in advance, if at all possible. You will be very busy the last month. Any reaction to the shots is short but inconvenient if you are in the packing-moving process.

Children receive several types of immunizations during childhood: **measles, mumps, rubella,** the **DPT series** (diphtheria-pertussis-tetanus) and **polio.** Travel immunizations for children up to ten years of age should be administered by your pediatrician. He will know the schedule of other immunizations being given and the proper timing and dosage for the travel ones.

The doctor administering vaccinations must record these on the *International Certificate of Vaccination as Approved by the WHO* (PHS-731). **Double-check** that his signature **and** "approved stamp" are beside **each** entry. If either is missing, you will be greatly annoyed and inconvenienced at some far away immigration checkpoint where the immunization is required. Although blood always should be typed before any transfusion, you may wish to record your blood type in the certificate of vaccination.

Hepatitis. Viral hepatitis A, sometimes known as infective jaundice, is an infection of the liver. Its source is contaminated food, infected water, unclean foods and poor sanitary habits. It has an incubation period from 15 to 50 days (average 28-30). Symptoms are poor appetite, tiredness, nausea, fever and upper abdominal discomfort. Depending on your doctor's opinion, gamma globulin can be given to prevent Type A hepatitis; it does not guarantee absolute protection; it has short duration validity. The best preventative measure is good hygiene by the food handler, thoroughly cooked shellfish, food stored properly and boiled water.

Malaria. If residing or traveling in an area where malaria is a problem, ask your physician for recommendations. There is more than one form of malaria, each requiring specific preventative medications. An increase of chloroquine-resistant malaria has necessitated new drugs to treat these strains. The U.S. Center for Disease Control has a special 24-hour malaria information service: (404) 639-1610.

Malaria is spread by the bite of an infected mosquito. The disease is characterized by cycles of chills, fever and sweating; it is long-lasting and can reoccur. Pills can be taken to protect against most strains of malarial infection. Your doctor or pharmacist will tell you the specific timing for taking any medication. Generally, pills are taken two weeks before departure, during the stay in the country and for a short time after leaving the country. Pills are available that can be taken daily or once a week. You can decide if it is easier for you to take a pill each day or remember the once-a-week variety. The incubation period for malaria is ten days. If you forget a daily tablet you should be all right; if you forget the once-a-week pill you risk greater exposure to the disease.

Other preventive measures for anyone residing in a malaria area include keeping yourself well-covered after dark when mosquitoes appear, use of an insect repellant on your skin, use of mosquito netting around beds and an insecticide spray in the bedroom.

Polio. Polio is preventable by proper vaccination. Adults as well as children should be immunized. It is still prevalent in some areas and at least a primary vaccination and booster should be received by all international travellers.

Rabies. This inoculation is recommended when you will be living in an area where rabies is a serious threat.

Tetanus. All travelers should be vaccinated against tetanus, a bacillus-caused disease sometimes known as lockjaw because of its rigid and spasmodic muscle contractions. The preventive injection can be valid for ten years. Booster shots are advisable when indicated. The TAB injection can be combined with the tetanus vaccine (TABT).

Tuberculosis. If small children will accompany you or if there is a possibility of pregnancy while abroad, ask a pediatrician about the BCG vaccine. It is not readily used in the U.S. but is a standard immunization in other countries. Drawbacks are decreased value of periodic skin tests (Tine test), short-lived protective benefits, lack of standardization techniques and occasional severe side effects. A preliminary Mantoux text should be given first to determine any degree of natural immunity.

Typhoid and **paratyphoid.** These are diseases resulting from poor sanitation usually transmitted by a bacillus in contaminated food, milk or water, uncooked and unwashed food. Both are characterized by red rashes, high fever, bronchitis and intestinal hemorrhaging. There are two types of vaccine: one is against typhoid only and the other (TAB) is against typhoid, paratyphoid A and paratyphoid B. Annual injections are needed for continued protection.

HEALTH INSURANCE POLICES

Make sure your medical insurance policy provides adequate protection for you and your family while you will be overseas. Medicare does not cover medicine bills outside the U.S.

Medical information resources are listed in the *Appendix*.

LEARNING THE LANGUAGE

The avid tourist may say you don't have to know the language of a country. It's true -- English is well known in almost all *tourist* business transactions. The salesman whose livelihood depends on selling what a tourist buys -- be it a native trinket, genuine gem, beautiful basket, antique or "antique" -- learns the necessary words and ways to communicate and sell. But few tourists have had to deal with a car that won't start in Reims, finding the way to the orthodontist in Sao Paulo or searching for spices in the local (not super!) market in Colombo. You may need not only verbal language but also arm gestures, facial expressions and body language! Most relocated Americans are charade experts!

Language study is absolutely essential for international assignments. It requires effort and time, but it greatly eases your cultural adjustment and the frustration that comes when you are not able to communicate. In order to live and mix with the people of the country more than in polite situations, you need to know their language. The rewards will be the ability to meet everyday needs, the security of being independent, the sense of belonging and the opportunity to understand the new culture. Don't be fooled when you're told English is the second language of a country. English may have been a required subject in school but those young enough to have taken the classes may never have spoken a word outside the classroom. (They may have been reading *MacBeth* in English Lit which won't help with your needs!) Don't count on English in the local market, at the hospital or with the car mechanic!

Hopefully, time will permit some language instruction before you depart. Even 20-30 hours will help immeasurably. It can get you over the hump of, "I can't learn a language." Corporations sending families abroad usually offer language study to both the employee and spouse and make any needed child care allowance for the lessons. In most cases, the wife interacts with the local people and has the most need and use for instruction. She will have to tell the electrician about the water heater problem, understand the cost per catty or kilo from the woman in the fish market and read the labels on food products. The businessman will have the help of the office staff in conversations and written letters and an interpreter when necessary.

Rudimentary knowledge of the local language is invaluable, not so much for communicating as for creating a good impression. Your willingness to use greetings and a few simple phrases can smooth any transaction with local people, even if you later switch to a combination of English and sign language. On your own, from almost any travel guide book, you can learn "good morning" ("afternoon," "evening"), "please," "thank you" and "excuse me." You'll need such phrases immediately on arrival for a "thank you" to the taxi driver who takes you to the hotel and a "good night" to the bellman who brings the luggage to your room.

A variety of possibilities for instruction exists. A tutor offers individual attention and can be most helpful in giving appropriate situation skills as they are needed. When the tutor is a person from the host country, this gives you the benefit of a true accent and, additionally, an opportunity to learn cultural aspects firsthand.

An intensive course or total immersion program offers full-day instruction for two or more weeks. If going to a country where no English is spoken or understood in daily situations (e.g., Russia, Saudi Arabia, Japan, Algiers, Brazil, Greece and Turkey), this type of study is mandatory.

Tapes and records can be purchased to expose you to the sounds of the new language and the basic phrases. For long-term learning, this method has the disadvantage of no pronunciation correction. Great self-discipline is needed to learn by this method.

If you know long in advance of the actual move, an adult education language course may be possible.

And plan to continue your language study as quickly as possible when you reach your destination.

Learn the Money, Too

Before you go, become familiar also with the currency of the country. You will need this immediately -- to pay the taxi driver and tip the bellman. You also need to be able to count change! The American way of giving change, counting from the cost of your purchase, is not universal. Some simply count out the total of the change; some expect you to know your change will be accurate and you can insult them by counting it. Cash registers are unknown in many places and receipts may not be offered to help you.

It's possible to get money packets for most foreign countries at many U.S. banks. Whenever you are traveling, it's a very good idea to take some of the currency of the country with you. Let children become acquainted with the coins before they arrive -- something to do on the flight over!

ORGANIZING THE DETAILS

An indexed, loose-leaf notebook for moving details is an indispensable aid for "getting your act together." Jot down questions, things to purchase, people to call, appointments, the family immunization schedule, etc., etc., etc. Keep the list of moving expenses with receipts in an envelope in the notebook. Everything pertaining to the move will then be in one place instead of tattered notes in scattered places. It can greatly reduce frantic searches for some tidbit you know you wrote down "somewhere." A calendar for organizing your days and scheduling things to be done is also helpful.

So many things are involved in any move. As quickly as possible, you will need to get uninvolved from responsibilities and commitments outside the family.

CHANGE OF ADDRESS

Don't Say It, Write It

Write letters to give notice of your address change -- don't telephone -- you want a record of the notification. Send the letters as far in advance as possible. A general letter which can be photocopied and then the addressee and appropriate information filled in will make the task easiest for you. Here's a sample:

Organizing the Details 43

> Date
>
> Regarding (insurance policy no. 1234), effective February 29, 1990, all mail should be sent me at the following new address:
>
> _____
> _____
>
> Please send all correspondence via *international air mail*.
>
> Sincerely yours,

Keep a copy of each letter sent. You can photocopy the completed letter, use carbon paper as you type it or fill in a photocopy. In spite of your careful change of address notice, rest assured some computer (or human!) will goof and use your former address and a 25 cent stamp. That's when you write them: "In my letter of August 3, 1989, I informed you of my change of address but...." A copy of the letter will remind you of people and services to be notified when you move in the future. If there is a special reason for making the change of address by telephone, such as a utility company, make a note in that aforementioned notebook of the call, date and name of the person to whom you give the forwarding address or moving notice.

Notice of the address change can be given credit card companies and charge account stores with the payment of your bill, using the form sent with each monthly statement. Make a note in your moving notebook of the date on which you do this. If it is a local store, it is important this information is in writing; resist the temptation to telephone. You will want to keep some of these accounts open for use during interim visits to the U.S. Also, they establish your credit rating which can take time to re-establish in the future.

Make a list of regular billing dates for recurring expenses -- taxes, mortgage, personal insurance, household insurance, etc. Penalties and interest for late payments can be avoided by marking your calendar to expect the bill and following up if it does not arrive when it should.

Stockholder Companies

Depending on your destination, it may be possible to have stock accounts transferred to an international branch of your broker firm. Merrill Lynch, Drexel Burnham, Goldman Sachs, Shearson Lehman Hutton and others have offices in many cities of the world.

Changes of address for companies in which you hold stock can be sent to the company itself or to a bank transfer agent. Your stockbroker may be willing to take care of this. If you want dividends deposited to a stockbroker account, include this information in the letter. You also can arrange for your bank to receive the dividends. Give deposit instructions to the dividend-issuing company being sure to include the bank account number to be credited.

In your change of address letter to companies in which you hold stock, you must include the sentence (if true), "I am a citizen of the United States." If the company does not have this information and they are mailing a dividend to a non-U.S. address, taxes are usually withheld. The inclusion of this sentence will preclude additional letter writing by you for clarification and bookkeeping corrections. Here is a sample letter:

Date

Supersure Corporation
711 Lucky Street
Rainbow's End, State of Joy 20001

Subject: Stock Account No. 000123 for
        I.M. Onthego, SS No. 313-131-0000

    Effective October 10, 1989, please consider this letter your authority to send all dividend checks for the 100 shares of Supersure Corporation in my name to:
        Security Bank
        Fortune Building
        Fort Knox, Tennessee 11111
These checks should be marked for deposit to my account number 011-204599.

    Please send all reports, notices and other correspondence to me at the following address:

_____
_____

    The foregoing instructions are to remain in effect until further written notice from me.
    I am a citizen of the United States.

                        Sincerely yours,

Forwarding Mail

U. S. post offices have a special card on which to advise them of a forwarding address. List all family members.

The post office will not forward mail to an international address. First class mail is sent domestically for one year after which it is returned to sender. Second class mail is forwarded for three months.

Employers may suggest mail be sent to them for forwarding until you are in your new residence. At that time you will have to be sure everyone is notified of your new mailing address.

Personal Mail International, Inc. (PMI) offers a multitude of helpful services, including mail forwarding, to anyone living overseas. They winnow mail to save you postage and unwanted mail, keep a confidential log of mail forwarded, send you fax notice when certified urgent mail is received, notify you weekly if no mail was received, provide bi-lingual labels to speed delivery, forward mail to other family members at other addresses (e.g., your son at college) and more! Send for information on all their services:

PMI, Inc
P.O. Box 311
Mendham, New Jersey 07945
Telephone: (201) 927-4722, 1-(800)-548-3622

Whom to Tell

Your list of people and places to notify should include:

- banks

    Notify all appropriate departments (some banks don't do it all for you): checking, loan, mortgage, safe deposit box, savings, trust.

- credit card companies and services

    American Express, Diner's Club, Master Charge, Visa, car rental agencies (Avis, Hertz, etc.), gasoline companies (Exxon, Shell, etc.) Many have worldwide facilities. Hold onto one or two of the widely-accepted cards -- they may be useful in your new location, certainly as you travel, and often in emergencies.

- department stores and mail order firms

    Don't cancel all your charge accounts. Write the companies

of your change of address and ask them to keep your account open for ordering by mail and when you visit or return to the U.S.

- insurance companies

    automobile, homeowners, household goods, life, medical, personal liability, etc.

- accountant
- lawyer
- stockbroker
- state and county tax offices

    Notify these offices in any state where you own property and have tax liabilities.

- employer of spouse

    Advise of address for mailing of W-2 form.

- landlord or property owner if you are a renter

    Arrange for refund of any advance deposits (e.g., security or pet deposits).

- community affiliations
- church, social clubs
- service companies -- garbage collector, furnace oil company, pest control services
- newspaper and other delivery services
- voter registration office
- blood bank
- alumni organizations, professional memberships
- periodical subscriptions, book clubs

    Overseas magazine postage rates are considerably higher than within the U.S. Consider having issues sent until money for the additional postage runs out. Depending on where you will be, you may or may not wish to continue subscriptions. (International editions of Time, Readers' Digest, Business Week, Newsweek, etc. will reach you sooner if you subscribe to international editions.)

- friends

    Depending on the time of year you are moving, you might be able to send November Christmas cards with your new address.

Utility and Service Companies

Electric, gas and water companies need to be notified about discontinuing service and a time arranged for reading of meters. Arrange for any monies due you, such as rebates on unused service plans or return of deposits, to be sent you or your bank. Ask the name of the person to whom you are speaking and in that moving notebook, make a note of this along with the date called. It is still advisable to send a written notice of the forwarding address.

Let telephone service continue through the very last day you may be in the house. If you will be there after the moving men have loaded the van to clean up or do odd jobs, you still want to be able to make and receive calls. The telephone company doesn't have to come to your house to disconnect service.

Arrange to pay utility and other bills which may arrive after your departure.

INVENTORIES

Household Inventory

You may never have thought of taking a household inventory -- or want to now. It's not only advisable but necessary. Moving is an efficient time for this accounting. The possibility of damage and disappearance increases during a move and an inventory is needed in order to establish an insurance value for shipment and/or storage. It is valuable also for insurance purposes in case of fire, robbery or other incidents.

The inventory should be dated and include all household items, date of purchase, cost and replacement values. Any receipts of purchase should be attached to the inventory pages.

Depending on your relocation destination, you must decide whether to store or take high-value or sentimental items.

If you have art pieces, antiques, special porcelains, rugs, other valuable collections or items, you may want the help of an appraiser to establish values. An appraiser can be hired to take a quick look through your house to tell you general items that should be given a value; he or she can be hired for a set fee to appraise a whole household or by the hour for special items. Have your inventory as complete as possible before you call the appraiser so you utilize his or her time to best advantage. Request the appraisal as far in advance as possible to allow time to arrange the insurance coverage needed during the move and when you are relocated.

Photographs should be taken of special items such as art pieces, antiques and jewelry. It is a good idea to take pictures not only of individual and groups of items but also of the rooms of your house. Panorama pictures will remind you of the many things you have in case there is loss by fire or burglary, long periods in storage or a lost box in shipping.

One copy of the inventory should be in a safe place other than your house. Keep a copy of it at home. And keep it up to date! There is more information about keeping a list of items purchased while overseas in the *Potpourri* chapter.

Personal Inventory

A personal inventory, including information on all family members, should be made also. This can be left with your lawyer, in a safe deposit box or in a sealed envelope with a family member or company officer. The information also will help you recall people and places to notify of your change of address. A sample inventory is at the end of this chapter. Any list should include:

- bank account numbers for all checking and saving accounts with names of individuals authorized to sign checks and withdraw funds
- bank information on safekeeping accounts, loans, mortgages, credit cards, trusts
- safe deposit box location
- social security numbers
- passport numbers
- real estate records -- location of property owned and related papers
- insurance policies, issuing company and address of issuing agent
- names of lawyer, accountant
- stockbroker and stock account numbers
- IRA, Keogh plan numbers
- location of will
- driver's license numbers
- credit card account numbers

After arrival at your new location make a supplementary or similar list of information: bank accounts, insurance policies, alien registration numbers, charge accounts.

BANKING

Consider transferring or setting up an account with a U.S. bank which has offices in your new location. The major international banks are Bank of America, Chase Manhattan and Citibank. They have full service branches worldwide which handle checking accounts, credit card payments, foreign exchange transfers, savings accounts, interest posting, safe deposit box rentals and investments.

When establishing an account, you need to decide about joint account versus separate accounts, who can authorize transfers and whether to have regular transfers to your foreign account or to make transfers on the basis of need and exchange rate. Keep in mind that extensive travel by one partner in the new location may necessitate change in the way you have handled family finances previously. Both husband and wife need access to a source of funds overseas.

If you can transfer to an international bank, don't close your present account. It will be valuable as a financial reference, as a depository for U.S. dollar checks and as a source of funds from which to replenish your foreign bank account. You may want checks without an address or with your overseas one.

Whether you change accounts and/or banks, visit an officer of your bank who can take care of your banking requirements while you are away. This high-level contact is important. A letter addressed to that individual will receive personal attention -- it's much more efficient than a pre-printed envelope address to Mail Teller, Bank of My City. Get the individual's business card with telex or fax numbers for expedient contact. Your spouse should know the name of this individual as should an attorney or person holding signature authority. Some banks will charge you automatically each month for the privilege of maintaining an inactive account.

You may want to arrange a power of attorney for someone to have access to your safe deposit box. (See *Power of Attorney* section of this chapter.)

You will need cash during the move. Decide on an amount and get this in travelers checks. It's not wise to carry large amounts of cash anywhere. Until you have a bank account in the new location, it may not be possible to cash personal checks quickly. Travelers checks are accepted worldwide and are an immediate source of money. Both husband and wife should have these checks, especially important if the employee expects to travel shortly after relocating.

Get a small amount of money in bills and coins of the country where you are going -- for convenience but also to familiarize yourself with the money before arrival. Play games with the children to help them become familiar with the money also.

INSURANCE

You undoubtedly have insurance coverage of several types: automobile, health, liability, life, household and perhaps workmen's compensation. Each insuring company needs to be informed of your coming move. Find out if any present coverage is applicable or valid for your move abroad. You may be due a refund on some policies. Arrange for any reimbursement to be mailed directly to your bank with notification to wherever you are. This will avoid several weeks' time in receiving the money and the inconvenience of having the check sent abroad and then having to return it to the U.S. Overseas banks frequently are unwilling to accept foreign checks for deposit and if they do, up to three weeks can be required for clearance of the check. Also, there may be a charge to convert the money to their currency.

Many countries give an **automobile insurance** discount -- sometimes as much as 60% -- for claim-free periods. To obtain this discount, a letter from the automobile insurance company (or companies) stating how many claim-free years have been accumulated for each family driver must be presented. Get the letter before you go so there will be no delay in obtaining any possible premium credit.

Be sure your regular **personal accident policies** continue during your move and residence abroad. They should include worldwide coverage.

If your **medical insurance** is through your employer, get claim filing information and forms before you depart. When you will submit claims personally or when you have an individual policy, telephone the company to talk with the head person of their customer service department. You want a manager or supervisor --

not a claim adjustor. Explain you will be moving overseas and want his/her name as someone to whom claims and letters can be sent directly. Frequently claims are returned with an identifying number and no indication of who handled the matter; when there is a question you will get a quicker response writing to a specific person rather than to the general address of the company.

You need to have complete up-to-date information on the coverage of your medical insurance plan. Will you be covered while traveling worldwide? Learn from your contact the exact procedure to follow in sending bills from an international location. Do they need from you the U.S. dollar equivalent for the foreign currency billed? When you submit a claim, enclose a deposit ticket from your U.S. bank with your account number on it. Notice of all payments made should be sent you by the insurer.

Medicare programs do not provide payment for hospitals or medical services outside the U.S.

Telephone your **dental insurance** company and get the name of a person to whom you can send claims. Get a supply of claim forms.

This would be a good time to review your **life insurance** coverage if you have not done so for a long time.

Household insurance most often covers household items only while they are in your house; when they leave your premises they may not be covered. Understand the terms of your policy and arrange for adequate protection during the time it takes the shipment to reach the destination point *and is again in your home.* You will need insurance coverage for items left in storage. Insurance companies generally cover valuable jewelry and special items under separate policies, called floater or scheduled property policies, and they require appraisals of current value. Jewelers from whom you have purchased an expensive bauble, bangle or bracelet sometimes will update the appraisal at no additional cost to you. Other jewelers usually charge a percentage of the value as their appraisal fee.

MEDICAL INFORMATION

All family members should have a **medical examination.** Do it early to allow time for recommended treatments or special tests.

In the case of **special doctors,** such as an orthopedist or orthodontist, ask your doctor for the name of someone in his field in your new city. He may be able to give you a name in a directory only but there is a chance he may know someone.

Get **medical records** for all family members. *Take with you* a record of your children's physical examination. These are usually necessary for enrollment in schools overseas and should be available on your first visit to the schools.

Have your doctor give you a *typed* copy of any **prescription drugs** used by family members, using *generic name* and strength. Rarely is it possible to have a U.S. prescription filled outside the U.S.; however, you will have the specific, legible information about the medication to show a doctor in the new location.

Take with you an adequate supply of any prescription drugs currently needed until you can establish yourself with new medical service. *All medicines should be carried in their original labeled containers* showing what they are if a customs inspector asks. If you need to take medication containing habit-forming or narcotic drugs with you, take a doctor's certificate attesting to that fact. To ensure you do not violate the law, consult the embassy or consulate of the country for precise information before leaving the U.S.

A **medical alert bracelet** should be worn if you have allergies, reactions to certain medicines or other unique medical problems. Consult *Useful Addresses* in the *Appendix* for places to obtain this and also information for groups with international medical services.

Have your eye doctor give you a copy of **eyeglass prescriptions** and contact lens information for all family members. It is wise to have a second pair of prescription glasses. Put the prescriptions with the papers to be carried with you. Glasses can be lost or broken and it will be a bit inconvenient if the prescriptions are in an inaccessible shipping container.

A small **emergency first aid kit** to be taken in your suitcase is recommended, especially if you are traveling with children. It can eliminate a frantic search for a drugstore in an unfamiliar city and finding new products perhaps with labels in unfamiliar German, Greek or Japanese! Suggested items are:

- aspirin
- sterile cleanser for wounds (e.g., Bactine), antibacterial cream (e.g., Neosporin), bandaids or other dressings, adhesive tape, scissors, tweezers
- medicine for diarrhea (e.g., Imodium AD, Pepto-Bismol, Kaopectate) and motion sickness (e.g., Dramamine)

- a digestive pacifier (e.g., Gelusil or Mylanta)
- antihistamine (for insect bites)
- antibiotic (e.g., Tetracycline)
- sore throat, cold and cough preparations
- thermometer (It is possible to purchase one with both Fahrenheit and Celsius. The latter is used universally outside the U.S.)
- optional:
  - sun cream, insect repellant
  - fungicide for athlete's foot or other skin afflictions
  - water purifier (if your destination or a stopover point is a country where you know water purity will be a problem)

You may wish to take in your shipment a one volume or paperback **medical reference book**. Your doctor may be able to recommend one.

If you are a member of a state **blood bank**, you should consider continuing membership as a non-resident when you have declarable relatives in the U.S., for example, children in U.S. schools or dependent parents. Contact your local group for details on this type of membership. Also, ask if you can donate blood prior to departure or during a U.S. visit to meet future obligations. By agreement of the American Association of Blood Banks, anyone having taken malaria medications is ineligible to donate blood for three succeeding years.

There is no worldwide association of blood banks. If you require blood while in a foreign country, ask if replacement in like amount is possible. Any medical bill should be itemized in detail giving such information as laboratory fees, blood and transfusion costs. Your U.S. health insurance company will require this information. It will save time and effort to get it at the time of billing.

DENTAL RECORDS

Dental graduates from the University of Pennsylvania and Northwestern seem to have located worldwide! However, all the family should have any recommended dental work and cleaning done before departure.

Ask your dentist for all family dental x-rays and other information he feels you should have, perhaps regarding an orthodontic program, periodontal care or fluoride treatment. Although dentists always seem to like to take their own x-rays, it is helpful to have previous ones for background information and comparison.

SCHOOL INFORMATION

Visit your children's schools to obtain records. The school may be willing to send academic transcripts if the overseas school is known; in any case, take a copy with you. By federal law, school records of a child up to 18 years must be given to the parent if requested. After 18, the student must request the records and receive them or authorize a parent to receive them. A release form for academic transcripts and records should be signed for each school and each student so future requests, such as at time of college application, can be honored.

Meet with the teachers and counselors of all your children. Ask their recommendations for transferring them to a new school. Request samples of their math and science work; these can assist with class placement. Give teachers your departure date to allow for possible completion of work or exams.

Most international moves necessitate private schools for children. While American ones will be predominantly American, certainly there will be other nationalities and your children will meet people of many cultures. These schools may or may not have a predominance of American teachers. Other possibilities which may be available include: English-language school other than the American system; schools of other nationalities, such as German or French, which have an English "stream," and church-affiliated schools. Investigate all possibilities. Ask people who have lived in the area for their opinion of the schools. In most cases, early application is needed to private and boarding schools to assure placement. Your employer may be able to assist with information on the choice of schools and in securing enrollment. Pre-schools also may be limited in space available. Apply to them as early as possible.

Private schools require entering students to have a physical examination. Take a copy of your children's medical reports with you and their latest examination information.

The Scholastic Achievement Tests (SATs), and others, are given at specified cities throughout the world. If schools in your destination city do not offer them, contact College Entrance Examination Board, 45 Columbus Avenue, N.Y., NY 10023-6992 (tel. (212) 713-8000) for location of testing centers and dates of tests.

ACCOUNTANT

Depending on the extent of his services and intended role, items needed by your accountant will include:

- copies of recent tax records (if he doesn't already have them)
- a contact with the company who handles salary payment and tax withholdings
- name and address of your attorney
- name, address and telephone number of business or investment partners

Price Waterhouse, Ernst & Young, Deloitte Haskins & Sells, Peat Marwick Mitchell and Arthur Andersen have worldwide offices and can give assistance in filing U.S. and host country taxes. Check to see if your company retains the services of one of these accounting firms. They are often retained to give pre-departure briefings on tax matters.

TAX RECORDS

U.S. law requires financial records be kept for five years. Tax records for this period should be taken with you as well as any records for pending claims beyond the five year period. If you have an accountant, this information can be left with him but you may wish to have copies to refer to. Arrange with your accountant deadlines for getting information to him. If you plan to handle your taxes personally, get the address of the regional Internal Revenue Service (IRS) where you will have to file as an overseas resident. Look inside an overseas tax instruction booklet or telephone 1-(800)-424-1040 to get the address.

If a tax refund is expected, make arrangements for it to be deposited.

ATTORNEY

Your attorney should be advised of current obligations outstanding, any pending business investments he may have to handle, a list of individuals who owe you money along with proof of their debts and name of a family member or company contact who can always reach you.

Power of Attorney (POA)

A power of attorney is legal permission for another person, known as an "attorney-in-fact," to conduct your business in your absence. A *general POA* gives unrestricted powers to the attorney-in-fact to deal with all your property and business in any fashion. Because this is so broad, it should be used only in emergency situations. A *limited POA* restricts the authority to a specific item, such as sale of particular automobile, closing a real estate transaction or making an investment change. It should not grant more power than is necessary. It can have time limitations.

Obviously, a POA should be given to a most responsible person such as a relative, trusted friend, professional associate or personal lawyer.

Since it is a powerful legal document, consult with a lawyer about its use. A POA must be written, signed and notarized. Most states require cancellation of a POA to be done in writing. It is good practice to destroy all original copies.

For federal income tax matters, the IRS will provide a Power of Attorney and Declaration of Representative (Form 2848). Most state income tax departments will furnish similar forms on request.

WILLS

A review and update of your will is essential. If you or your spouse do not each have a will, write them immediately. An attorney's help is imperative. He needs to understand the laws of the country where you will reside with respect to your property rights and assets so you are assured the will can be executed in your state in the U.S. He must know about inheritance and government taxes in the foreign country of residence and how they could affect your estate. Failure to have a valid will that can be executed in the U.S. can be catastrophic.

When there are minor children in the family, a legal guardian should be designated in your will. Take with you a separate notarized letter stating who the guardian is and give a copy to the guardian. In some countries only parents or a legal guardian can take a child out of that country.

A letter of last instruction, to be attached to the will and/or given to a family member, is recommended. This would state your funeral wishes as well as special items you wish certain family members to have.

The original copy of your will should be in your safe deposit box or left with your lawyer. Take a copy with you.

DRIVER'S LICENSE

Take your valid U.S. driving license with you. In many countries the license must be at least three months old and you must have resided in the country of issue during those three months.

A valid license is needed to obtain a license in another country without taking a written or road test. (Just as U.S. tests are in English, expect written tests to be in the language of the country you are in.) In countries where there are long lists of learners waiting to take required tests, you could be at the bottom of the list and not be able to take the test for months -- even a year. In addition, some countries require all new applicants for licenses to take driving instruction and this also can involve a long waiting time -- and knowledge of their language!

Make a note of your U.S. license's expiration date so you can keep it current -- when possible (the issuing state will do this in absentia) and when desirable (you will be returning to the country issuing the license).

Children under 18 years rarely are allowed to drive in countries outside the U.S.

An **international driving license** is not really needed abroad when you have a valid U.S. license. Some countries, such as Mexico, Iceland, Iraq, Nigeria and the People's Republic of China, do not accept it. When it is acceptable, there are time limitations for its use (from one month to a year). When it expires, the regular driving license issued in the U.S. must be produced. Before you dash out to get one, learn from the country's embassy whether it is needed or even acceptable. When you travel on vacation between countries, you will find that most accept your individual country's valid license.

If needed, the international driving license can be obtained from an established U.S. automobile club. Two photographs and a valid driving license are needed. A small fee is charged. It can be obtained abroad also.

PASSPORT PICTURES

There will be many occasions when each family member will need pictures -- driver's license, visas, identification cards of various types. Order at least a dozen copies and ask for the negative. Take the pictures *and* the negatives for each family member *with* you.

PETS

Usually it is possible to take your dog, cat, bird or tropical fish with you. It may be a little difficult or inconvenient with those latter two, but possible! There are many questions to be asked of the embassy of the country to which you will be going.

- Is an import permit or visa required? a picture? (Yes, it can happen!)
- What are the health regulations for entry? How close to departure must examination and shots be scheduled?
- Are there medical records or papers that must accompany the pet? How many copies of any papers are required?
- Is it necessary to have required papers translated? Must papers be legalized by the embassy before departure?
- Is quarantine required? If so, what facilities are available?
- Is there any duty to be paid? (This could be based on breed, size or something else.) When and where is it payable?
- Are customs facilities for clearance of pets open on Sunday or holidays? (Remember that Sunday is not the holy day everywhere -- it's Thursday in Pakistan -- and Washington's birthday and the Fourth of July are not celebrated outside the U.S. but the Lunar New Year and the *Fete de la Reformation* may be!)

- Is an official approval of documents or veterinary examination required on arrival? (Again, remember about holidays.) How do you make the required appointment for this? On flight day, have the airline telex or fax destination authorities to confirm the arrival of your pet and to have the proper person present.

It is preferable to take your dog or cat as accompanying baggage. This necessitates making shipping arrangements and reservations. A few airlines permit a very limited number of small pets in airline containers in the plane cabin. Most are transported in the cargo area. Airlines have kennel containers of various sizes. There is a charge for them. It may be possible to rent one but you don't know the health of previous occupants so this is not recommended unless you can obtain it in advance and clean it to your satisfaction. Request the kennel by the size of your pet. An Irish setter can't scrunch into an "average" size cage. Let your pet become accustomed to the shipping crate or kennel a week before shipping.

Your pet needs identification on its collar along with an emergency telephone number. Attach a card to the kennel itself with your pet's name, complete destination information, time when last fed, any sedation information and that emergency phone number. Telephone the transporting airline for their specific procedure and timing for putting your pet on board.

Water your pet just before departure but do not feed. Eating close to flight time can cause air sickness. Water can be put in the kennel. Do not tranquilize your pet without your veterinarian's approval and his recommended medication and dosage.

If your pet must fly separately from you, your veterinarian or the local SPCA can assist with the shipping to the east or west coast embarkation point. The American Society for the Prevention of Cruelty to Animals (ASPCA) has a shelter at Kennedy Airport for traveling animals. They can care for your pet during stopovers and can kennel dogs. Contact them for all their services and charges. ASPCA Animalport. Air Cargo Center, Kennedy International Airport, Jamaica, N.Y. 11430, telephone (212) 656-6042.

Remember to make travel arrangements so your pet will arrive on a weekday to avoid the possible problem of customs facilities not being open. This could mean no care, no food. If you will not be present when the pet arrives, make arrangements for immediate pick-up. Ask the embassy the arrival procedure when quarantine is required and make arrangements for the transfer of your pet to a local government officer or veterinarian. Forward all necessary papers to the officer or person abroad who will handle this.

FLIGHT RESERVATIONS

Make your travel plans as far in advance as possible. Use a travel agent knowledgeable in international travel. If traveling with an infant, tell the airline and they can reserve an appropriate seat and portable bed. Hopefully, you can schedule a few days of relaxation en route.
Reconfirm your reservations. Don't forget the one for your pet.

HOTEL RESERVATIONS

Hotel reservations should be made also as far in advance as possible to assure getting into the hotel you want. If you will have an extended hotel stay, this is very important. In your choice of hotel, consider such factors as proximity to the office or the school for your children and a downtown central location or one in a less busy crowded, noisy area. The latter may not be as convenient but offers a more relaxing atmosphere. If children accompany you, you may want to have a hotel near a park or one with a swimming pool, especially if it is a summer move or one to a tropical location.

Special accomodations such as adjoining rooms, a suite, baby crib or high-chair should be requested when making the reservation. If taking your dog or cat, ask if the hotel accepts pets and confirms this on your reservation. Ask someone in your company to reconfirm that everything is ready for your arrival.

You may need rooms for an indefinite period of time when your housing accommodations are unknown. Give yourself a long allowance of time in the departure date you give the hotel. They may be fully booked when you seek an extension and it's terribly inconvenient to have to shift your unpacked belongings unnecessarily.

When a long hotel stay is anticipated, you may want a kitchenette or efficiency accommodation to have the means to prepare a simple breakfast or lunch. This is especially desirable when small children will accompany you.

REGISTER WITH CUSTOMS

Foreign-made cameras should be registered with a U.S. customs office. If there is a local office, take your camera and all lenses there. They will record serial numbers and give you a copy. If this is not possible where you live, do it at the customs office in the airport where you will get the international flight. Keep a photocopy at home and carry the original with you, perhaps attached to your passport or in the camera case, whenever you are bringing the items into the U.S. This can prevent inconvenience and duty charges.

Other foreign-made articles taken abroad are subject to duty and tax on return unless you have acceptable proof of prior possession. Documents such as an insurance policy, jeweler's appraisal or receipt for purchase are reasonable proof of prior possession. Items such as tape recorders, binoculars, radios, stereo equipment and jewelry which can be readily identified by serial number or permanently affixed markings, may be registered at a local customs office before departing the U.S. If it is not possible to register them, be sure you take abroad with you receipts for these items. A telephone call to a customs office before you go will tell you which, what, where and how!

MISCELLANEOUS

In a very few countries presentation of your college diploma is needed to obtain a work permit. You can inquire about this from the country's embassy. If a spouse intends to work or attend university classes, a copy of the diploma and transcript should be taken with you.

Make copies of all family birth certificates and, if appropriate, marriage and divorce certificates. Know whether you need certified copies. These valuable documents may be needed in case of adoptions, birth of a child abroad, certain permit applications, etc. A naturalization certification may not be copied so special care should be taken with it.

If you are responsible for an aged family member, get his or her social security number, contact information for his or her attorney and name, address and telephone number of neighbor or family friend. Give that person information on how you can be reached abroad.

THINGS TO DO CHECKLIST

Travel Arrangements
   __passports __visas   __permits
   __flight reservations
   __hotel reservations

Pets
   __entry info from Embassy   __health exam   __inoculations
   __travel reservation

Household Items
   __household inventory completed   __photos taken
   __personal inventory completed
   __repairs completed
   __appliances cleaned
   __appraisals obtained
   __safe deposit box inventory made
   __foreign-made camera registered with customs

Medical
   __physical exams scheduled   __records/x-rays obtained
   __inoculations scheduled - self __spouse   __children
   __copy of prescriptions
   __dental exams scheduled   __records/xrays obtained
   __eye exams scheduled   __copy of prescriptions
   __second pair glasses

School
   __application made to new schools
   __records obtained   __physical exam report received

Lawyer Items
   __will updated
   __power of attorney
   __sale of house
   __guardianship letter   __sale of car

Accountant has all needed papers__

Stockbroker has all needed papers__

Driver's licence valid__   Insurance claim-free letter__

Insurance - all coverage reviewed for
   __medical   __life
   __household shipment   __storage items

Organizing the Details 63

PERSONAL INVENTORY CHECKLIST

A summary of personal information should be made and a copy kept in your safe deposit box. You may also wish to give a copy to your attorney or leave in a sealed envelope with a relative or with your company in event of an emergency.

Social Security Number

    Husband   Wife
    Children

Passport Information

    No.   Place   Issue Date   Expires
    H

    W

    Children

Birth Certificate Information

    H   Place   Issue Date

    W

    Children

Marriage Certificate

    No.   Date   Place

Naturalization Certificate

    No.   Date   Place

Car Information

    Serial No.   Registration No.
    Policy No.   Insurance Company

Driver License

               State or Country   Expiration
    H
    W
    Children

Credit Cards

    Company   Account No.

Insurance Policies

    Company   Policy No.
    Address
    Type of Policy   Expiration Date

Wills

            Date   Where Original Located

    H

    W

Lawyer

    Name and Address

Accountant

    Name and Address

Bank Accounts

    Bank   Account No.
        Address
        Type of Account (checking/savings)
        Single Name   Joint with

    Safe Deposit Box
        Located in

    Vault Storage
        Located in

    Safekeeping Account
        Located in

    Mortgage Loan
        No.   Bank

Stockbroker

    Company
    Address
    Agent

PACKING
AND MOVING

Moving is never easy, no matter how organized you may be. It's a time of change and inconvenience -- sometimes chaos! -- which involves breaking up the home, the unsettled transition period and the re-establishment of home in a new place. Make it as easy as possible for yourself and family with good pre-move planning. Your company may assist in many of the areas mentioned in this chapter. The items discussed are to alert you to all the considerations necessary to permit your shipment to reach you without problems. Check things off in the margins!

Before you start the packing process, learn the import restrictions of your destination country. An experienced mover should have the current information. If he doesn't have answers to your questions, you or he needs to telephone the customs section of the destination country's embassy. To preclude future shock and frustration, it's essential to know:

- What imported items are dutiable?
- What items can be taxed? (There can be a difference between duty and tax.)
- What items require a license? Ask the procedure and cost to obtain required licenses, such as for rugs, cameras, television, new fabrics for drapes, etc.
- What items are restricted in quantity? (e.g., appliances)
- What items are prohibited? (e.g., narcotics, pornography, gambling objects, religious objects, guns)

- What time restrictions are there for arrival of household goods following you into the destination country to be duty-free or untaxed? Can you bring in more than one shipment in the time limit (e.g., an air shipment and a sea one)?
- Is it required to take all items brought into the country out again?
- What documents are required for entry of household goods, such as bills of lading or insurance? Must they be original papers or are copies acceptable?
- Is an inventory required? If so, is the inventory of your mover sufficient? (They sometimes list "carton" or "miscellaneous" which may be insufficient identification.) Is a translation of the inventory required? before you arrive?
- Are serial or model numbers of electrical items and appliances required for customs clearance?
- Are there any papers which must be legalized by the embassy or consulate before your departure?

Most countries allow duty-free importation of household goods that have been used for a period from six months to one year prior to shipping. There are lots of variations, however. For example:

- Duty on certain items makes them prohibitive to import. Consumable goods, such as foodstuff and toilet paper, are subject to a tax and duty in Turkey as high as 300%.
- Pianos and antiques may be considered luxury items and have a high tax rate.
- Austria and Scandinavian countries require household goods correspond to the social and financial status of the owner.
- Brazil, China and the Philippines limit specific items to which a family is entitled duty-free, such as only one air conditioner, one television, one radio and one carpet.
- Germany requires a signed house or apartment lease before duty-free entry of household goods is granted.

Government bureaucracy and the requirements for documentation can be discouraging, even overwhelming. In Indonesia approximately 30 separate permits and papers are required before household goods can pass customs formalities! Sometimes an "expeditor" can take care of such technicalities for a fee. (Often it's a necessity!) Because entry requirements change without notice, in certain countries it's essential to hire a customs broker to get your shipment through the myriad of details.

An overall recommendation concerning whether or not to ship your household furniture and furnishings and appliances is difficult. Many people are happier surrounded by their own things; others prefer not to take the risk of shipping or they recognize a possible problem in a change from a dry, cold climate to a tropical one. Cost is another factor. Shipping an entire household is expensive but replacement is also, and the quality and style may not be as acceptable as what you have. The choice may be an individual one or it may fall within the framework of employer policy.

THE COMPANY MOVE

Moving has become a regular part of corporate life. Be sure you understand, beforehand, all aspects of the company policy for your international move: who pays for what, who insures what and for how long; what is the policy on taxes and tax equalization, on the sale of your home, appliances and cars, on relocation expenses, on school allowances for tuition, books and transportation; what can and cannot be shipped and the return move policy.

Many companies provide little guidance on moving other than the setting of maximum weight or volume allowances on household goods. The decision of what should or should not be included in the shipment is left to the individual. Moving with a company offers a better than ordinary chance of finding someone within the company who has lived in the assigned country who can offer suggestions on the move -- what to take, what not to take, what to expect.

Your employer, most likely, will have recommendations concerning movers. Companies who transfer a large number of employees are valued accounts by movers -- it means repeat business. You should expect and get good service from them. Any complaint should bring fast action.

On the basis of the answers you get when you meet with the recommended moving company and recommendations you can get from others, make your preference known to your employer. The cost estimate has to be a part of the analysis for the selection but hopefully your reasons and choice will be accepted.

Corporations who do a lot of moving of employees' household goods are often self-insured. In any case, verify that there is coverage from the moment items are taken from your home until they are in your new one, i.e., door-to-door. It should be all-risk, comprehensive insurance, with full value protection, without a deductible clause based on replacement costs for all your items. If taking valuable items, special insurance may be necessary and you should negotiate for complete coverage. Have adequate insurance for items put in storage.

You will need a record of moving expenses, with receipts, for your company and for U.S. tax purposes.

PROHIBITED ITEMS AND SPECIAL REGULATIONS

Moving company policy and federal, interstate and international laws forbid transporting certain flammable goods: matches, ammunition, paint and other incendiary matter. Transportation of plant life outside the U.S. is usually prohibited. Moving companies may refuse to ship furs, jewelry and valuable collections. It is not advisable to ship laundry detergents; many contain bleach, ammonia or harsh chemicals that can ruin fabrics (upholstery or clothing), if spilled or leaked. It also is not advisable to ship liquid in bottles, aerosols or candles. Damage can occur through breakage, leakage and melting.

All countries have entry regulations on specific prohibited items. These rules change so ask about the latest ones. Usually there are restrictions on importation of wines and alcohol. Amounts are sometimes limited, sometimes prohibited completely, sometimes taxed at very high rates. As stated above, it is dangerous to ship liquid in bottles because of possible breakage and damage to other goods. Also, liquor presents a pilfering temptation.

Tobacco is usually limited to small quantities. Narcotics are prohibited completely. Firearms and other weapons are also restricted items and if allowable will involve complicated procedures. Know regulations before you ship. For instance, an antique pistol with firing pin removed and which has not been used for over 100 years cannot be imported into Japan. Even a pistol-shaped toy is prohibited in Singapore.

Pornography is another restricted item. Different countries interpret pornography in different ways. Printed material may be allowed entry but the censor may obliterate offensive areas of pictures. In some African and Middle Eastern countries the bare arm or leg of a female is considered injurious to their morals and offensive to religious beliefs -- even in an art history book!

Trademark regulations restrict the entry of some goods which originate in specified countries. It is sometimes possible to remove the trademark and avoid a problem.

Know before you go! Each country has specific no-no's. Here are some unusual ones:

- Games and devices that can be used for gambling are forbidden in some Middle Eastern countries. Saudi Arabia and France, among others, prohibit importation of playing cards.
- India forbids importation of world globes and Singapore walkie-talkies.
- Britain won't accept duvets filled with feathers of certain disease-prone birds.
- Religious articles such as bibles, crucifixes, statues or material relating to religions other than the Moslem religion commonly are prohibited in Arab countries.
- Oriental carpets are forbidden in Brazil.
- All food items are quarantined when brought to Australia: packaged and canned items, baby food, fresh meat and dairy products.
- New Zealand and Ireland prohibit hay and straw and items going there should not be packed in these materials.
- Holland and France, while not prohibiting importation of gold and silver articles, require them to be packed and inventoried separately and subject to special customs inspections.
- Thailand, China, Greece, Italy, Germany and other countries restrict the export of certain valuables, antiquities and precious metals. Unless these articles are registered upon entry, and it can be proven the articles were imported by the owner, they may not be permitted to be re-exported.

THE MOVERS

Your mover should be experienced in handling international moves. At your home talk separately with at least two moving company representatives. You want a reliable company who is able to service and control the entire move from door-to-door.

Choose a mover who is well recommended by someone you trust and who impresses you favorably. It is unwise to make a decision based on a cost estimate.

The mover will have advice and helpful suggestions. And you will have umpteen questions! Your questions must be answered satisfactorily so you feel confident your belongings will be handled safely and unnecessary problems or frustrations are avoided. You need to know:

- What specific experience has the mover had with shipments to the country where you are going?
- Are there customs or security problems taking shipments into that country? Is payola or theft a problem in that area? If pilfering is a problem, can boxes be banded? Can you be present when the customs office opens containers or boxes?
- What specific papers will be required? (This could be a visa, a work permit, lease and/or residence permit.)
- What special handling will be needed -- crates for pictures, glass or marble tabletops? How will valuable items be handled -- antiques, silver, art objects, heirloom pieces?
- Can the mover "tropicalize" a piano, if necessary? (Or would it be better to sell or loan it?)
- Will he take up carpeting, take down drapes and rods, disconnect appliances or disassemble play gym sets?
- What recommendations does he have regarding storage of refrigerator, freezer, washer, dryer, microwave oven, television? If possible, you may want to "store" antiques with a family member or friend.
- Is air conditioned storage space available by the mover?
- How much time will be required for packing? Rather than have your house inundated with six packers each doing his own thing in a different room, request just two or three packers for a longer time so you can keep in touch with what is going on, make your own list of some box contents, watch as certain items are packed, check labeling, etc.
- Are packers experienced, regular employees and not daily hires?
- Are water and humidity-resistant cartons available? This can be important if moving to a wet or tropical climate where mildew can be a problem. These cartons are manufactured

Packing and Moving

with a heavy paraffin wax formula which impregnates the entire surface of the carton.

- Will boxes and furniture be containerized at your house or taken elsewhere for this? A lift-van pack at your house is recommended. An interim loose-pack into a truck means additional handling and chance for damage and loss before containerization.

- Are containers guaranteed to be waterproof?

- What shipping options do you have -- air freight or sea freight? (Conference line ships run on set schedules; other carriers are less expensive but may take longer.)

- When will household goods arrive at destination?

- How long will it take for clearance through customs after arrival? Does mover have a specific, affiliated destination agent "over there" to handle customs procedures and paperwork and supervise delivery and unpacking of shipment?

- Are storage warehouses available or could containers be left outdoors? Seaports, especially in warm climates, are notorious for allowing shipments to sit outdoors. If you will have a long wait to get housing, you may want to delay shipment so it will arrive as near as possible to the time you are ready to move into your housing.

- What insurance coverage does the mover have on your belongings? Is it on replacement value, weight or something else? Is there a deductible clause and if so, how much is it? All-risk comprehensive insurance may be expensive but it insures you for full replacement value, not a depreciated amount. The mover may be able to arrange this full coverage for you. You will need to supply him with a detailed inventory with values.

- What is cost estimate? An estimate will include:
    - cost of origin service (packing materials, time, local transport to port)
    - insurance
    - cost of air/ocean freight
    - cost of destination service (transportation from port of entry to your door, customs clearance, unpacking, setting up and location of furniture, removal of packing materials)

Port taxes, port handling charges, pier or warehouse charges, customs broker fees, transport from port to bonded warehouse and storage charges can be over and above the mover's charges.

- A written estimate should be given to you. What does estimate mean? What percentage of cost variation can be expected? How and when is final price determined? Domestic moving costs will be calculated on weight and value of household goods; costs for a transoceanic move are based on volume (cubic feet) and value.
- When and how is payment made?

When you have selected the moving company, get the name, address and telephone number of the destination agent in the new location.

June, July and August are the busiest months for movers. This means you must plan as far in advance as possible. This will assist the mover schedule your shipment to reach its destination at the time wanted.

BEFORE THE PACKERS COME

As preparations get underway and as the packing and moving days approach and begin, be alert to the apprehensions of small children. They have their own small traumas giving away pet hamsters and turtles, seeing disorder and household changes. Remember to make them a part of the move as much as you can. They can sort through playthings, check games to be sure all belonging parts are included then tape the box shut.

The packing aspect of moving involves much thought and many questions. What will be shipped, stored, carried with you, go air freight? The decisions take time and will involve cluttered living areas, organized piles, inconvenience and confusion. The more organized you can be for the packing days, the easier the unpacking and getting settled will be. The following suggestions are given to make these days as smooth and painless as possible.

In a move from Davenport to Dusseldorf you can expect some degree of similar climate. This would not be the case going from Minneapolis to Manila. With the humid tropical climate of the Philippines, heavy wooden and upholstered furniture, wall-to-wall carpeting and delicate antique pieces would not be appropriate.

Consider storage of some items if you are moving to an area involving a dramatic change. A fur coat is virtually useless in New Delhi. It is also an item very few people would have and therefore local commercial storage will be unavailable.

Find out all you can about the type of housing you can expect. If you move from a house in Houston to a high-rise in Hong Kong, you will need less furniture than in your split level with its eat-in kitchen, family room, guest room, basement and two car garage. You certainly won't need your lawn mower and play gym set!

Schedule your packing so you can have a few days in town after it is completed. If it rains on the day everything is to be moved into the van, you have some leeway to wait for better weather. And, a couple of days to catch your breath before takeoff will be greatly appreciated!

Getting Ready

There is no way to avoid the busy days and nights to get ready. Start as early as you can. Many aspects can be done far in advance of moving day -- the inventory, change of address letters, Salvation Army pick-up of unwanted items, etc. No matter how well you organize ahead, the last week will be filled with many things to be done. As you think about all the errands, the little cleaning jobs, small but annoying household repairs, consider hiring a neighborhood teenager to help a few afternoons or on a weekend.

Regardless of whether or not you are taking any or all of your belongings, a move is the time to do a complete housecleaning and reorganization. Start with the areas you dread the most -- the ones you've been meaning to get around to. After the hardest job is done, the other areas will seem a cinch! Do one room or area at a time. Then you feel you've really accomplished something. Ruthlessly attack closets, drawers, cabinets, room contents, the attic, basement and garage. Some things will fall into the sell-now-replace-later category. Worn out, outgrown, unused or out-of-date clothes should be given away or discarded. Don't put off this decision by moving them! Call your favorite charity and donate unwanted items. Ask for a receipt of valuation for the items as these amounts are tax deductible. Be ruthless also about cleaning out the medicine cabinet. Use masking tape to seal any bottles with liquid you absolutely must take with you.

Everything should be clean regardless of whether it will be shipped or stored. This means clothing, drapes, rugs, blankets, linens and upholstered furniture. A small soiled spot can grow mildew in a dark storage container very quickly and whether you are unpacking six weeks or six years later it is something you want to avoid -- yes, indeed! Consider the cost of cleaning versus discarding an article.

Make a note of rug measurements to attach to the clean, rolled (not folded) rug or jot the information in your moving notebook. This will tell you if it will fit in a new location without the cumbersome job of unrolling and fitting. Ask the cleaner to use a desiccant as he rolls the rug up to help keep it dry. If rug is to be stored, ask to have moth or camphor flakes sprinkled on it as the rug is rolled. Cleaned rugs should not be wrapped in plastic; if anything, paper.

Taking drapes with you? Have them cleaned before you go. They may be wrinkled on arrival but they have to be pressed when remade or rehung. This beats finding a reliable cleaner in the new location -- and that could be a big problem when you unpack in Reykjavik or Karachi. Remove any hooks before cleaning. Write with an indelible pen on the pleater tape "center right" and "center left." Also mark the tape to indicate where each hook is inserted. This will save you the awful misery of trial-and-error efforts to rehang them. Take a dozen extra hooks so, if needed, you can expand the area to be covered. Other countries may not have your type of hooks. This also means you should take rods for use with your drapes unless you can find out your type is available.

All appliances going with you should be in good condition as service may not be available or reliable.

Small and large kitchen appliances need to be cleaned before storing or moving. Washer hoses should be drained of water. The steam iron should be empty and dry. New appliances, and sometimes appliances that appear new, often are subject to high import duty so they must be taken out of factory boxes and used. Take brochures for the appliances you ship. They contain maintenance information and any pictures can be useful to household help. If a new appliance is needed, buy a "basic" one; it will be easiest to repair and easiest for domestic help to use. Think about all the options on a U.S. washer or dishwasher! The fewer decisions to be made the better!

Empty the refrigerator and freezer and thoroughly clean and dry it *at least* three days before it will be stored or packed. Use a baking soda-water solution to scour each ridge of all the rubberized gaskets as well as all shelves, drawers, trays, surfaces and corners, evaporator pan -- the whole thing! Drain icemaker and filter lines.

Charcoal has absorbing qualities which will minimize musty odors and help prevent mildew. Place about two pounds in an old pillow case or other porous cloth and put it in the refrigerator and freezer just before they are wrapped or crated. Dry coffee grounds and silica gel have the same ability but it takes a considerably larger quantity. You'll really have the caffeine jitters if you try to drink coffee to get sufficient grounds to be effective in your 17 cu. ft. fridge! Also, compare the price of a five pound can of coffee and a five pound bag of charcoal! All shelves, drawers and other removable parts should be wrapped and packed separate from the refrigerator.
If refrigerator is to be stored, have it packed so door remains ajar.

Before you decide to ship it, find out if your stove will match the voltage of the country or work on their gas. Rarely is this the case. You should not operate a stove through a transformer.

Clean garden tools. Because there is danger of pest infestation from soil left on shovels and the like and grass accumulated under lawn mowers, some countries require this cleaning -- Switzerland, Australia and New Zealand, for example. Lawn mowers should be emptied of gasoline and oil. Drain your garden hose, roll it up and pack or store in a plastic garbage can.

Certain items may not be available in your destination country. If your company regulations allow, stock up on whatever the "short" item may be: toilet articles, spices, coffee or educational toys. Your favorite toiletries will probably be more expensive overseas. Take along an oven thermometer, oven timer and smoke detector (and batteries for it), useful items that are difficult to find in some countries. When prepared baby food is not available, you may want to take a blender. American sheets are so varied and pretty and can be used in many ways: for window and shower curtains, bed covers, cushions, etc. Sheets are generally less expensive in the U.S. than elsewhere.

Take a good supply of basic clothing and shoes for children but don't overbuy. You might misjudge sizes and seasonal needs or your children may want to dress like their new friends. Regarding women's clothing, you may want to do some shopping depending on where you are going. Keep in mind that generally people are tall in Scandinavia, short in Spain, have fat feet in Germany and petite ones in Asia. If you have favorite U.S. shoe brands, have an adequate supply until you make a return trip to the U.S. Walking shoes, for any destination, are a must.

Do you do a lot of sewing? Along with your sewing machine, you may want to include patterns, thread and other sewing notions.

If going to a place where you will use a dressmaker or "sew-girl," include a pattern book. They make their own patterns, all they need is a picture.

Although the electric power may be different in other countries, it is perfectly possible and safe to use your vacuum, stereo, kitchen appliances (including refrigerator), sewing machine and electric tools with a transformer. The electric drill or mixer may be slightly less speedy and the electric knife may vibrate a little more slowly, but they can be used. If voltage is similar to the U.S. (110), the 60 cycles must be the same in order to use the electrical item without a transformer. An electrician can advise the correct size transformer to use with each appliance.

Consider the feasibility of purchasing household appliances "over there" if you know they will be available. GE, Whirlpool, Hoover and others are international manufacturers. This will eliminate voltage problems, heavy transformers and possible confusion by household help who are not familiar with imported ones. If you do take appliances and will use them with transformers, before packing make a list of the appliances and the wattage for each one (found on the plate with the serial number). You then can purchase the transformers soon after your arrival and have them in the premises when your shipment arrives. (See *Appendix* for approximate appliance wattage information.)

If you need to purchase a hair dryer, curling iron, travel iron or razor, get one with convertible voltage so it can be used with both 110 and 220 current. Almost all hotels have special dual bathroom electrical outlets for razors but few have them to permit use of dryers and other high wattage items. Many hotels have hair dryers and irons available for guests. Most can supply plug adapters.

There are advantages to purchasing a washing machine (and other appliances) in the new location:

- It may be more economical.
- You can be assured of service.
- Resale possibilities are good.
- You can obtain one that will fit the space available.
- U. S. washers have hot water inputs but connections may not be available and, if not, can be expensive to install. Non-U.S.-manufactured washers usually have a water heating element.

- In areas where washing is often done daily and a lot of it by hand, the typical 18 lb. U.S. washer may not be practical.
- Locally made appliances may be used more easily by local servants.

The phonograph turntable and tone arm need to be anchored. If moving to a country where the electric power is not 60 cycle as in the U.S., you will need a pulley adjustment for the turntable. This is also true for a tape drive. Have this done by a dealer before you leave. It will be more convenient to find one through your present telephone book Yellow Pages than in a new community where your brand of equipment may not be available or the telephone book is not in English.

A shortwave radio may be wanted if you will be in a non-English-speaking area.

A 110 volt electric typewriter will need a pulley change to handle cycle differences as well as a transformer for voltage adjustment. It is a simple job for a dealer to exchange the pulley. Keep the old one to reverse the process when you return.

Lamps can be taken. Proper wattage bulbs can be purchased in the new location and adapter plugs will enable your plug to fit existing outlets.

If taking a vacuum cleaner, take a supply of bags and a spare belt or two. Take extra covers for your ironing board and extra filters for your coffee maker.

When moving to a high altitude location, take along a cookbook for this situation. You will also want to include a pressure cooker, an extra safety valve and gasket rings.

Take batteries out of flashlights, radios, tape players and toys. Take salt out of shakers. This applies whether they will be stored or shipped.

Retrieve loaned out items -- the pie plate you took to the neighborhood party, the saw you loaned your brother, the bicycle tire pump the kids loaned a friend. Things being cleaned and repaired must be picked up. Return library books and other borrowed items.

Group similar things together as much as possible -- bed linens, decorative pillows, lamp shades, books, room accessories. There is less chance of a lovely tablecloth being packed with medicine cabinet articles if you do some preliminary organizing. It is also a help at unpacking time. You can delay unpacking some boxes until you are really ready for them.

Gather delicate and valuable objects in one place. The packers will give them special attention if you point them out and ask them to take particular care.

Before you pack any boxes yourself for whatever reason, check with the mover. Most likely, they will not be covered by his insurance. The mover will need to approve your packing or repack the boxes in order for them to be insured. Ask before you act. If you do pack any boxes, limit yourself to non-breakable items. For a summer move, a week before the packers arrive, turn on the air conditioning and leave it on until the packing is finished. Also use dehumidifiers if you have them. Dampness and humidity are the top causes of damage in shipping so do your part to have everything as dry as possible before packing begins. Along this line, do not wrap things in plastic. You may think it is good waterproofing; however, where there is a water problem such as a container being left outdoors in the rain, it is doubtful the plastic will help and humidity trapped under it can cause mildew problems. Delay the van loading if it is a rainy day.

Going to a tropical area? Could your shipment be held in storage for several weeks in summer weather? A few mothballs in boxes containing shoes, leather items and books can help prevent mildew. Spray the interior of chests, empty drawers and cabinets to guard against insects and even mildew. Vaseline on metal fittings before shipping or storage will help prevent rust. A small piece of camphor placed with silver items retards tarnishing.

As household packing day comes, you must make decisions about what you will take in your suitcases. Set aside, if possible, a spare room where all items to go with the family can be collected. Write yourself notes of items to be included and tape the list on the door or another obvious place. Don't forget clothes not yet returned from the cleaner or things still to be used that for some reason cannot be put in the room at the moment.

Try to pack so you will not have to open every bag at every stop en route.

Jewelry, stamp and coin collections, special papers and other valuables you will store or personally take with you should be put in a safe deposit box. Do this early, before the packers begin, so the items are safely out of the way and you aren't moving them from one place to another in the pre-move days. You won't have to worry about their safety or that they might be packed.

All U.S. airlines require an identification tag on the outside of luggage. Other countries may or may not require such tags so remember to mark all your pieces. How miserable it is to lose a piece of luggage. Put stick-on labels with identification information *inside* all suitcases and on those other pieces you frequently carry -- briefcase, carry-on cases, suit carrier, camera case, basic traveling purse, pocket secretary or travel folder with tickets and passports. Don't forget your eyeglass case and your child's carry-on. The address should be that of your destination hotel. Remember to update the address when you are relocated.

When you are taking most of your belongings but some are going in storage, have the movers come one day to take the storage items and the following day to begin the other packing. This lets you double-check all those things you want in storage are gone and you don't have to be concerned something will be misplaced. Make a list of stored items.

Your packers are professionals. Leave the dishes in the cabinets for them; let them disassemble the beds and take the pictures and mirrors down. You have lots of other things to take your time and effort!

Moving Without All Your Possessions

Perhaps you will take only a limited amount of your belongings. If going for just a couple of years you may want to look at it as a special experience, take advantage of what the country offers and not concern yourself with the worry of things to take. Perhaps your company's policy permits you to take only a certain weight allowance. If someone tells you to take nothing, saying "It's all there," *don't believe them*. You will have to do your own investigating and the best source will be someone who has lived in the area recently. Two factors need to be emphasized.

First, in order to feel at home in your new surroundings, familiar things are important. Although most overseas moves are limited to a few years, you want to feel "at home" and not suspended in a temporary place or camping out. Ask yourself, "What will make the new place like home?" The "things" will vary for each family. Maybe you will want paintings and family pictures, or certain books; another person will want special flower arranging containers or *objets d'art*.. The "things" may be ones you want to have with you or ones you don't want to duplicate because of cost, such as a typewriter or hifi equipment.

Along this line, as much as possible, you will want to be the same host or hostess as you are in the U.S. Take those serving items -- dishes, silverware, serving pieces, linens -- that will enable you to entertain in your individual way.

The second important point is to weigh those things you are considering taking. To be told you can take 600 kilos or 900 pounds is perplexing. You need to determine those things you "must" have and weigh them to know what additional "would like" items can be included in the shipment.

The pre-weighing must be done a couple of weeks ahead of moving day. Use a kitchen-type scale, not a bathroom scale if you really want to take full advantage of your allowed or self-imposed limit. A smart moving company will be able to loan you a scale of the proper type. If not, borrow or buy one -- it's vital to do the pre-weighing when you have a weight limit.

Set aside one room in your house and assemble the things you want to take in that room. Sort things into areas of (1) "must" go, (2) "would like" to include and (3) "perhaps if weight allows." And be sure you put everything in the room. Those tools in the basement that you're sure you will remember will be in storage before you realize you forgot to put them in the "to go" room. If there are items you need until the last minute, make a list of them, tape the list to the door of the "to go" room and be sure on packing day the items are included.

It's really impossible to weigh clothing and it really isn't necessary. Estimate clothing for two people will weigh 400 pounds. When the packers arrive, have them pack the clothing items first and weigh the boxes. You know how much weight you are allowed and having pre-weighed your other things, you will know how much additional can be shipped.

What to Take

After selecting and weighing the items mentioned above, you need to decide if you want to take dishes, silver, glasses, kitchen items, table and bed linens. Remember that sheets can be attractive and inexpensive as room and shower curtains, bedspreads and chair covers. Here are some thoughts to help your decision-making.

- Don't skimp on children's things -- they will outgrow the toys, books and teddy bears put in storage. Also, having these familiar objects in the new place eases acceptance of the change and unknown. If going to a developing country, you will want to take a good supply of paper and pencil activity books, crafts and games. Some new toys or books to be brought out when your children are having a "low time" are also suggested. They, too, will experience culture shock.

- Depending on your children's ages and on what you can find out about their schools, consider including an encyclopedia.
- Take an atlas and a dictionary.
- Unless you know cribs and playpens available in the new location will have lead-free paint, include yours in the things to take. (Also be aware that toys for your little ones, who seem to want to taste everything they play with, may not be decorated with lead-free paint.)
- Take a car seat for your baby or young child. This may not be available and to have one sent may mean a long wait and high duty. You may want to get the type that can double as a backpack and high-chair.
- If your family has been using the same bed pillows for 15 years they may not like initiating new ones. An orthopedic mattress for an ailing back may need to be included. Pillows, bed linens and towels may be expensive or limited in choice in the new location.
- Take favorite kitchen knives, cookbooks, special cooking dishes and implements, cookie sheets and muffin tins. If you will have household help and especially in a non-English-speaking country, cookbooks with pictures are useful.
- Liquid measuring cups with cup and metric gradations are available in the U.S. but not in all other places. A small kitchen scale with both ounces and grams will be useful. Take a measuring spoon set.
- Consider purchasing electric appliances "over there." For any you decide to take, include brochures.
- Use some of your cleaning cloths to wrap items you are taking. You need them instantly on unpacking and the few you include will come in handy before you buy or accumulate others.
- Wall brackets for shelving may be hard to find in some out-of-the-way place when you are not taking your furniture. Take a selection of brackets -- you can get some kind of shelves there.
- Catalogs from mail order companies you use, e.g., Sears, J. C. Penney or Talbot's.

82 MOVING ABROAD

- Get your special hair coloring formula from your hairdresser.
- Take traditional holiday items. For example, Jewish festival or Christmas decorations. (Your 110 volt tree lights can be used with a transformer in a 220 voltage area.) A live evergreen Christmas tree in Dubai is wishful thinking and you may wish to take one of the "evergreen" plastic type.
- Take a few basic hand tools.
- Your local telephone book is often helpful to have.
- Do not take:
    - light bulbs -- unless the country has 110 voltage.
    - electric clocks and clock/radio combinations -- unless the country has 110 volt *and* 60 cycle electricity. (They won't keep accurate time.)
    - an American television system - unless the voltage *and* transmission system are the same. Most foreign broadcasting systems are incompatible with the U.S. system.
    - video cassette recorder

Things to Take with You Personally

A carry-with-you checklist is at the end of this chapter. In addition to the special items to take personally, you might want to include:

- copies of insurance policies
- first aid kit
- measurements of appliances and large pieces of furniture (sofas, dining room table, buffet, dressers) to help you in house or apartment hunting
- non-electric travel clock
- bottle opener, knife for cutting fruit, cheese, etc. and can opener for use while in hotel. (A Swiss Army knife can be purchased with scissors, screwdriver, corkscrew, bottle opener and more!)
- enough baby food, diapers, formula and bottles for a few days immediately after arrival -- also, favorite blanket and toys.
- Be absolutely certain you have a copy of all pages of every document involved in the shipment:

- the mover's complete inventory
- your inventory of items shipped
- any required translations
- insurance papers
- receipt for unaccompanied baggage
- name, address and telephone number of destination agent (It should be on the mover's bill of lading.)

Storage of Valuable Items

Many banks have safekeeping vaults for valuable items too large for safe deposit boxes or that you do not want to put in storage or ship. Don't take with you special or valuable objects you cannot replace if lost or stolen. If you have inherited Grandmother's sterling silver, a pattern no longer made, this may be an item for the vault. Pack these items yourself in boxes, crates or perhaps suitcase. The bank will band your container. Yearly rental fees for space is small. Keep a list of what is there.

PACKING AND MOVING DAYS

Schedule the packing to allow several free days before your departure. An unexpected problem, such as rain, can be accommodated and you will still have a day or two to catch your breath and say goodbyes.

All packing, and unpacking at the other end, should be done at your residence. If at all possible, containerization should also be done at your home. Call the moving company the day before you expect the packers to confirm that everything is scheduled to proceed as planned.

The packing process means confusion. You will have to find the right balance between having your pre-schoolers in the house on packing and moving days and having a friend, relative or babysitter keep the children. If people offer to help you, let them. If you prepare children adequately, they may not object to leaving you and home when they know changes are taking place. It certainly will be easier for you to give full attention to the packers and all that's going on.

Be at the house all the time the moving people are there. Last minute decisions will have to be made and you can be sure what is supposed to go is packed -- and other items not packed by mistake. Usually the first day the packers come is the last night you stay in the house.

Just as you will appreciate a mid-morning and afternoon break, so will the packers. Suggestions you make to them go better with Coke or a cup of coffee!

Keep a couple of marking pens handy. You can code boxes for the room they should be put in at your destination. This helps greatly when delivery men at the other end do not speak English. You also can buy adhesive-backed tape in many colors. On the sides of cartons put blue tape for dining room, red tape for bedroom no. 1, yellow tape for kitchen, etc. You may want to make notes of special items in certain boxes. Use that moving notebook so all information is in one place!

Your possessions are valuable to you for many reasons. Experienced packers know and respect this. Tell them which items need special handling. If they seem careless and do not heed your requests, speak to supervisor in charge of your move without delay.

Crumpled packing paper in a silver chest and desk drawers will stop items from moving. Try sweaters or towels in bureau drawers.

Silver items should be wrapped in a soft cloth before being wrapped in the packing paper. If you don't have specific cloths you can use old T-shirts or soft cleaning cloths.

Pack one box with some basic needed-right-away-items for that first day: silverware, a few dishes or paper plates, skillet, paper napkins, cups, teabags or instant coffee, bed linens and towels. Mark it in a way it can be identified quickly. You might also include a clock, pliers and a screwdriver.

You will hear pros and cons regarding whether to ship clothes in wardrobe boxes or lying flat in cartons, on or off hangers. The moving company may have a definite policy you have to follow. In any case, consider these facts. When clothes are put in wardrobe containers, they must be squeezed tightly together with no room for movement to avoid dropping from their hangers and lying in a heap. If a wardrobe bar bends, breaks or shifts from possible pressure on it or the box, the clothing will be in a jumble. Pressure by hangers on some fabrics, such as suede, can leave an impression that cannot be released. There is a high potential for damage to fabrics when hangers are in the same box. Flat packs take less cubic footage.

As curtain rods come down, put the various support pieces and screws in a plastic bag and tape the bag to the rod. This is true also for shelf systems, dresser mirrors, headboards and side rails.

Boxes should be labeled in meaningful terms: kitchen, Tom's room, basement, reference books, lampshades, bedroom linens, etc. Avoid "miscellaneous." It's almost impossible to recall what things you included in such a catch-all category a week later -- or three years hence when the box comes out of storage.

All furniture and boxes will be inventoried by the mover and a gummed identifying tag placed on each. On the moving company inventory, the condition of your furniture will be listed. You should accompany the person doing the evaluation. If you are not there to comment, you will find that everything -- including the newly cleaned rug, two month old sofa and new end tables -- will be listed as SO, SC, F and W (soiled, scratched, faded and worn). Be sure you understand the conditions on the inventory you will be asked to sign. If you disagree with the condition stated by the mover, make a notation on the inventory page before you sign it.

If taking a limited amount of things and the majority will be stored, have the packers come to do only the packing of the items to be shipped on one day. The storage packing should be started another day. This will give you a chance to check that everything you want to ship is packed before everything starts to disappear at once. It also will give you half a day to do some of the personal packing for the trip.

Regarding the suitcases that will accompany you, pack these and as soon as possible take them to the hotel or motel where you will be staying before departure. If they are still in the house when the packers come, boldly label them. *Don't move* or lock them in a closet so there will be no confusion about them or other items you personally are taking. In the U.S. each airline passenger is allowed two checked pieces of luggage and one carry-on piece (with size limitations). There is no weight limit. If you have several pieces of luggage that must accompany you, check to see if it would be more economical for them to go as excess baggage or accompanying personal effects (at a cargo rate).

The loading of the van requires advance planning by the movers. Furniture and heavy items should be on the bottom. Tables should be placed with legs up. Void spaces should be filled or stuffed to prevent movement. Although you cannot supervise this aspect, watch as much as possible, at least on special items and when the van is being closed.

When everything is loaded you will be asked to sign a bill of lading. It will show the destination, date of expected arrival, declared value of items being shipped and the size and/or volume of the shipment. It should have a contact address of the destination agent and, if known, your future address. A copy should be given to you. The bill of lading should be in your name or the name of your employer as shipper. The name of a destination agent is not always accepted by customs offices and they may not accept title transference on a bill of lading. Your mover should be aware of such details.

You also should be given a copy of the insurance policy for your shipment before the van leaves your house. Check the valuation figure.

Read every line of all papers you are asked to sign. Understand the conditions you are asked to accept and the obligations you assume. You can write a notation on it if needed, e.g., I disagree with the condition description of furniture.

During those last hours when the boxes, crates and wrapped furniture are being put into the container, you may be able to do a little housecleaning. Leave cleaning materials for a last box or borrow them from a neighbor. Better yet, consider hiring someone to come the next day when the house is empty. It is so much easier to clean when you do not have to work around stacks of boxes and people coming in and out of every room.

If your house will be vacant for a while awaiting a renter or new owner, you may wish to notify police it is unoccupied.

EXPORTING A CAR

Obtain information and details regarding importing a car from the embassy of the country. Only new cars can be taken into some countries, only used ones into others. Some countries will not permit you to sell an imported car in their country. Import duties and taxes frequently are imposed on cars and they can be substantial (astronomical in Chile, where they are 340%). Duty can be determined on weight, horsepower or some other basis. Sometimes exemptions or lower charges are made if the car has been owned by you for a specified period of time. If it has been owned by you over a year, check to see it is possible for the car to be shipped as "household goods" and no duty charged.

You must have required papers, complete with required stamps of approval or consulate legalization, proof of ownership and insurance, in your hand before shipment is made. Prior to shipment, the condition of the car should be well documented, witnessed and the statement approved by you and the insuring company. Generally, cars are "stripped" before shipping to avoid theft, however, insurance coverage should include protection against pilferage as well as damage.

Make note of the car serial and motor numbers to take with you. Also, carry an extra set of keys with you.

Know what requirements your car will have to meet to be licensed abroad.

- Are the U. S.-required sealed-beam headlights acceptable?
- Is special equipment required -- new windshield wipers, seat belts?
- Must tires have certain treads or depth of tread? Are studded snow tires permitted?
- What are exhaust emission laws?
- Is steam cleaning of engine required? If you have this done prior to shipping, be sure you have acceptable certificate to show it was done within any required time limit.

It will be more convenient, possibly required, to take care of these items before you leave -- and most likely cheaper.

When your car may arrive at the foreign destination before you have gotten your local (foreign) driver's license, an international driving license may assist in clearing overseas customs.

Take a brochure of the car showing all technical data and specifications to assist clearance.

You also may want to take a repair manual and depending on the country, some of the ordinary spare parts such as fan belt, spark plugs, air filter, radiator hose and touch-up paint.

The often repeated know-before-you-go advice applies when shipping a car, motorcycle or motorbike.

PAPERS TO TAKE WITH YOU

Hand-carry:

___ Passport ___ extra pictures ___ negatives
___ Immunization record
___ Flight tickets

___ Jewelry and valuables

___ Copy of will(s) ___ Letter of last instructions
___ Birth certificate(s)
___ Marriage certificate
___ Guardianship letter
___ Divorce decree
___ Child custody documents

___ Power of attorney
___ Driver's license ___ Insurance claim-free letter
___ Copies of insurance policies

___ Travelers checks
___ Personal checks
___ Currency of the country
___ Bank books and records
___ Credit cards

___ Medical records ___ Prescriptions ___ Prescription drugs
___ Eye glasses ___ Prescriptions
___ School records
___ Diplomas/transcripts ___ employee ___ spouse

___ Address book
___ Pet papers
___ Personal address book
___ Receipts for foreign-made items ___ camera ___ other items
___ First aid items
___ Inventory of stored items ___ safe deposit box ___ vault
___ Pocket/purse dictionary
___ Travel clock

___ Moving papers:
    ___ mover's complete inventory & bill of lading
    ___ your inventory of items shipped
    ___ any required translations
    ___ insurance papers
    ___ receipt for unaccompanied baggage
    ___ name, address, telephone number of destination agent

ORIENTATION: PRE-MOVE AND AFTER ARRIVAL

It's Essential!

Orientation is the most certain way to make the international assignment successful for the individual and for the company. You need to know what to expect -- and what will be expected of you.

The culture of a country influences all elements of daily life. Background information is essential to understand the new ways of where you will be. Differences should be anticipated *and* you will need to develop respect for the differences without being judgmental.

The several indispensable phases of orientation are:

- **Corporate briefings.** These include the scope of the assignment as well as the policies and assistance for housing, medical needs, cost of living, taxes, schools, home leave, etc. -- the necessary details enabling you to accept the assignment and to make the move.

- **Pre-move orientation.** This equips you with the knowledge of why things are the way they are -- the culture, the history. Cross-cultural training prepares people for the differences they will face in every aspect of daily life and the impact on professional as well as personal lives. It gives positive steps to deal with possible problems in an alien culture. For the business person it provides an understanding of work practices so he can be effective and achieve maximum results for the company.
- **Language skills.** Communication enables you to cope *and* to feel like a belonger.
- **On-site orientation.** This offers practical assistance and information to make you functional, self-reliant and self-confident in your new home and culture.

All are essential!

MOVING ABROAD

AND

AND

Airplanes are marvelous in transporting us quickly from continent to continent. Unfortunately, the transition of individuals is not so quickly made. It's unreasonable to assume you can prepare for the international move and not be physically and mentally fatigued from all the details to remember and emotionally drained by the parting from family and friends. To be "here today" and "there tomorrow" leaves no time to adjust to the strenuous weeks you've been through and all that is ahead. Highly recommended are a few days of rest and relaxation somewhere en route to recoup and regroup.

The Flight

The second phase of your move -- getting from here to there -- is a short one. First comes the airline check-in, perhaps getting your pet to the cargo area and the security inspection before you board. These checks are made worldwide and can include personal inspection as well as x-ray and individual examination of carry-on items. (The security x-ray machines for hand luggage are not always safe for photographic film, especially high speed types.)

On any transoceanic flight, you will be shown how to use a life vest. Check to see yours is in its proper place. Special vests and instructions are provided for children -- ask for them. In case oxygen masks are necessary, put yours on first then one on your child. The same is true for the life vest. It assures the child it is all right if he or she sees mother or daddy do this. Also, you will be able to give full attention to the child if yours is in place. Wear the seat belt at all times when seated -- unusual, unexpected big and small bumps do occur.

Set your watch to the destination time early in the flight and think in terms of the new time. How easy it can be to sleep between Los Angeles and Tokyo, arrive in Tokyo at 8 p.m., go to bed two hours later and expect a good night's rest. Sleep or nap during the hours that will allow you to get off the plane and be somewhat in phase with your new time schedule. If you use a blanket remember to put it under the seat belt. Then, if you're sleeping and the *Fasten Seat Belt* sign goes on, you don't have to be disturbed as your buckled belt will be obvious.

Drink lots of water on long flights -- one glass for each hour of flying time is recommended. Because there is very little humidity in the plane cabin, your body experiences dehydration. Alcohol greatly dehydrates the system and should be avoided.

After the usual hurried last days before departure, you probably will rejoice at the thought of sitting six (probably more!) hours uninterrupted. Don't just sit. Walk the aisles occasionally; it's good for the circulation. Try not to cross your legs for long periods of time.

Ear-popping is a common occurrence during takeoffs and landings. For an infant, have a bottle available. Chewing gum can be helpful for children. If the usual swallowing and yawning techniques don't work for you, ask a flight attendant for help. They know other simple tricks to try to alleviate the problem.

On Arrival

Your arrival and the ensuing procedures may be very quick or the first test of your patience in the international arena! If there is an outbreak of cholera, typhoid or other health problems, authorities will require inoculation before entry is permitted and you must present proof of immunization. In a rare few countries an agricultural check is made.

There are three stages to getting out of any airport.

Immigration. Immigration forms (requesting name, passport number, destination, local address and reason for traveling) are usually distributed on airplane flights for completion before arrival. At the immigration desk your passport is checked and stamped. Your name is processed through the country's records as a person not sought by the government for any reason. There's no cause for worry. It's a routine procedure in almost all countries.

Claiming your baggage. Any air traveler has wild tales to tell about hours spent waiting for suitcases. Patience! Any damage to luggage must be reported immediately to the airline representative. Many international airports have carts available to help with luggage. Look around to see if people are using them and where they get them. Also observe others to see if the cart can be taken through the customs inspection to the transportation area. If not, porters are usually available.

Customs inspection. This procedure can be very simple -- a wave of the hand to go on -- or annoyingly bothersome -- opening every piece of luggage. In England, Switzerland and other countries there are self-determining red (stop, I have something to declare) and green (go, I have nothing to declare) exits. Spot checks can be made when you elect the green door. All too frequently there is no posting of what items you are supposed to declare. So unless you have found out in advance, make inquiries of an official to help speed you through the inspection lane.

Most countries have restrictions on tobacco, liquor, firearms and drugs. Many have additional regulations on plant life, food and books. Inspectors may ask how many cameras, watches, radios and how much foreign currency you have. Be prepared to open everything, answer questions (cheerfully helps!), show your passport again, present proof of onward transportation or financial sufficiency or guarantee of such by letter from your employer, squeeze shut those suitcases again and hoist the whole shebang back on the cart. You've arrived!

A bit of the local currency is immediately needed for transportation and tips. Remember to bring some with you. Airports have a money exchange desk or a bank where you can exchange money but what a chore to lug all the luggage, keep track of the kids and wait in line AND they may be closed when you arrive!

Some hotels have cars and buses to pick up their guests. Ask at the airport information desk about such services. The charge, if any, can be put on your hotel bill. Taxis, buses, airport limousines and rental cars are other obvious possibilities to get you to your hotel. When taking a taxi, ask the "starter" -- or someone -- the approximate charge. From Narita International Airport to downtown Tokyo by taxi is about $175! The bus is $25.

You may be required to leave your passport at the hotel reception desk overnight so it can be checked by authorities. This is a routine procedure.

Hotel Days

Few people arrive at their international destination rested and relaxed. After reacting to all the information and suggestions in the preceding pages, it could be considered impossible! Adjustments will start immediately so let's first consider some aspects of hotel living.

Unlike the U.S., in many parts of the world a service charge, usually 10% to 15%, is automatically added to hotel *and* restaurant bills. Additional tipping is not necessary in such places. If it is a country where tipping of service people is customary, bellmen and doormen usually are given a small amount for their services. Also, you can leave the small change (the nickel-and-dime variety) from meal bills on the service tray. If you will be in the hotel for a long time, it may be proper when departing to leave something for the maid or room boy. In a very few countries, tipping is prohibited or objectionable (for example, Yugoslavia and Japan). Consult a local information book or resident to find out local customs. Where permitted, tipping should be in amounts appropriate for the country.

In almost all instances the electric dual voltage outlet (110 or 220) in the bathroom is *for razors only*. Hair dryers and other items that require more power (i.e., higher wattage) cannot be used in this outlet. When in doubt about the current for any items, call the housekeeping department or reception desk and ask. If you have a hair dryer, curling iron or travel iron that works on 110 or 220, be sure the switch is set to the correct current before plugging it into a socket.

For any items with a different current than that of the hotel, ask the housekeeping department for a transformer. They also can supply plug adapters for your electrical items whose plug does not fit the wall outlet. If you will be a frequent traveler to various countries, you may want to purchase an "international adapter" so you have the convenience of being able to fit the plugs of your items into a great variety of outlets -- even the light bulb socket when all else fails!

Locate the nearest fire exit to your room. This should be done in all hotels you stay in during all your travels. Walk the route you would take and keep in mind it might be filled with dense smoke in a real emergency. Count the doors and make a mental note of anything between your room and the fire exit that you could identify if groping in the dark -- potted palms, radiators, chairs and spittoons!

Hotels can assist in obtaining emergency medical help. Many have baby equipment and babysitting service. Stamps (at cost, unlike the U.S.!) are usually available from the concierge or reception desk. Most countries have economical, self-stamped aerogram stationery just right for reasonable length letters to the family and friends "back there" who are wondering about you "over there."

Incredible surcharges are often put on long distance calls from hotel rooms. Ask, and avoid unpleasant surprises.

Telephone books throughout the world give more than just telephone numbers, for example, bus routes, postal rates or typhoon precautions. Almost all countries have directories with commercial sections, many with the familiar Yellow Pages. Check for an all-purpose emergency telephone number to call police, ambulance and the fire department. The number 999 is used in many European and other countries for emergencies. Usually a coin is not needed to call an emergency number. (In New Zealand and Australia, "down under" as it is fondly called, the number is 111! and water goes down the drain counter-clockwise!) While you are discovering what, how and where, why not call the American Chamber of Commerce, American women's or men's club and ask for their information for newcomers.

Did you bring your baby's silver feeding spoon and fork? Put them away immediately. It's too easy to put them on a room service table and forget them.

Things To Do

There are lots of things to do during your hotel days until housing is found, your shipment arrives and ordered appliances and furniture are ready to be delivered.

Read the daily newspaper -- several of them, if available in English. This will give you the broadest exposure to political concerns, what is going on locally and internationally. Want ads can be useful to find housing, used cars, secondhand appliances, language tutors and household help.

Locate a good book store. Undoubtedly, you will find books on your new country that were not available in your hometown. If you are in a country where food items will be different from those you knew in the U.S., look for food books with pictures to identify the local fish, fruits and vegetables.

Buy the most detailed pocket map of your new city available. The tourist-type distributed in hotels will quickly prove inadequate. Government tourist offices publish maps and they will be available from book stores and hotel newsstands (kiosks). Some maps will be so detailed they show buildings, one-way streets, street block numbers (even building and house numbers), walking paths, public transportation routes -- all helpful bits of information. The Michelin guides for many European cities and countries are outstanding in their content. You can learn to get around from just reading the map in your room -- from an alternate way to the office, to the shortest way to the license bureau, names of major boulevards and avenues, even the location of the opera house.

Tourist offices have complimentary brochures and sometimes weekly newspapers with information on local transportation, coins, restaurants and things to do. Pick up any of these to help orient yourself with your new surroundings.

Telephone the destination agent of the shipping company to give him your telephone contact number. In most cases, customs clearance cannot take place until the importer is in the country. Also tell him you want unpackers (and the number) the day *after* the shipment arrives. For some unexplainable reason, agents often are surprised by this request.

One of the first practical necessities is to open a bank account. If there is a U.S.-affiliated bank, most likely procedures will be familiar. Don't take this for granted, however. When you are told to sign the required cards and forms, it is assumed you know their bank procedures and information is not volunteered. Ask about minimum balance, writing checks, itemized monthly statements, return of cancelled checks, service charges and how money transfers are handled. If a U.S. bank is not available, don't let that slow you down but do ask about all of the above aspects. In some countries a husband has to accompany his wife in order to open a joint account; the marriage certificate may be requested. Additional information on banking is in the *Potpourri* chapter.

Visit the schools your children will attend and be sure all registration details are completed. If it's summer time, ask them for information on play groups, recreational centers, swimming pools and the like that your children could enjoy. Investigate play groups and pre-schools for your young children. Depending on the number of English-speaking families, availability and space may be a problem. Many an American mother has started a neighborhood play group to remedy such a situation.

Many countries require registration of foreign residents. (You might as well get used to the fact that, as unpleasant as it may sound, you will be called an alien, non-citizen, foreigner or expatriate.) Ask a government administrative office the requirements, time limits in which registration should be done and documents you need to present. Are pictures, of a specific size, required? What is the fee? In some cases, this registration or special permit is a prerequisite for obtaining a driver's license, owning a car or securing housing.

Register at the American embassy or consulate. This enables consular officers to locate individuals in the event of an inquiry from family, friends or business associates. Because of the Privacy Act, information will be made available only when authorization has been given by you. Registration enables the U.S. government to know the location of American citizens should there be a natural disaster or political emergency. In the latter case, the consulate will notify all registered citizens of the emergency and suggest steps to be taken. Registration aids you in obtaining a replacement passport if needed.

It can be convenient to get your driver's license while you are still in the hotel. The U.S. is one of very few countries where driving is permitted by individuals under 18 years of age. Before you go to the licensing office, know all the requirements. Read the detailed information in the *Getting Around* chapter also.

In addition to the obvious housing search, you can use hotel days effectively to inquire about applications for gas, electric, water and telephone service. Find out where local offices are for possible radio, television, road and dog (!) taxes. Make inquiries about insurance needs -- household, automobile and, if you anticipate having household help, workmen's compensation.

You can begin your search for sources of drapery fabrics, rugs, housewares and hardware. Just before moving from the hotel, shop for the household basics -- laundry detergents, paper products, cleaning items, salt, mustard and so forth.

Learn which post office will serve your address and register for delivery of mail. If you've been recently married or divorced, give all possible names that could appear on your mail.

In addition to tending to the necessary aspects of relocating, you will want to orient yourself to the city. Take that map in hand

and, where possible, start exploring. "Where possible" is taking into consideration the map is in English (and not unreadable characters!), and there is no personal safety problem. Getting lost (but only reasonable so!) is a good way to discover a new city. You will find English spoken at major hotels if you need help. Sometimes police speak English; sometimes they don't. It's a good idea to carry a card from the hotel to show a taxi driver in case you walk farther than (or stray from!) your planned exploration. Also carry your spouse's business card with his address so you have some identification as well as his telephone number.

Use buses or trams to get a view of the city and to help orient yourself. Follow the route on your map and mark it with notes about parks, markets, sports areas, etc. Get to know your city, its landmarks and neighborhoods! A visit to a supermarket and drug store will reveal familiar foods and items and certainly lead to the discovery of new ones and substitutes. When you have a delivery date for your shipment to your apartment (or flat!), notify the building superintendent and reserve the elevator.

While you're taking care of re-settling details during those hotel days, don't be so pre-occupied you don't take time with your family. A zoo is appealing to all ages. Parks and playgrounds give young children a chance to use some of the endless energy they seem to generate in a hotel room and are restrained from using by "shhh-ing" parents. A new set of crayons and pack of paper, chalk and lap blackboard, book or toy found on one of your discovery walks will help pass hotel hours. Make weekends a time to do special things with the children. The family unit is so very important and the all-consuming details involved in a move and new job should be put aside for some family activities. This helps the moving experience to be a positive one.

There are so many details to attend to! There is so much for both husband and wife to learn, discover, experience. Do take time out together to relax and share all that is happening. Get a babysitter, reserve a table for two and enjoy each other and all that's going on.

MOVING ABROAD

THERE

COPING WITH CULTURE: ADAPTING TO CHANGE

Living abroad -- anywhere -- is different from "home." How different will depend, of course, on where you are going. Some of the differences will be exciting and beautiful and some could be unpleasant or unsettling.

Each city offers new sights, smells and sounds. Not many Americans have seen bicycle-riding chimney sweeps -- with top hats, spiky brushes and implements -- as you can see in Zurich. Kodak film containers may now hold a personal treasure in the "pierced" ear of a Masai man in Kenya. Roasting chestnuts on a Paris street corner offer a pleasant aroma but this is not so of the durian fruit sold along Malaysian roads or the night pots on Shanghai curbs. You may be surprised to hear the *Tennessee Waltz* emanating from the Taipei garbage truck, a pleasant sound compared to the continuous honking of car horns in Istanbul.

Each country presents new insights and challenges. Each one has its own art and artifacts, traditions, values, manners, beliefs and laws -- maybe even superstitions, myths and legends. These are the recognized elements of culture. However, just as much a part of culture is understanding the people and what makes them "tick" -- what is important to them, what turns them off, what motivates them, what makes them comfortable and uncomfortable, how do they show emotion, how do they occupy their time.

Americans tend to associate culture with other countries and not their own. Yet we, too, have a definite culture and it varies depending on the area of the U.S. you call home. Your American assumptions, attitudes, patterns of behavior and patterns of thinking -- your cultural values -- will be obvious as you are introduced to and evaluate new ones. Living abroad requires an understanding of the new environment and you must view it objectively against your own cultural background. You will not be overwhelmed by the move if you anticipate differences and recognize you must cope with them.

Daily behavior from country to country can be affected by family honor, loyalty and other values, age, social class and its inherent education and occupation opportunities, sex and religion. Anywhere you live the variations in thinking, attitude and manner of doing things require investigation. The businessman needs to be cognizant of these factors as he presents a new marketing technique in India or Korea and the woman as she prepares to entertain a vegetarian or chopstick user. As many as 85% of the world countries are agricultural with considerable differences among them. Contrasts between the U.S. and Western Europe will appear minimal compared to other places. People moving to "the continent" generally feel comfortable with the thinking, the ways, the manners. Elsewhere differences and adjustments are much greater.

"Culture Shock" -- It's a Normal Part of Moving, Anywhere

A move within the U.S. usually means rapid friendships and easy assimilation into community life because of common customs, resources and language. The changes involved in an international move include alteration in everyday routines and schedules, lifestyle, manner of speaking, patterns of behavior, social expectations, social and job responsibilities, foods and eating habits and, most importantly, your network of relationships.

Culture shock is the impact of differences -- perhaps subtle, perhaps disturbing -- when you are transplanted to a new country. The familiar 'props' and cues of your surroundings are gone. Your natural, automatic responses are now wrong. It's "psychological disorientation," according to Kenneth Oberg, originator of the culture shock phrase. It comes as you find yourself amid unexpected, unfamiliar situations and try to handle them -- reading street signs, riding the bus, dealing with your new secretary or the servants, living with bureaucratic red tape, learning where to shop, bargaining for groceries, finding an dentist, etc. Each individual is affected differently and to different degrees. There's no need to feel unique; no one is immune from it -- even if you've lived in several other international locations. It's not a sign of weakness and no one should feel inadequate, abnormal or "guilty."

It takes time to get settled. Plan on six months -- or more -- until you are really "at home." Accept that the breaking-in period can be painful and it will reduce any self-imposed pressures and resulting stress and frustration.

Phases in the Adjustment Process

1. The Honeymoon

On arrival there is an excitement and enthusiasm toward the new adventure! It is natural to be attuned to the similarities and captivated with the differences. It doesn't seem as bewildering and unnerving as you expected!

2. The Honeymoon is Over

Then comes the period of disenchantment, disintegration and discouragement! It doesn't happen all at once. It's an accumulated response to all the "foreign" differences around you. All those enjoyable aspects of Phase 1 are now inconvenient, stupid, even threatening.

You can expect to feel a sense of isolation and not belonging, of impatience with the "locals," alienation and, very likely, a sense of depression. Surrounded by the unfamiliar and unpredictable, it is a time of personal upheaval and vulnerability. You feel the genuine loss of relationships, family and "things," perhaps it's only a telephone book in English. The feelings of loss of support and inadequacy are most acute as you work to establish your usual routine. It happens to the businessman at work, the children in school, the homemaker. Little day-to-day, mundane things become monumental and frustrating: communicating trouble, transportation trouble, babysitting trouble, shopping trouble, etc., etc., etc. This period of helplessness is difficult. Your energy -- physical and nervous -- will be drained.

The symptoms of this very negative stage can be *everything!* They're generally both physical and emotional: fatigue, nervousness, overeating, irritability, aggressiveness or timidity, tendency to complain and criticize, withdrawal from attempts at social contact, loneliness, feelings of superiority or inferiority, fear of being cheated, unreasonable obsession with cleanliness, longing to be "home" or wherever you were last, irrational anger, hostility at the threats to your self-identity, impatience. *Yes, just everything!*

It's absolutely the worst of times. The cultural differences are all revealed. You feel confused, alone and lonely. It's very easy to feel sorry for yourself -- don't! And don't stay home -- it's the time when you need to be with other people, which means initiative and effort on your part. You really will have to exert yourself when you don't feel like it. Finding things you like to do -- an aerobics class, computer club or whatever -- will give a feeling of continuity and people to do them with. Inquire if there's a newcomer's group in town and find out what's going on at the community church.

Fortunately, there are better phases to follow so don't get trapped here. Community resources are usually available to assist. If you need help, do get it.

3. Re-Adjusting

This is the period of acceptance and readjustment.

You don't break into an established culture strictly on your own terms. Your attitude towards the new environment must change to accommodate the differences. Don't set unrealistic expectations. Do something about any negative feelings. Most importantly, speaking the language increases your coping capacity.

Now you understand the "foreign" culture and why the local people behave and think they way they do. You can accept the realities of the new environment. Your self-confidence returns and you're able to cope with the differences. A suitable lifestyle again develops.

4. Back to Normal

The feelings of understanding and acceptance in the final phase enable you to appreciate your new culture and participate in it. The hostility is gone. Your enthusiasm is back -- as well as your sense of humor! You've made the essential adjustments! Friendships and personal sources of satisfaction have been found.

Expectations

Expatriate communities are usually family-oriented. This means the single person experiences greater loneliness than others and should be prepared for this. It's vital to find opportunities to be with people. Adjustment is greatly eased by having someone to talk to and ask questions of. A Chamber of Commerce interest group, fitness center, athletic activities, hobbies -- and a sense of adventure -- will be helpful. Hopefully, the families in your corporate community will be sensitive to your needs and quickly include you in their activities.

In a family international move, culture shock affects women more than men. For the employee the work situation is familiar; there is continuity in the job and a supporting office staff who insulate the physical adjustments; professional qualifications are readily accepted. The new challenges are exciting. Not so for the wife. The homemaker is frequently frustrated by the new challenges and all she is leaving behind -- family, friends, neighborhood, possibly job and certainly innumerable intangibles. The everyday routine is altered, sometimes dramatically, and she must establish a new identity, probably to all the people she meets. No one knows whether she has had a career, is a mother of six, served on the board of directors of your local symphony, is a horticultural authority or a master bridge player.

Often there is a let-down feeling when the house is finally settled and a period of loneliness when the children are absorbed in school activities, the husband busy with his work and new friendships not yet established. You must take the initiative to meet people. There is no need to be alone in any new country. All those "expats" you meet were once newcomers and undoubtedly you'll find friendly and sympathetic people ready to help you overcome relocation difficulties. The process of developing friendships will be discouraging if you wait for people to seek you out and entertain you.

Many people find setting personal goals aids tremendously in feeling better about their new location. Be sure to include a time limit for achieving them! These might be to study the language, explore local customs, find your way to the medical center, discover a way to play tennis, take an education course, develop a new interest or volunteer your services. There are many ways to belong and get involved.

Even if you're the kind of person who normally avoids clubs and organizations, in moving overseas it is essential to be outgoing and a "joiner." In addition to being a source of friends, groups such as the YWCA and community clubs publish interesting newsletters, helpful shopping sheets, service addresses, etc. Children and adult activities offer ways to meet people and make friends. *Get involved!* It's natural to gravitate to fellow countrymen because they understand you. It's comfortable and easy to rely on the American Club weekly bridge foursome or bowling team. Don't limit yourself to an American group, however. Instead, be imaginative and find ways to learn more about the country and meet its people. Most areas offer a great variety of opportunities: regional cooking classes, community service, art study, etc. In those instances where you are required to live in a "company compound," you will need to be especially resourceful to develop sufficient interests and a variety of friends.

Americans are accepted abroad generally. In a few places the acceptance is cordial. Don't be offended by what you may feel is indifference; the lifestyle in some countries is oriented toward family and home rather than toward neighbors and newcomers. You can be sincerely flattered when you are invited to someone's home, but don't let that stop you from inviting your neighbor for tea or coffee some afternoon.

Anticipate Adjustments

Adjustment means change -- and challenge. The following chapters deal with subjects requiring practical changes from your usual routine and ways. Here are some other typical challenges you may face.

- It's impossible to know or anticipate all the big and little frustrations you can expect in moving abroad -- finding a toothbrush holder in Bombay, full length mirror in Korea, seatbelts in Nairobi or baking powder in Montevideo.
- The "automatic" American household with multi-faceted telephones, computers, microwaves and VCR's is a far cry from two week mail service to the U.S., frequent power failures, non self-cleaning ovens, boiling water to purify it and unreliable telephone services.
- One's concept of privacy differs everywhere. A Chinese may ask how old you are, your salary and how much rent you pay. In other cultures it is improper to ask such personal questions (including asking them of a Chinese!). Political discussions are improper at certain times and places.
- Americans are accustomed to personal space around them and may not be prepared for close physical proximity elsewhere in conversations as well as being jostled by the crowds on buses and streets.

- The lack of independence for women is a major adjustment in several countries. They may not be allowed to drive a car, ride public transportation, go out alone and have to wear clothes that cover their arms in public. Moslem countries may forbid religions other than their own which can add a sense of frustration.
- The image of the U.S. by the local newspapers, radio or television will be different from what you are accustomed to from ABC, CBS, NBC, PBS, AP, UPI and *The New York Times*.
- Thanksgiving and July 4th will be working days unless you are in U.S. government service abroad. Christmas in tropical Kuala Lumpur by the backyard swimming pool contracts completely with the snowdrifts you know in Kalamazoo. (And you always swore you would never have a plastic tree!) This means you must work hard to keep special family occasions.

Importance of Language

The fact that you are a minority in your community is realized instantly when English is not the common language. You will always be an outsider but more so when you cannot communicate. Hearing a language with unfamiliar sounds and unrecognizable words certainly makes you feel isolated at a time when you can be trying to find alternate ways of doing nearly everything.

You must learn the language. Excuses of "don't want to spend the time" and "too old to learn" are inadequate. Ability to speak the host country tongue will enable you to be independent, a natural part of your pre-move life. Ability to speak gives emotional comfort and self-confidence and most of all, coping skills. Hostile feelings can be eliminated through understanding and communicating. Being able to communicate is the single most important aspect of the feeling of belonging and being "at home."

Knowing the non-verbal language of behavior patterns (body language) will help avoid embarrassing moments.

Don'ts and Do's

- Don't pass judgment too quickly -- you need time to understand.
- Don't complain about your host country. Negative comparisons and criticism will not be appreciated.

- Don't try to impose your values on someone else or expect people in the host country to think as you do.
- Don't insult or shock people by your behavior. You need to know their standards and be sensitive to them.
- Don't be rebuffed by impersonal attitudes. Friendships across cultures develop slowly.
- Don't wait until the house is settled to start meeting people -- getting psychologically adjusted is more important than being physically settled.
- Don't go "native," and don't call the local folks "natives" -- just as in Hawaii you don't say, "When I get back to the States....." -- you're there. In Mexico and South America, don't refer to yourself as American forgetting they are also.
- Don't keep talking about "back home" or "In the U.S. ....." Home is where you are *now* and it is an injustice to yourself and family to regularly refer to where you have been. It could imply you wish you were back there. Besides, many of your new friends also have moved and left familiar things and adjusted to the changes.
- Do be willing to compromise and adapt. Be a positive person! Don't surround yourself with negative people -- they're contagious!
- Do learn to accept and live with the differences -- no sense spinning your wheels. The country has a long established "system" that was going on before your arrival and will continue after you depart.
- Do share your reactions, problems, feelings and experiences. Challenges can be eased by encouraging friends, supporting partners and family.
- Do recognize stress symptoms and situations -- for yourself and all family members -- and respond with understanding.
- Do keep your cool. When you show anger, you and the "victim" lose face. If you shout at the taxi driver, he may never again stop for a foreigner.
- Do learn the do's and don'ts of the country -- from cultural customs to legalities.

Few people get bored with life abroad -- there is something new each day! Sometimes good, sometimes not so good! Once the moving-in miseries are forgotten there will be many good and memorable personal experiences.

Especially for Her

So many times the international assignment involves more business entertaining (time!) than you presently know. The culture of the country where you are located will determine how much. Most commonly, the spouse is not included. As much as you will miss your spouse's presence to share the hours and parental duties, recognize that these are part of expected business responsibilities. They are seldom social evenings, instead a continuation of business meetings and he is still "on duty" rather than having a relaxing time. In truth, he would prefer being at home with you for an informal, casual evening .

Business travel is not easy, certainly not restful. A lot of time is spent getting to and from airports, a lot of hours getting to and from destinations. A week's trip to Munich, Milan, Paris, London and home is obviously strenuous. (Where did the laundry get done?) The ten-day trip in July from Japan (summer) to tropical Singapore then Sydney (winter) probably involves a lovely hotel but lonely nights and full meals with associates and clients at least twice a day. (But there was time to get the laundry done and jog in the morning!)

The stay-at-home spouse will be challenged in fulfilling home and family duties. It's important to be understanding and supportive of your husband's obligations. Quite likely, there is a marked increase in your free time and it's essential to find a good balance of satisfying activities to fulfill your interests and occupy your time.

Especially for Him

Your arrival at the office is anticipated, everything is ready and there's assistance for all your needs. Your wife arrives and instead of being "somebody," according to the travel documents, she is "wife" or "dependent." That is not an easy transition. The brunt of settling the home in an unfamiliar place is hers while at the same time she is trying to establish her personal identity. That also is not easy. It takes time to get connected again. She needs your understanding and support.

International assignments often involve travel for the businessman. This can mean additional responsibilities and stress for the spouse. She is left to cope with the car that won't start, meet the arriving relatives at the airport, deal with a landlord problem and the unexpected emergency. She is perfectly willing to do all that is needed but sensitivity to her role will help greatly.

The overseas experience is rewarding in many ways. Most couples and families say the resulting closer relationship is one of the very best aspects. Communicating, sharing and understanding by each individual will assure the international assignment is personally successful.

HOUSING

As you would expect, housing varies worldwide, as do standards of living. Finding housing abroad very likely will be your first adjustment and compromise. Your choice may be limited by availability, budgets and costs. To avoid disappointment, don't go with preconceived requirements and glamorous ideas. It's far better to be pleasantly surprised.

A short time with a couple of real estate agents will show the typical housing you can expect as well as shopping and recreational areas, what driving is like, distances and traffic. All these factors will influence the decision on where to live.

There may be spacious houses on landscaped, private lots or high-rise apartments in a crowded city. It's possible in the Philippines to find space and gracious surroundings but not in Japan where land is very precious and the lifestyle very different. You may have to alter your thinking and pattern of living a bit to change from a house to an apartment or from a quiet suburban area to a traffic-clogged city. Americans are accustomed to many-room houses with the latest mechanical conveniences but housing in other parts of the globe may not offer the familiar entrance hall, built-in closets, eat-in kitchen and other features you are leaving behind. The change to an apartment can mean adjusting to hearing piano lessons being practiced, the aroma of a neighbor's dinner preparations or children's running footsteps (hopefully not tricycles!) overhead. Flexibility will be needed in many ways wherever you will be.

How to Find Housing

Companies may have current leases on houses or apartments and your choice may be stipulated or limited. You should be prepared, however, to do a lot of legwork and comparative shopping.

Ask business associates and others about rental agents they know, have used, liked or disliked. A good firsthand recommendation is very helpful when you are in a strange location. You want a competent realtor. Also ask for information and opinions on housing from other Americans who have recently been through the residence-finding process. You may get conflicting information but it is useful, nevertheless, in making evaluations.

- Know the company's housing policy and allowance.

- Before you register with any real estate agent, inquire about charges. Know who is responsible for the agent's fee -- you, your company or the lessee. A fee may be charged even if he doesn't show or find anything for you.

- Verbal contracts may be binding so seek competent advice before you proceed.

- Legal advice is mandatory before signing any agreement, contract or lease.

- Find out if the price a real estate agent gives you is a firm price. In some countries the rent the landlord asks is not necessarily what he expects to get and you can bargain. You also may be able to negotiate a trade-off -- possibly a renovation.

At first, look at all possibilities even though they may not be suitable, exactly what you had in mind or within your budget. You will soon learn how to evaluate descriptions by agents, which can be misleading -- the eat-in kitchen could be a counter for two and you have five children. Seeing all types of housing helps confirm the important features for you, the justification for rents and compromises you may have to make. Don't disregard a house because it is not in the area you think you want. The positive features of the house may compensate for its location.

Read newspaper classified ads for housing. Some will have special days for real estate listings. Consider placing your own ad. The grapevine can be a source of information of people leaving. Ask people at organization meetings, at church and when you go for school interviews. You also can get an input on rental agents, good and bad, and the general attitude on housing in the area.

Take a notebook whenever you look at housing. Jot down the name of the agency showing each place, the specific address and, in the case of apartments, the apartment number. Another agent may show you the same one or a different one in the same complex, and you will want to compare information. Take descriptive notes about house space, features you like and dislike. It is so easy to forget details after seeing several apartments or houses in one day let alone after a two-month search. Also, as you see other available housing, your ideas and wants may change. The notebook can save duplicate visits with different agents and your comments will help organize your thoughts about places.

Housing Considerations and Questions for Realtors

- How far are you from work? What is commuting time? Is a carpool feasible?
- What public transportation is available?
- What is the distance to schools? What school transportation is available?
- How close is shopping for every day needs? In many areas, food shopping is a daily procedure at local markets rather than large familiar supermarkets.
- Are children of your kids' ages nearby? Are play facilities available for young children?
- Does it matter if you are in a neighborhood with no others who speak English (if that is possible)? Because you live among the nationals, it does not mean they will accept you or that it is their custom or desire to get to know you other than a polite "good morning."
- Is there construction in the neighborhood that will present a problem (dirt, noise, workmen)?
- Is the electric voltage and amperage adequate or adaptable for your appliances (U.S. or otherwise)? Is there an adequate number of electrical outlets in each room? Is the power supply and wiring adequate to allow additional outlets?
- Is hot water heating capacity provided? This may be one unit or individual water heaters (known as geysers) in the kitchen, bathrooms and laundry area.

112 MOVING ABROAD

- Is the clothes washer hookup adequate? Is there hot water available or is it necessary to have a washer that heats its own water? Is power adequate for a clothes dryer?
- Who is responsible for electrical problems? heating? plumbing and air conditioning repairs? hot water heaters?
- What are approximate monthly costs for electricity, gas, water, heat and telephone?
- Is immediate telephone service available? Don't assume a telephone left in a house or apartment will remain. Connections can take months in some places so do ask for continuity of service.
- Are light fixtures, television antenna, curtain rods left in the house?
- What refurbishing will landlord do before you move in? Generally this is only painting of walls, polishing of floors and minor repairs. Will he repaint after two or three years? What freedom do you have to make renovations at your own expense?
- Does landlord provide a regular pest control program? If not, will he fumigate before you move in? Has house ever had termite problems?
- Who is responsible for exterior maintenance of plantings, lawns and flower beds? A landlord can arrange for upkeep more easily than the new occupant. What freedom does renter have to add flower beds or install a playgym?
- What is rent payment schedule? Is advance payment requested? If so, what refund obligation does landlord have? Can house or apartment be sublet?
- Are there government or other taxes in addition to monthly rental?
- Is a security or damage deposit required? a key deposit?
- Is there allowance for normal "wear and tear" or are you required to redecorate or return everything to the state it was when you moved in?
- In an apartment building what laundry facilities are available?
- What parking is available at apartments? Is a parking space included in the rent or is an additional fee charged?

- Is there an assessment for building maintenance for apartments? This could include such items as janitors, guards, elevator servicing and general upkeep.

Before any lease is signed it is recommended an electrician visit the premises to give advice on electrical capacity. It is especially important to have wiring checked by an electrician before installing large appliances. Old premises can present problems as they may not be wired to handle more than one major appliance or one or two air conditioners at a time on a given circuit.

"Unfurnished" will mean different things in different places. It may mean no stove, refrigerator, floor coverings, kitchen cabinets, light bulbs, light fixtures, curtain rods or towel racks. If a house is furnished, discuss the possibility of renting it unfurnished or partially furnished and rental adjustment. If you move into a furnished or partially furnished accommodation, a full inventory should be attached to the lease before it is signed.

When You Think You Have Found Housing

- Carefully inspect the premises and agree with the owner on any repairs to be made.
- An inventory with the landlord is a protection for you. This can include such items as keys, number of electrical outlets, damage spots, loose wallpaper, chips, cracks and scratches, broken windows as well as all items left in the house. The condition of everything should be listed so you will not be held responsible for something you did not do. You and the landlord should each sign and have a copy of the inventory.
- Check the reliability of water pressure by turning on a downstairs tap and observing if there is sufficient pressure in an upstairs bathroom. Flush toilets. If necessary, would the installation of a water pump correct any problem?
- Check heating unit.
- Look for any signs of water damage near windows or doors that would indicate leakage problems.
- All air conditioners and electrical items left in the premises should be checked to determine if they are in good working condition.

Maintenance items and repairs should be taken care of before you move in so the landlord is responsible for them. In many instances, once you move in all the problems and expenses are yours. Know who is responsible for what after you move in.

Window screens are unknown in some countries, and ones where you would think they would have them. If it's any comfort, those small indoor lizards keep down the insect population!

If you will be living in a apartment and have small children, you will be concerned about guard rails on windows. The landlord may have a solution to this problem so ask what is usual for the building.

Inquire if there are regulations regarding chimney sweeps or water heaters. Your fire insurance may be invalidated if you do not have required inspections.

A "Leave House"

Many people are reluctant to leave their house or apartment vacant for extended periods of time so they try to find someone to live in their home while they are away. A "leave house" or "leave flat" can be available for a few weeks or a few months. Many times it comes with household help, sometimes with a car and a pet! Hotel rooms are quite limiting after a week's time and to be in a normal house situation, fully equipped, is a great relief, especially when there are children. If you're having a difficult time finding housing or if you have a long wait until yours will be available, you might want to try a leave accommodation. Depending on your location, some real estate agencies specialize in this type of rental.

The Lease

Companies usually sign leases for their transferees and, if not, assist in the procedure. They must approve any lease before it is signed. If you as an individual are required to sign the lease, know your obligations. A lawyer should check your lease. Just as for a driving test, the lease undoubtedly will be in the language of that country. Ask for translation into English.

Always pay rent by check, not cash.

Does the lease contain a release clause with no penalty when adequate notice is given in the event of a transfer from the area? Are you permitted to sublease?

What is the cancellation clause of the lease? The lease may be renewed automatically unless you write to cancel or change it. One or two month's cancellation notice, *in writing*, may be required. Send any such letters by registered mail.

Before You Move In

Don't move in until the lease is signed by all parties. Don't move in until repairs, improvements and alterations agreed upon with the landlord are complete. If you move in and pay the rent, the landlord will believe you are satisfied.

As soon as you have found your housing and signed the lease, arrange for telephone service. Sometimes there is a waiting period and the sooner you apply the sooner you will have the equipment. There is always someone you need to reach, starting on moving-in day! It may be necessary to arrange separately for an international direct dialing account. A deposit is usual in most places. Wall connections may be sparse and until furniture is arranged, you won't know where you would like to put the phone. Ask about cord lengths; they can vary from 39" to 13'. If you request a long cord at the time of line connection, you can save money by avoiding a second visit to make the change.

Get the name, address and telephone number of utility companies (gas, water, electric) from your realtor. Ask if they can arrange for service. Advance deposits may be required. Be sure wiring is in good condition and gas supply is adequate. Request utility companies to check, before you move in, so it is the owner's responsibility to make needed repairs. Learn where fuse and meter boxes are and what to do in case of emergency. Are there special emergency numbers to call the utility companies?

Water heaters may have to be bought or possibly can be rented from the gas or electric company. For safety reasons, proper ventilation is required for gas heaters. Be sure you know how they operate and precautions about use. They should be maintained and checked periodically. Fire insurance may be invalid if not routinely inspected.

When you are in an area where there are other foreign families, it may be possible to buy a secondhand washer, dryer, water heater, stove, refrigerator, etc. from someone transferring elsewhere.

Unpacking

Your passport may be indispensable for customs clearance thus requiring you, as shipper, to be in the country when your shipment arrives. A work permit, lease or residency permit is required in some countries before release of the shipment. You may have to be present for the clearance, which can be at a warehouse or at your premises. If your presence is not required, get advice on whether it would be advisable and possible. Triple-check beforehand that you have all the required transportation papers, inventory lists (possibly translated) and other required documents to avoid delays and frustrations. It should be no surprise that all duties, taxes, service and storage charges must be paid before goods or shipment will be released or delivered to you.

Examine the shipping container carefully. If there are obvious damage spots or water stains, call the insurance agent and request his presence before the container box is opened and removed. He must be able to establish who is responsible for damage.

As individual boxes are brought into your house or apartment, check for obvious damage and to see if they have been opened. Check each item and numbered box against the mover's inventory sheets. Keep a list of any missing carton numbers. Furniture should be checked for damage as it is brought into the house.

As soon as household goods are delivered, shipping insurance is terminated. Make sure you have additional insurance so coverage is continuous.

To make it easy for yourself and the mover, have furniture and boxes carried directly to the room where they will be used or unpacked. If language is a problem, give a number to each room. Write it on a large piece of paper and tape it to the door jamb then stand at the entrance door, find the identifying information on each box and do your best with fingers or fumbling with the new language to tell in which room the box should be put. If you color-coded your boxes, workers can find the blue, red or black rooms identified by pieces of the same colored tape on the door jambs. Movers generally will lay rugs, put furniture where you indicate and set up beds.

When all the shipment is in your house, you may be asked to sign a delivery receipt. Be sure it is only that and not an acknowledgment for all your inventory or the unpacking. You must read the fine print on the pages you are asked to sign, delete or comment as necessary. If the papers are not in English, require a written translation before you sign them. Don't let a driver or moving company agent tell you signing a paper is only a formality. You may be signing a document saying everything is OK when you haven't opened a box.

Just as half a dozen packers can be overwhelming, the same is true of unpackers. Where do you put all the dishes, glasses, books, shoes, linens, nic-nacs, tools and clothes until you have dressers in place and cabinet shelves cleaned? Arrange for two or three unpackers so you can keep up with them and put things away. Make a list of any damage as you unpack and a notation on the inventory pages. The moving company should remove all empty cartons and packing material.

You may not want all boxes opened and unpacked immediately. Is the insurance valid if you do the unpacking? To protect yourself for items you unpack later, on the inventory sheet beside the number of the carton, write "subject to inspection for concealed loss or damage" or "condition at time of delivery unknown."

In some countries it is customary to tip moving men. Find out if this is (or is not) the case where you are and the proper amount. Give the total tip to the "chief" to distribute.

Know how to file a loss or damage claim and to whom to send it. What is the time limit for filing? Be sure *every* box has been opened and *everything* is unpacked before you file the claim. The moving company at the point of origin should receive a copy of any official claim and you should keep a copy of all related papers.

Keep customs entry papers in a safe place. You may need them when you depart from the country.

Settling In

Arranging your young children's rooms the same as in your former home will help give them a secure feeling. Let them help unpack their things. It will keep them busy and give them reassurance about the move. Then you can give your attention to getting the essentials unpacked in the kitchen, bedrooms and elsewhere.

A caretaker or concierge in apartment complexes can be most helpful those first days and weeks as you learn how various things are usually done. He often can give you the names of people to call for assistance. Ask him or neighbors about trash pickup days, repair services, nearest hardware store, household help, babysitters or a good produce vendor.

It's a great feeling to be surrounded by familiar things again. It does take time, however, to get everything arranged -- and rearranged! -- to make it home. Despite all the big and little things to be done, take time out and make weekends special. Plan an exploratory trip, maybe a hike and picnic, an outing to a nearby park or a new restaurant.

Just as soon as you **can** -- *note*, **not as soon as you are settled**, get yourself involved. This can be in a community group, church, language lessons, an activity for yourself or something for your children. It is up to you to take the initiative. Even if you are not usually a joiner, it's essential to discover ways to meet people and establish friendships.

Housing Miscellany

The company relocation allowances given employees are intended to compensate for many minor expenses, alterations and needs. These can include updating wills, new driver licenses, house cleaning when you move out and before you move in, remaking drapes and so forth. In addition, a foreign service incentive payment sometimes is given in recognition of the inconveniences and difficulties of living and working abroad. A common reaction is to hoard this money rather than using it to ease adjustments and to permit you to purchase familiar items. Everyone will be happier if you buy the coveted jar of peanut butter, a new chew bone for the dog and telephone the folks in Philly occasionally -- all within the intent of overseas allowances and benefits.

Regarding household needs, buy familiar items when you see them. Your favorite imported ones may not always be available. Cake mixes may be out when cream cheese is in. Depending on where you are, you may want to buy in quantity. It may be the only shipment of cheese for six months. (Many varieties can be frozen.)

Don't be shy about asking for an item you don't see. Americans are accustomed to self-service but other countries may have less sophisticated marketing and often little space. Not only may you find the wanted item you will also get language practice!

If you are told an item is unavailable, keep asking friends and acquaintances about it. They may have found it in an unlikely place or may be able to suggest a substitute. Get to know your local neighbors. They can show you many things you would not discover and give you insights only a local person can.

And you will have to learn to substitute. What you want for a dinner party may not be available. You may have to plan your menu *after* you go to the market. Imported food items are costly so you will want to try foods of the country as much as possible. It will save money and, better yet, the item will be available year-round.

Cuts of meat differ all over the world and this is a big adjustment for the housewife. Not only may you not recognize a chuck roast or eye of the round, but in Asia chickens are "chopped" into bite-sized pieces -- the familiar breast, leg and wing are unrecognizable.

Your daily food shopping may be at stalls or small shops, each one selling a specialty -- spices, fish, vegetables, dairy items. The absence of one-stop shopping at supermarkets and drugstores means much more time will be required. After a few trips to do the grocery shopping, you will learn whether you should take bags with you, wheel a little cart behind you or be prepared to pack your own items -- bring and bag!

Unlike the U.S., many stores, shops and service stations will not be open on Sunday, and perhaps not on Saturday. Learn the hours of the ones you will use and plan accordingly. It's so frustrating to dash out on an errand, arrive and realize the shop is closed from 12:30 until 2:30 and it is 1:15.

A few countries have dual voltage -- both 110 and 220 current. That can really blow your mind -- as well as your socket! Where this is the case, label all sockets with the information on power. Household help and children will need instruction -- and reminders. Take care not to overload electrical circuits which will result in blown fuses. Have extra fuses on hand for emergencies, however. See the *Appendix* for electric appliance wattage and transformer precautions.

Check due dates on utility bills. They will not be 30 days hence everywhere but "on presentation" or "within seven days." Late payments may mean quick disconnection, reconnection fees, fines and most of all, inconvenience.

If you purchase a clothes washer abroad, there are several factors to consider. Before purchasing, understand the spin cycle information. If a washer spins at 120 rpm rather than 750 rpm, it will take two days in the dryer for a load of towels. Washers that heat their own water can take as long as 90 minutes for the "short cycle." Washing programs may have 90 C. cycles (194 F.). This will make your dingiest car-washing cloths dazzling white and the size 42 T-shirt a size 10; perma-press items can be permanently destroyed after a cycle at this temperature! Know what your machine is capable of before you start a wash cycle. For dryers that cannot be vented to the outside, tie an old nylon stocking over the exhaust tube to catch the lint.

Ask for written estimates when renovations or repairs need to be made to your furniture or premises. You may want to confirm an order in writing. You will have a better chance for quality workmanship when repairs can be done at your home and you are present to make suggestions -- with a smile, of course.

When ordering custom-made furniture, get a copy of the order with all measurements and specifications. Attach the receipt for any down payment. Expect the finished item will take longer than promised. "Next week," *mañana* and "as soon as I can," are easier to accept if anticipated. Don't accept anything that does not meet your original specifications. Insist it be redone or your down payment returned. If you can express your exasperation in a pleasant way, you have a better chance of getting it done the way you want.

While you are trying to decide what furniture to purchase or if the waiting period for ordered items is a long one, a couple of big plants will make voids in a room less obvious as well as give an established and comfortable feeling.

Interior walls in one location can be wallboard and in another cement block, stucco or wood. Before trying the hooks you brought with you that might chip the paint or crack the wall (or seem to bend the hammer!), see if there is a local variety for hanging pictures and wall decorations.

Regular fumigation is necessary in some areas, especially tropical ones. Pesticides and poisons may be stronger than ones you know. Take special precautions, especially when there are pets in the family.

If your new area experiences periodic loss of electricity ("brown-outs") or water, set up an emergency contingency plan.

A neighborhood watchman who supposedly checks to see your gate is locked at night, rejects unwanted salesmen and performs other guard duties is common in Brazil and other locations. He sometimes is part of "the system" and it is better to join in than fight it.

CHILDREN

In an overseas move, parents and children typically spend a lot of time together. A close relationship develops when you rely on each other and share learning about your new country, its ways and customs. Your attitude is everything! It, and your emotional state, will greatly affect how changes are accepted.

Many things will be different for your children. The personality of some will permit them to fit in without a moment's hesitation. For others, parental support and understanding will be needed to ease and speed adjustments and help them master apprehensions about differences.

- Your children may blend unnoticed into a European city and other parts of the world but there are countries where they will "look" different. This may cause feelings of uneasiness.

- If moving to the Southern Hemisphere, school may begin in July and end in March. This can be hard to accept when you've just finished a school year in June.

- Children may have new freedoms and restrictions. Your nine-year old will be offered wine in an Italian restaurant and your 12-year old can buy beer in Germany, but your teenager cannot drive in France, and elsewhere, until he is 18.

Over-protection can rob children of the fun of exploring and discovering. Because they are more carefree and daring than over-anxious parents, children often will try the public tram or bus system before you and order nasi goreng at the hotel coffee shop -- just because it's different or sounds exotic!

Parents need to be understanding of the possible stresses for all ages. Everyone experiences culture shock to some degree at some time. Talk with your children about it, what it is and its causes -- missing family, friends amd familiar things, new manners to learn, new language, new school, new social life, new expectations.

Encourage children to express their concerns and anxieties. Continuous communication, including the expression of negative feelings, is essential. The negative attitudes should be analyzed and action to remedy them instigated.

Make time to be together; it's essential. You'll never really be able to know how your children are handling, coping or feeling if you try to communicate on the run.

Individual country courtesies will be different, but anyone living in a foreign country is expected to conform to the social courtesies of the country -- whether you feel like it or not. A good rule is to observe how people behave; act accordingly and you will not be embarrassed. Children need to be aware of correct manners for the country, especially what can be offensive -- from loud voices to style of dress. In many areas, relationships and accompanying "protocol" are more formal than in the U.S. For instance, handshaking is expected, by children as well as adults, on meeting *and* parting in many countries. The behavior (good or bad) of children is a reflection on parents, the parent's corporation, on the United States and fellow Americans, and it should reflect favorably on all. Being a "goodwill ambassador" is far better than being an "ugly American."

If you live in a city, there may be no neighborhood as it is known in suburban America with friends, playmates and a play area readily available. The family as a social unit must compensate for the absence.

Almost always in a family overseas assignment the father has business commitments and trips taking him away from home for short and long periods. Fathers must take time for children -- for the children's and the mother's sake. The papers in the briefcase can wait each evening until you've read a story to your little ones -- and certainly on the weekend while you help coach the Little League team or attend the school fair. Togetherness is important.

Mother is the lightning rod of the family, the shoulder to lean on, the stable "something." Communicating and sharing with your children is so essential. Those first weeks, at least, be at home when they arrive from school and ready to listen to what has happened that day. "Boy, is David stupid," is often an introduction to a frustration. Talk openly with your children. Participation in the PTA and the mother's club, attending school dramatic productions, athletic events and other programs enables you to meet parents, and students, and learn more of what is going on. Get involved! School is the "community center" for your adolescents so give it your support.

Finding activities should receive "top priority" attention and the kids may need your encouragement.

- Investigate YMCA's and YWCA's for programs, craft and swimming lessons.
- Indian Guides and Scout groups offer activities.
- Music, dance, art and photography classes may be started or continued.
- Collecting stamps or coins are "naturals" when living abroad.
- Go places. See things. Whenever you take small children to a museum, the zoo, park, shopping or other such outing, plan a meeting spot in case you get separated. You may find it hard to describe your child in a foreign language to a sales clerk, museum or park guard but the kids can find the kiosk selling popsicles or popcorn at the main entrance door if pointed out ahead of time.

Young Children

Young children who are adjusting to a new environment may cling to mother and not want to let her out of sight. Mother is security and they are asking for reassurance. "Can't you see I'm busy?" will not be understood or accepted by a toddler surrounded by unknowns. As quickly as possible, establish a familiar routine for eating, exercise, play and sleeping. Look for similarities in your new surroundings -- from squirrels to playgrounds or an ice cream parlor. Familiarity brings confidence. Spend extra time playing and reading with them. Plan ways they can meet other children.

Play groups and nursery schools provide good group experience. Investigate all possibilities and enroll your little ones. Neighborhood children may be in school already and the lack of available playmates makes children at home more dependent on mother for entertainment. A nearby play-school often will introduce your children to playmates. Once a "buddy" is found, it won't be long until your four year old will be trading tricycles with his new friend down the street and wanting to invite him to his birthday party. Families frequently meet their neighbors and benefit from the friendships begun by their pre-school children.

It can be easy to start pre-school children in a local nursery or kindergarten. They are at an age of easy integration, are uninhibited and learn words and phrases quickly -- unlike adults who only feel secure when their sentence structure, verb tense and pronunciation are correct! If children then go on to public school you may need to supplement their English reading so they will be able to integrate into U.S. schools when that time comes.

School Age Children

Public schools may be impractical or impossible for older children as classes will be in the local language and fluency is necessary. An intensive, several month program to learn the language sufficiently to integrate would be required. For teenagers you also must ascertain that academic requirements for entry into U.S. universities or colleges will be met.

The mobility of corporate families means international schools have high attrition rates. Some classes have 30%-50% turnover. Students are accustomed to accepting newcomers, much more so than will be the case on the return move to the U.S.

Wherever your children are enrolled, ask about medical emergencies and first aid procedures. If a child has a medical problem such as asthma or an allergy, it is important to write a note with appropriate information and emergency instructions to be kept in the child's file and nurse's office. Also, give the school an emergency telephone number in case they cannot reach you at home. This could be the father's office or you could have a reciprocal arrangement with a friend or neighbor to help each other in such circumstances.

You can help ease the transition to school by visiting the individual teachers of your children. Be frank about academic, health or emotional problems your children may have. This is the time to ask what is expected in classes and the common areas of adjustment to the new school.

Regrettably, but realistically, discipline and drug problems are universal. How are discipline problems handled? What drug and alcohol problems do exist? You want to be alert to social problems that can affect your children. It's essential to discuss these matters with them.

Show your interest and concern in the happy integration of your children by meeting again with their teachers after a couple of weeks. Don't wait for the mid-year conference time; you want to be ahead of any problem situation. Is the child's class placement correct? Has he made good social adjustments? Is tutoring necessary or advisable? Tutoring not only can help academically but also can bolster a child's morale. Discuss the strengths and weaknesses of your children as both of you see them. Discuss interests and see if there is a related activity that hasn't been found yet. Getting off on the right foot can preclude later problems.

Encourage children to participate in familiar activities. The weekly school newspaper may need your daughter with her writing skills and the band may need your son's musical talents to expand the trumpet section. It's an ideal way for them to make friends and to feel they belong. The same will be true when they move to another place or return home. Being involved in the newspaper, band, dramatic group or whatever offers immediate entry possibilities. Sports are an excellent way to meet people. The possibilities for familiar competitive sports often are not available overseas; however, it's an opportunity to try something new that may not have been possible at a former school.

When language study is not a required subject, encourage (insist, if you can) your children to take any available classes. For older children an introductory course on the history, religion and government of the country is also recommended. Being able to talk with the people who are neighbors and knowing various aspects of their culture will make them feel more comfortable, give an additional dimension of understanding and offer opportunities for friendships.

Teenagers

The teen years present the hardest period of adjustment. For teenagers who are already experiencing physical changes and emotional stresses, moving is an extra complication. Many of the problems resulting from a move lie in transferring personal credentials. Your teenagers will be leaving established relationships, the accompanying prestige and empathetic friends. Be alert to signs of problems: sloppy habits, loss of self-respect, non-acceptance of the different cultural values, moodiness, depression and withdrawal, which can take the form of academic under-achievement, cutting of classes, no after school interests, disruptive behavior and poor family relations.

Getting Ready for College from Abroad

When your child enters 10th grade, it's time to think about college entrance requirements, SAT and achievement tests. These tests are given at specified centers in many countries overseas. You may have to travel, however, to a different city than where you live. U.S. bookstores offer quite a selection of practice and coaching manuals. These are especially recommended if your child is not in an American-affiliated school. *College Entrance Guide for American Students Overseas*, available from College Board Publications, Box 886, New York, NY 10101, has helpful information.

When submitting college applications from abroad, work closely with your child's school to be sure all required transcripts, tests and documents are sent before deadlines. Non-U.S.-affiliated schools may not have guidance counselors familiar with application packets. Your follow-up may be necessary to assure everything needed arrives on time.

Rewards

The overall rewards and benefits for children living overseas are many. They will mix with and learn from the people of their new home country as well as meet other nationalities through schools and groups. The exposure to other cultures broadens adaptive skills as well as increases understanding and tolerance.

Opportunities to travel increase geographic knowledge. History becomes more real when you actually have been to the Tower of London, East and West Berlin, the Acropolis, the Great Wall of China, Corregidor and the Yucatan. Visits they may make to Kenya, Katmandu, Machu Picchu, Bontoc and elsewhere will really put them into settings -- and cultures -- very different from Western ones. In addition to family jaunts, most schools plan excellent reasonably-priced trips during school holidays. (Wouldn't you enjoy tagging along on a ski week in the Andes, to the Loire Valley's chateau country or pony trekking in Kashmir?) Even your young school-age children will impress you in later years with their recall of knowledge gained by such exposures. Teenagers, especially, capitalize on their international experiences. They develop self-reliance and are more secure people with realistic views of the world. Carry-over friendships develop and it is truly recognized that "it's a small world!"

LEARNING MORE LANGUAGE

Forget your inhibitions about speaking and begin at once using the language skills you've acquired. Most people will be understanding -- and helpful -- when they hear you try to use their language. By reading the menu you can gain more vocabulary from your first day in the hotel. Many will have an English edition and you can use it in conjunction with the one in the local language -- provided, of course, the language utilizes a,b,c,d, etc!

When there is a long transitional hotel period, start language instruction while someone else is making the bed and preparing the meals. The need to handle daily necessities commences immediately after you leave the hotel. Begin your lessons early!

Until you know how to get from here to there, don't worry about counting to a hundred by fives! You want to learn the meaningful words and expressions for everyday situations. It's the practical, conversational language knowledge that will enable you to ask directions to get around, make appointments, buy food from the local market, instruct the barber or the household help and talk with the repairman. Feeling able to cope in routine situations will decrease the isolation and frustration associated with lack of communicative skills.

Second to the daily "working" language, learn the pleasantries of conversation that will let you greet neighbors and chat with the green grocer. This will show your interest in being a part of the community and will be recognized -- and appreciated -- by the people with whom you meet and talk.

Whether you are the host or guest, you also want to feel comfortable in social situations. In many areas of the world, men speak English but wives have not had the opportunity for language lessons. It is always awkward -- miserable, in fact! -- only to be able to wear a smile and nod your head unknowingly for a whole evening. You will really feel the "foreigner."

You can help yourself in several ways in addition to formal instruction.

- Memorize useful shopping phrases: how much, where is, how do I, etc. But you also have to be ready for the answers! One ingenious person took a Sears catalog with her to Geneva and memorized the phrase, *Qu-est-ce vous avez quelque chose comme ça?* When she went shopping she clipped a picture of the wanted item from the catalog, showed it to the salesperson and asked her memorized question which translates, "Have you anything like this?" What a great idea!

- Listen to people talking -- on the bus, in the market, the neighborhood children -- anywhere!

- Scan newspapers and magazines.

- Listen to the radio and watch the television, if you have one, especially the news and weather and support your interpretation with confirming information from newspaper reading.

- Make your shopping list in the new language.

- Use a dictionary to prepare to handle situations such as a plumbing repair, instructions to the gardener or a trip to the dressmaker.

It's important to remember also that English may be a "foreign language" to the person you are asking a question. Speak slowly. Ask a *simple* question. "Where is the drugstore?" It should also be a *single* question. "Is the drugstore on this street?" will enable you to be understood and to find one more quickly than, "Is the drugstore on this street or is there another store nearby that sells toothpaste?" Negative questions always cause confusion and should be avoided. "You have sandpaper, don't you?" and "This is the way to San Jose, isn't it?" are examples of perplexing questions to a person with a little knowledge of English. Either could bring you an affirmative *or* negative answer!

Use simple words when you are trying to communicate with someone who understands only a little English. You also will find sign language and synonyms helpful, for example, ladies room, loo, lavatory, toilet, rest room, comfort station, W.C.!

Everywhere in the world people tend to move or shake their head in agreement with someone talking. (In India the soft rolling of the head from side to side means yes, not no!) It's human nature. This may mean, "Yes, I agree with you," or "Yes, I hear you -- but, I don't know a thing you're saying!" You may be able to tell whether you are understood by the facial look, the reaction or response -- or the lack of reaction or response!

The world is fast becoming a do-it-yourself place as you can realize from supermarket shopping, ticket-dispensing machines for public transportation, coin-operated machines for stamps and coded ones for banking matters. Nonetheless, as an outsider and newcomer you need to be able to communicate in the everyday situations of living in a foreign country and you want to feel comfortable with what is happening around you. Not being able to communicate creates a barrier and is a major frustration, one you can avoid by learning the language. It will do so much for your confidence if you can cope. It will avoid any feelings that you are being cheated, and you will be recognized as a participant not a stranger. Start your language lessons early!

Body Language

Facial expressions, hand gestures, touching, posture, eye contact, displays of affection, smiles and laughs -- all are ways of communication and the interpretation of each varies greatly depending on where you are. Winking, blinking, nodding, waving, pulling the ear, crossing the arms -- outside the U.S. these all may have meanings different from ours. Body language is subtle but carries profound meanings. It's important to know what you are saying without speaking!

Many books are available on the customs and manners of individual countries. *Do's and Taboos Around the World*, the delightfully entertaining book by Roger Axtell, is a wonderful introduction to international communication. In addition to its "international gesture dictionary," you'll learn about customs and etiquette as well as our American baffling jargon and idioms.

THE EXECUTIVE ABROAD

Cultural Understanding

Understanding cultural influences and proper business approaches are essential for effectiveness and success in an international assignment. Occidental and oriental manners and customs vary tremendously. The American businessman frequently greets an associate with a hearty handshake, a friendly pat on the back and an invitation to join him for lunch. All three of these gestures are improper in other cultures.

How do you learn the cultural language of business? Read all you can before the assignment begins. A professional pre-departure orientation program may be required, definitely beneficial and certainly recommended. Debrief in-country associates and those who have recently returned. Sitting down to listen and talk to someone with expertise is much more complete, efficient and interesting. It's important to learn the specific do's and don'ts so you won't offend. For example:

- In Mexico, Japan and many countries of the world, getting right down to business is not done. Personal rapport comes first.
- In Holland, as soon as a guest arrives he is offered some type of refreshment. It is required politeness to accept and take a sip of the offered drink. You can request tea or coffee if you prefer them over something alcoholic. In the Middle East it certainly will not be alcoholic but perhaps boiling hot tea in a tall glass!

- When invited for a business lunch or dinner in Finland, business is not discussed until after the coffee is served. In all countries it is best to wait for your host to bring up the subject of business. Often it is truly bad manners to mix business with social times.
- In Arab and other Moslem countries, the left hand is considered unclean as it is used for bodily functions. It is therefore offensive to give or receive things, particularly food or money, with the left hand.
- Throughout Asia, physical touching can deeply embarrass -- from a well intended assist to avoid a safety hazard as you cross the street to the intended compliment "job well done" and accompanying pat on the back.
- In some countries, the form of greeting may be other than a handshake (a bow in Japan, hands folded in front of chest in Thailand, etc.). To imitate a national or religious gesture is improper. If the person is acquainted with Westerners and knows a handshake is customary, you may find a hand offered to you. Always wait to see if a woman initiates the offer of her hand. Keep in mind that a Moslem man will not shake hands with a woman.

The businessman's greatest challenge is learning and understanding new values. Patience, tact and flexibility are required many times as you deal with different cultural traditions and beliefs while establishing cultural rapport. Recognize national sensitivities. Don't judge other nationalities by American standards and don't try to change people to the American way.

Religious influence is powerful in most developing countries and it is essential to know religious customs.

- Throughout the Moslem world Friday is the holy day; Saturday and Sunday are work days.
- Religious customs influence eating habits. Be aware of these when inviting someone to join you for a meal at home or in a restaurant.
- Some religions forbid alcoholic drink.
- In Indonesia during the several week Ramadan holiday, it is a period of daytime fasting. During fasting periods it is rude to offer food, drink or tobacco and you should avoid taking these yourself in public view as much as possible.

Most importantly, learn the work attitude and the way things are done in the countries where you are doing business. For example:

- Countries with warm climates tend to be less aggressive in their business approach. Many have a lack of concern towards punctuality, from being late for a meeting to a promised delivery deadline. You may have to learn to live with the *mañana* of Spain or the *bukrah* of Saudi Arabia.
- Faults sometimes are attributed to Fate (what will be, will be) or even a deity (Allah or otherwise).
- Nepotism is common throughout much of the world. And it can be the efficient way to get something done. It can affect everything from hiring practices to filling purchase orders. Uncle Pedro may be the fastest way to get the office air conditioning system repaired. Kinship can be as important as religious beliefs.

Communicating Effectively -- Verbal Language, Body Language

A cultural approach is needed in daily work situations and especially in problem-solving. As you get to know your associates and the people with whom you do business, you need to explore many aspects. How do they view discussions? Is there free exchange of divergent thoughts? What techniques persuade? How veiled is disagreement? How do they give and receive criticism? What embarrasses them? Do you have to work through people who arrange things? Is payola a usual part of doing business?

Stop -- look -- and listen. Observing people gives great insight. Every culture communicates through unconscious non-verbal behavior. Body language is "spoken" by eyes, hands, feet and posture. What do facial expressions mean? Is eye contact essential, shunned or embarrassing? The eyes are most revealing: do they show boredom, excitement, shock, irritation, lack of understanding? Notice the way others greet people -- their superiors, their inferiors, the importance given to protocol, hesitations and expressions. What gestures are acceptable? unacceptable?

The ability to listen is a crucial element in international business. This skill enables you to know what is going on beneath the surface. People unknowingly reveal themselves through overtones, omissions, evasions and emphasis. All are signals requiring interpretation. This is an important factor in dealings with employees and with clients.

Listen also to silence. It can mean disagreement, displeasure or lack of understanding. Asian people do not like to give a negative reply. To disagree can be a breach of etiquette, therefore you may get silence or an oblique answer. Courtesy is more important than a clear response. It is known as "saving face." This is a cultural difference and not a means of deceiving or being evasive.

Oriental people have a natural poise. They often remain comfortably silent. In many places, loud voices are offensive as well as embarrassing. The American compulsion to talk (too much and too loudly!) should be avoided.

Accustomed to making quick, independent decisions, the American businessman can be considered rude by such directness. In Asia he will find business negotiations are not accomplished quickly. The Japanese, for example, will discuss a subject, get everyone's viewpoint, take a consensus and then make a group decision -- not in one meeting but many! -- a slow and annoying procedure. Patience and respect of their sense of timing is needed. Visible annoyance will gain nothing but loss of face for you. In some countries an intermediary (go-between) is customary. The American may judge this as inefficient unless he understands it is part of the cultural structure of doing business.

Learn the subtleties of the language so you can communicate knowing the other person's thought patterns.

Unless you have full comprehension of the language and its innuendos, an interpreter may be needed in business meetings. Brief him or her in advance. Let him know the purpose and goals of your meeting. Speak slowly and distinctly and without superfluous words or slang. (Not only difficult to translate, slang is easily misinterpreted.) Use short sentences, pause frequently allowing time for translation and reaction to your statements.

In the U.S. a great deal of business is conducted by telephone. In most other countries, however, face-to-face contact is required for all but the most routine business, at least between equals and with those of higher rank.

The informal mannerisms of Americans will not always be understood by your staff or secretary. Your sense of humor or kidding may not be comprehended and therefore misinterpreted. Sarcasm, jokes and joke-telling are often misunderstood.

Introductions, Business Cards and Titles of Address

The protocol of business introductions often necessitates having another individual introduce you. A desired meeting can be possible by pre-arrangements through your office or other business people with whom you are in contact. U.S. banks and Chambers of Commerce located worldwide can be valuable contacts for these introductions. The Lions, Rotary and Kiwanis clubs in many international locations are helpful for meeting local people as well as other American business people.

When introducing yourself, always say your name slowly and distinctly. Repeat it if you detect a difficulty in understanding. Personal names in many countries are quite different from Western ones. Whenever possible, get the names of people you will meet beforehand. Seeing names in writing aids pronunciation.

In Asia, the Middle East and elsewhere, it is usual -- and helpful -- to have your name, title and other information translated into the national language on the reverse side of your business card. Present your card with the local language facing the recipient. Handle a presented card respectfully -- don't stash it quickly in a pocket.

Professional titles and education degrees are important in many locations. In Germany, for example, Klaus Mueller who has an advanced degree is addressed as *Herr Doktor* Mueller. In Latin and South American countries, professional titles are used in addressing a person, such as *Licensiado* (lawyer) Gomez. Russian names have varying degrees of familiarity (for example, Ivan Ivanovich, meaning John, son of John) and you need to use the proper one. In England medical doctors and dentists are called Mister. Until you know or if in doubt, use Sir or Madam.

Wait until you are addressed by your first name before calling another business person by a given name. In Switzerland this may never happen! Even if men call each other by the first name, it is still proper to address a woman with Miss or Mrs. or its foreign equivalent until asked to do otherwise -- and maybe even then to continue with the more formal, respected prefix.

Time and Timing

Business appointments are expected to be made several days ahead in some cities. An impromptu call the day before is improper. It can be considered discourteous to change plans at the last moment. In Europe you are expected to arrive at the agreed appointment time. To be late is sometimes unavoidable but in England it is very bad manners. In South America being late is expected.

Learn if you immediately start with business or whether there is courtesy "small talk" beforehand and whether refreshments should be offered.

Lunch in hot climates may be two or three hours and it truly is a time to relax and not appropriate for business. In Granada, Greece, Guatemala and other hot climate countries, it is usual to go home to one's family for the main mid-day meal.

The American occasionally meets an associate for business over breakfast. In Europe, and elsewhere, this is not only out of order but considered an invasion of privacy.

Entertaining

In many countries entertaining most often is to establish a rapport and sense of trust, not to pursue business matters or make a sale. It can be discourteous to discuss business when you are a guest in someone's home or when you are the host.

Know about times on invitations. Are you expected to arrive early or promptly at the time stated? If you are the guest of honor special things may be expected of you, from toasts to promptness of arrival to the timing of departure. In Japan, Jakarta and elsewhere no other guests will depart until the guest of honor leaves and that will be early by U.S. standards; in other places he is the last to depart.

For dinner invitations if there is any doubt, ask if the wife is or is not included. Men-only entertaining is the norm in Japan, the Middle East and elsewhere. Club entertaining in England is almost always done without the wife.

Business Etiquette and Customs

In almost all European and Asian countries, it is proper and expected to see business guests to the office entrance or elevator.

The style of business dress varies worldwide, however, the business suit as Americans know it will be seen in many, many countries. Certainly in Europe and northeast Asia, the business suit (lounge suit as it is called in Britain) is required. In warmer climates an open-neck shirt without tie is acceptable with, and probably without, jacket; in Singapore a "safari" suit is worn by many men; in the Philippines the "barong" shirt is the cool way to do business.

Before You Travel

All countries have their **special holidays** -- some religious, some national, some traditional. When making a business trip, check beforehand to see if there is a holiday which could unexpectedly prevent your making the desired contacts or appointments. Ongoing travel reservations possibly can preclude rearrangement for a meeting after arrival.

Necessary **visas** must be obtained before entering a country. Some visas require a passport to be valid for six months beyond the intended departure date. It is usually possible for your travel agent to obtain visas.

A copy of your **itinerary** should always be left with your spouse: flight times, hotels with telephone numbers, including the international country dialing code. Emergencies occur infrequently but how traumatic if your 11-year old needs an unexpected appendectomy and your spouse doesn't know how to get in touch with you. Trying to get information from a telephone operator not fluent in English under regular circumstances is difficult and in an emergency exceedingly frustrating.

When you **exchange money,** check to see if you need to save the receipts. Some countries insist on seeing these before they will convert local currency to another one.

Learn the **gift-giving customs** and prohibitions of the countries you will visit. And know the policies of your company concerning gifts to and from foreign business associates. Most companies have rules about not receiving or giving gifts over a certain amount be they for you or a member of your family. National customs require gifts to foreign hosts be carefully selected. For example, in China a gift of a clock is associated with death; in Rio de Janeiro, a gift of handkerchiefs suggests you wish the recipient tears.

If you are in a country where **personal security** or political stability is questionable, know your company's emergency plan. On arrival in the country, visit the U.S. embassy or consulate and seek their advice and recommended precautions.

Your business traveling may require occasional **car rental.** Know if your personal or company driving insurance coverage is adequate or accepted. In New Zealand, for one, insurance policies other than those issued within the country are not valid.

> The frequent business traveler will be helped by having a "traveler's checklist." The sample one in the *Appendix* can be modified for your personal use.

BOOKS FOR THE INTERNATIONAL BUSINESSMAN

Managing Cultural Differences, Philip R. Harris and Robert T. Moran. 2nd ed. 1987. Gulf Publishing Co. These distinguished authors discuss the impact of culture on managers and business operations.

Going International, Lennie Copeland and Lewis Griggs. New American Library. 1986. Written by the producers of the award-winning Going International film series, this book gives advice on developing the strategy, style and sensitivity needed to succeed in international business.

The Economist Business Traveller's Guides. The Economist Publications. Prentiss Hall Press. A series of guidebooks for individual countries covering important aspects for doing business internationally: the political, financial and economic scene; business climate and framework; business etiquette and cultural awareness.

Do's and Taboos Around the World, Roger Axtell. John Wiley & Sons. 1985. An entertaining study on human behavior. It gives an understanding of cultural differences and nuances from protocol, customs and etiquette to body language, American jargon and baffling idioms.

The Traveler's Guide to European Customs and Manners, E. Devine and N. Braganti. Meadowbrook. 1984.

The Traveler's Guide to Asian Customs and Manners, Kevin Chambers. Meadowbrook. 1988.

International Business Gift-Giving Customs, A Guide for American Executives, Dr. Kathleen Reardon. 1981. Stanford University Dept. of Communication, Stanford, CA 94305-2070. $8.50.

GETTING AROUND: TRANSPORTATION

PUBLIC TRANSPORTATION ABROAD

Excellent public transportation is available in most world areas. Buses, trolleys, taxis, trains and ferries are abundant, safe, quick and cheap. Extensive subway systems can be found in Stockholm, London, Vienna, Tokyo, Hong Kong, Singapore, Caracas and elsewhere. Car rental agencies service many countries.

Tourist bureaus are a source of maps, routes and timetables. They can assist with answers about getting around.

How do you get a taxi? By hailing on the street, by standing in a queue or by telephoning? Is there an extra charge for this? Are taxis shared? It does happen in Istanbul and Mexico City, among other places, and you certainly would like to know this before your taxi door opens and several people pile in. How do you get a private taxi?

Waiting at a bus stop doesn't mean the bus will automatically stop for you. Learn -- by watching what others do -- if a hand signal is necessary. Several buses may utilize one stopping place. How do you know the bus you want stops there? How do you know the fare? Is exact change required? Are advance tickets or tokens used? Is a monthly pass available? Is there a transfer system? And how do you signal you want to get off -- pull a string? push a thing? and where is it? Is there a bus route map -- in English?

Local laws and attitudes regarding traffic offenses and accidents can make it unsafe or impossible for a foreigner to drive. Find out about accident responsibility laws. You may be in a country where a minor automobile accident can be a criminal offense and you are guilty until proven innocent, the reverse of the U.S. You may not be able to drive but need a driver. Other reasons for having a driver include traffic congestion, parking, costs of cars and their upkeep, insurance and risk of leaving a car parked unattended. In some countries it is expected that foreigners will have drivers. Consideration of all factors will let you know whether or not you will have a car and/or if you will drive.

DRIVING ABROAD

New traffic patterns, unrecognizable street names, international road signs, "priority of the right," a high density of bicycles, public buses and trams are all part of the transportation adjustments you can expect when you move abroad. In addition, driver temperaments and personalties will vary from reasonable to unbelievable to downright dangerous! Each city and country has its own driving "style" and mentality. The best way to cope: drive defensively. To do this you need to:

- be a considerate driver,
- be able to stop your car in time,
- keep control of your car and
- know how to handle driving emergencies.

This will enable you to handle errors by pedestrians or other drivers, poor road or weather conditions and unexpected traffic situations.

Inquire if there is a manual of car regulations with driving and traffic rules in English. The government may publish a booklet with this information; perhaps there is a commercially produced one. If the local driving test is available in English this can be most helpful. From reading driving instruction pamphlets and local regulations, but mostly from observation, you will become aware of the local driving peculiarities.

Getting a Driver's License

Getting your license can be as easy as sending someone for it or as exasperating as spending a full day yourself, shuttling between

various windows and offices. Before running off to get a license, know the requirements so you can save time and frustration.
- Is your passport, identification or alien registration card or residence permit needed?
- Does your valid U.S. license need to be translated into the local language? Must translation be certified? A consulate usually will do this for you, if required.
- What is the fee? Is cash required or a check acceptable?
- What size picture(s) is required? Must glasses be worn in the picture if normally worn?
- Is a medical examination or certificate required?
- Is an eye test required? Can it be given at the licensing bureau?

In most places it is required to have a license issued by the country where you reside. Undoubtedly it must be obtained within a specific time period particularly if you are permitted to obtain one by showing a valid license from another country. The international driving license is not an accepted license for a resident of most countries. Don't let your license expire. Renewal may not be possible without a very difficult test -- written, road or even mechanical. And, as in the U.S., the written test will undoubtedly be in the language of the country you are in. How's your Swedish or Portuguese?

The teenager who got his license in the U.S. at 16 will not be allowed to drive until he is 18 most everywhere else. Do renew the license in the U.S. if possible so that at age 18 it is valid and can be presented to obtain the foreign license without tests. In some countries there can be long waiting lists for mandatory driving instruction and then long waits until the required written and road tests are given. For example, in Hong Kong where the government wants to discourage additional cars on the road, these waiting times can be up to a year for the instruction and then a several month wait for the very difficult tests, which are usually failed the first time.

A time limit for notification of change of address is a common regulation. It can be from three days to a month. Know the law to avoid a possible penalty.

Registering a Car

A car dealer or motor vehicle agency can give you information on the requirements needed to register a car. Registration will be required within a specific time. Ask whether registration papers and/or insurance papers should, or should not, be carried in the car. If required in the car, make a photocopy to keep at home. Ask about any required plates or permits. European countries require a sticker designating country of licensing -- E for Spain, GB for England, CH for Switzerland, D for Germany, etc.

Read the registration document. It can contain information on number of passengers allowed in the car, inspections and renewal schedule. Reminder notices for re-registration rarely are sent -- you must remember.

Insurance

Adequate insurance is essential. Almost universally, car owners are required to carry third party liability insurance. Local authorities may require a minimum policy. In Europe an International Green Card is issued to show you have the required insurance coverage. This card is kept in your automobile. It is necessary for crossing the frontiers of many Western European countries. Always check the latest regulations before driving into Eastern European countries.

Insurers in some countries offer a substantial policy discount for prior claim- and accident-free driving periods. You will need verification letters from previous insurance companies to be eligible. It is best to obtain these before departing from the U.S.

Ask if property damage insurance is compulsory. You also should consider having collision, comprehensive, injury and medical insurance.

You Need to Know

- Are there road taxes? If so, how are they determined -- weight of car, horsepower, size of wheel base? When and where are they paid?
- Are maintenance or safety inspections required? How are they done? This could be by appointment and/or surprise spot-checks by police on the road. The inspection may be as simple as testing the horn, wipers and lights; it can be as involved as requiring a certain depth of tire tread and having body rust repaired!
- Is emergency road help available through an organization or automobile club?

- Is there a telephone number for road conditions in difficult weather?
- What is the law regarding use of seat belts? Are small children required to ride in the front or back seat?
- Is the number of passengers in the car limited by law?
- What are the regulations for bicycles and motorbikes? Do they require licenses, lights, reflectors, insurance? Is there an age limit for using them? Are they taxed? Be sure you and any child using them know the laws.

In Case of an Accident

The odds for accidents are greater when driving in a foreign country. Driving patterns are different, sometimes there are no speed limits or police don't enforce laws, there are more pedestrians, motorbikes, tram tracks and even such hazards as sheep, chickens, donkeys and camels! Mishaps can bring unimaginable legal complications.

- What are the requirements when there is an accident?
- When should you call the police?
- What information are you required to give the police or involved parties?
- Can you move your car? leave the scene of the accident?

If you leave the scene of an accident for safety reasons, go *directly* to the police station or U.S. embassy or consulate. Be cautious about what you say. Speak English at the police station and ask for an English-speaking officer. If someone is seriously injured, call the U.S. embassy immediately for advice.

Know in advance what to do in case of an emergency. Because you probably will be dealing with a foreign language and could be flustered by this, keep calm. Make no commitments. Failure to know and heed the law may nullify any insurance claim. Do not discuss insurance coverage with anyone except your insurance agent.

Helpful Hints

Do your introductory and exploratory driving on non-busy days, such as Sunday. Really study the street map ahead of time.

If possible, have a partner in the car to help with map reading. In cities everywhere, street names change or vanish at certain intersections and it helps to know this before you reach that point. Where street names are not in English, look for identifying landmarks. By all means, learn the way from your house to the nearest emergency clinic or hospital. Practice the "run" several times until you feel confident you can handle it with traffic and any emergency.

As a newcomer, whenever you are traveling by taxi, public transportation or private car, observe streets and intersections. Pay particular attention to traffic lanes at intersections. When driving, the pre-selection of your lane is important to getting to your destination without a traffic citation or extended detour through unknown streets. In Switzerland rental cars have a "T" (for tourist) sign you can place in the rear car window to excuse your hesitations and belated signals to change lanes! It's a wonderful deterrent to impatient, horn-blowing local drivers.

Observe also traffic flow and driving mannerisms. There is a psychology to driving in every country and written (and often unwritten!) rules to learn. In Manila, Kuwait and Caracas, for example, red lights and stop signs are no guarantee cars will stop. The double yellow line in the center of the road is ignored by drivers in Thailand -- and the U.S.! -- if one wants to enter a gas station, parking lot or driveway, but not in Europe where to cross it for any reason will get you a ticket.

On a few autobahns and throughways there are no speed limits! Elsewhere speed limit signs are few and far between or may not be evident and yet, most likely, there is a limit. Drive with discretion. A 50 painted on the road or an LSZ sign (limited speed zone) with *implied* speed may be new ways to you of indicating there is a limit.

Police may collect fines on the spot. Drive carefully or carry sufficient funds to pay the penalty. Be sure to get a receipt.

Driving on the left side of the road, as is the rule in Britain, Japan, India, Singapore and New Zealand, can be nerve-racking at first. The best clue to help adjust to this difference is to remind yourself the driver of the car is always next to the middle of the road. If not, and if it is not a one-way street or divided highway, you're in the wrong lane! Sitting behind the taxicab driver can help you get accustomed to the right-hand drive. The flow of visible traffic is a guide to being in the correct lane but when it is not present, you must drive very thoughtfully. Think -- *really think* -- before turning into any intersection or out of a driveway. Those are your most dangerous moments.

U.S. roads are marked with "yield" signs but this is not so in other countries. Many countries use few traffic lights and the "priority of the right" rule is common in Europe and other parts of the world. It is an understood, visibly non-indicated rule -- that you must know. It means a car coming from the right has the right-of-way, even when it is an oblique or perpendicular intersection and you are on the obvious main road. In England, there is an exception if you are in a traffic circle.

Few places outside the U.S. permit a turn (left or right) when the traffic light is red.

Know whether horn blowing is permitted or usual.

Consider joining an automobile association or touring club. Their services can include emergency road help, legal assistance, touring information and discount benefits.

Throughout the world, driving under the influence of alcohol is a problem and handled with varying severe penalties. The first offense can mean revocation of a driver's license for a year plus a substantial fine; it also may mean mandatory imprisonment, automatic cancellation of insurance or revocation of licenses for all family drivers. If asked to take a breatholizer test, the law may require you to do so. Best of all, don't mix drinking and driving.

In addition to parking meters which will vary in their time limits and charges, special unmetered parking zones, usually marked with blue lines, with time limits are found in several European countries. A "clock" card is placed by you on the dashboard indicating the time the parking space was occupied. Where used, these cards can be obtained from the local police station, motor club, tourist office or a neighborhood kiosk. In Geneva, Switzerland, it is illegal to deposit payment a second time in the same parking meter after expiration without going into circulation!

An unlocked car or one with keys in it can be against the law and also can nullify an insurance claim for loss or damage.

Throughout most of the world, gasoline is sold in liters (a shade over a quart) rather than gallons. The English imperial gallon is slightly more than four liters.

Safety Aspects

In European countries a red reflective triangle sign to be used in road emergencies is *required* in cars. It would be a wise requirement everywhere! It's surely more effective and safer than the piece of newspaper or plastic bag flapping out of the car trunk as often seen in Asia. The triangle should be carried *in* the car so it is accessible if the trunk cannot be opened because of a rear collision.

Few countries outside the U.S. require blinking yellow and red lights on school buses and passing a stopped school bus is legal. As a driver, beware -- and alert your children to the danger.

Countries have different regulations for car lights. Roads in France can be frightening with their rule to drive with parking lights only. It is extremely difficult to be seen or to see people and cyclists. Drivers in India depend on public road lights and do not use their car lights except as they personally judge them to be needed. You easily can miss seeing a stray animal, be it a cat in Katmandu or a camel in Jaipur!

Blinking of car lights from high beams to driving lights in the U.S. means, "I see you and don't want to blind you with my bright lights," or "Dim your lights, please." In Europe the blinking of lights is the way to say, "Watch out, I'm going to pass you." In some countries no one will have any idea what you're trying to say!

Some frequently seen international road signs are shown at the end of the chapter. Each country adapts signs so learn those in your specific area.

Road works

- *Danger signs are equilateral triangles* with a white background, red border and display a black symbol. They give warning of a hazard a driver may not become aware of in time, therefore they are telling a driver to slow down. Examples are: road narrows, men working, slippery road, pedestrian crossing and intersection.

No U turns

- *Instruction signs are round* with white background, red border and black symbol. These signs indicate a prohibition such as: no entry, speed limit, no left turn and closed to bicycles and motorbikes.

No through road

- *Indication signs are rectangular*, usually with a white symbol on a blue background. Examples are: priority over traffic coming in opposite direction, one-way traffic, no through road, priority road and hospital.

As complete as international signs are, you must still be alert: the road repair crew may put their *Men Working* sign just 10 feet before their project; oxen and camel-drawn carts can be distracting as can be men on motorbikes with guns (Switzerland's all-men army going to weekly rifle practice!). Pedestrian crosswalks throughout the world often are indicated by wide stripes painted on the street called "zebra" crossings. *The pedestrian on the "zebra" has the absolute right of way.* Flashing yellow lights also warn of pedestrian crossing areas. In cities in Japan you may see someone crossing the street, arm extended in front holding a yellow flag; there is a container on each side of the street to deposit the flag for another street-crosser. It may sound unusual, but it certainly is effective and gets the desired attention of drivers.

Unlike most of the U.S., many international cities have electric trams whose tracks are most commonly in the middle of the street. Usually there is a pedestrian island for boarding and discharging passengers. Do not pass a stopped tram when there is no landing.

Buses may have the right-of-way over moving traffic. It is usually a penalty to drive in a designated bus lane. In Bangkok, bus lanes are in the opposite direction to the traffic flow. This is a shock to the newly arrived tourist as well as a driver and pedestrian.

Getting Around 147

DANGEROUS CURVE	ROAD INTERSECTION	UNEVEN ROAD	RIGHT CURVE	LEFT CURVE
DOUBLE CURVE	DANGER	LEVEL CROSSING WITH GATES	OPENING BRIDGE	LEVEL CROSSING WITHOUT GATES
DANGEROUS HILL	ROAD NARROWS	MEN WORKING	SLIPPERY ROAD	PEDESTRIAN CROSSING
WATCH OUT FOR CHILDREN	BEWARE OF ANIMALS	INTERSECTION WITH SIDE ROAD	MAIN ROAD AHEAD	NO OVERTAKING
SPEED LIMIT (40)	CLOSED TO MOTOR VEHICLES	CLOSED TO MOTORCYCLES	CLOSED EXCEPT TO MOTORCYCLES
NO ENTRY	ROAD CLOSED	STOP AT INTERSECTION	NO LEFT (Right) TURN

International Road Signs

HOUSEHOLD HELP

Whether or not you have household help will depend on your needs, lifestyle, budget and, perhaps, the culture of the country. Some people do not need or want help. It may not be readily available; it may be too expensive. Few families in the U.S. have full-time help. It is common, however, in some parts of Europe and many parts of the Middle East. Foreigners are expected to be employers in most parts of Asia, Latin and South America.

Most countries have regulations regarding all labor, including domestic help. These will deal with minimum wage standards, social security-type systems, health responsibilities, insurance, working hours, vacation, holidays and notice periods. Contracts or work permits may be required. The obligations of the employer and the employee should be thoroughly understood.

Involved paperwork and documentation can be required when the employee or helper comes from another country. Just as you need a visa or permit to live in a new country, this will apply to any non-national seeking employment or residence.

GENERAL INFORMATION

There are several ways to find domestic help. The "grapevine" is a good place to start -- and usually the best. Ask friends, acquaintances and neighbors if they or their maid (or house boy) know of someone looking for work. Read bulletins boards at supermarkets, churches, clubs and other organizations. Read the "situation wanted" ads in the newspapers. Put your own ad in the classified section or on a bulletin board. When an employment agency is used, know the obligations of all parties as well as the fee structure.

Depending on the timing of your move and the housing you find, the present help of the departing family may be available. If the personalities fit and other aspects are right, this can be most helpful.

When interviewing help, discuss the job requirements carefully and have a clear understanding of expectations. Problem situations can be avoided by anticipating them.

Some countries require a registration or identification card for all residents. Be sure you know your obligations. When you have part-time or live-in help, ask to see their card. Keep a record of this information.

Stealing, particularly from foreigners, is common -- and acceptable -- in some cultures. It is an unpleasant aspect that must be faced realistically. Petty stealing can range from food to clothing. Find out if this is a problem or the-way-it-is for your location and take precautions. Never leave money in the house; jewelry should be in a safe deposit box and silverware carefully stored. When something is missing, first be sure it is not misplaced. Household help should know that any disappearance can mean termination of their job and possible other action.

Medical and liability insurance is recommended for any domestic help you employ.

Whether or not you have had household help previously, you are accustomed to keeping your home a certain way. Your ways and ideas may differ from that of your domestic help, and what was done to the satisfaction of a previous employer may be the opposite of what you want. However, be open to different ideas for doing things -- your way may not always be the best. There are many ways to remove stains, tenderize meat and slice a carrot. During the first month, it's important to give time and close supervision until the servant has learned what you expect. Actually showing what you want is often better understood than verbal directions. Reminders may be helpful, such as a sketch of a basic place setting. If you can find someone who has worked previously for a Western family, it is easier than having to train someone completely.

Communication can cause problems, especially when there is a language barrier. You want complete understanding about what you expect so it's up to you to communicate. It can prevent a problem later. Instructions should be given carefully, distinctly and without a lot of ifs, ands, buts and double negatives. Speak slowly. Discuss only one question at a time. Correct help so important things are done your way and on your timetable. Any criticisms should be made quietly and privately.

Be willing to bend a bit and to accept mistakes -- just keep working toward what you want.

In many countries, it's natural to respond giving the expected answer or to say yes. The latter is often done by nodding the head as if in agreement. Just observe yourself! This can mean, "Yes, I understand," or "Yes, I hear you." There's a big difference! Observe -- you will soon see if your help knows what you're talking about. Having the servant repeat instructions should let you know if you're understood.

Precautions

Instruct your help on the harmful things in your house -- cleaning items, insecticides, ammonia, etc. Mark the labels with a big red X as a warning. Tell your help to read (if she can) all labels before using the item. She needs to know about them for herself and also to keep the dangerous items out of the reach of children. Discuss the first aid items you keep. She should know you expect her to treat even the smallest wound, cut or injury. Have a list of emergency telephone numbers and instructions.

The most common household fires start in the kitchen, often with grease. Give instructions in ways to prevent them, and if a fire starts, measures to put it out (baking soda or fire extinguisher). Stress safety of children and others and how to call for assistance.

Your electrical appliances could be in jeopardy in the hands of servants. At the outset take time to instruct them in their use -- even if they say they already know how! A clothes washer with its many possible cycles and water temperatures can be most confusing. Tape a note to the washer with simple instructions, if it is a problem. (The note will disappear when it's no longer needed!) A clothes dryer can be an unknown appliance in some areas, especially tropical locations where outdoor drying is common. Give instructions on cleaning the lint filter after each use to prevent overheating and related problems.

Give instructions about transformers and which to use for specific appliances.

You cannot expect your maid to have the same sense of value or appreciation of your possessions. Tell her which ones are especially cherished and show the care you want them to have.

Instruct your maid on how to answer the telephone. When you are not there, she should always ask who is calling. She should avoid answering questions about when you will return unless it is someone she knows to be a personal friend or she has instructions from you. Keep paper and pencil nearby for writing down names of callers and messages. An emergency number list should be by the telephone. Also instruct her about answering the door. Unless you have told her the dry cleaner or repairman will come, she should not admit anyone she does not know or expect.

When more than one household helper is needed, your general maid may have someone she knows and can work well with as cook, baby helper or laundry help. Each servant should know their specific responsibilities: who answers the phone, locks the door at night, feeds the dog, etc.

Keep a notebook of all salary payments. Record each payment with the date paid and amount. The servant should sign to acknowledge any cash receipts. If your help cannot read or write, she should make some attempt at signing so you have a record.

When you find you have a non-harmonious fit or unsatisfactory working relationship and discharge is necessary, one month's notice is customary for full-time help, but check local laws and practices. Depending on the reason and the circumstances, it may be better to pay what is owed and have the person pack and leave immediately. When there is a problem, don't prolong a bad situation -- wipe it out and start over. In dismissing someone, especially an Oriental or Filipino servant to say, "I know you are not happy working for us," saves face for her and is an easy, acceptable comment from you. The final salary payment, with whatever termination money is given, should be recorded and acknowledged in the payment record book. Although you may not want to give a reference letter, if requested, you can at least write a letter stating dates of employment.

AU PAIR

An *au pair* is a young lady, usually 17 to 25 years of age, whose responsibility is to assist with small children. She may be given some light household duties also. This type of help is well known in Scandinavia and parts of Europe. In return for room, board and a small wage she cares for your children. She is part of the family with equal status (*au pair* means at par) to a family member, eating with you and participating in family trips and special occasions. It's essential that personalties are compatible between all family members and the *au pair*.

Be sure you know the entry formalities regarding registration, health examination and necessary permits. There may be specific rules about number of hours allowed to work, days off, minimum wage, health insurance and age. Some countries require language study by the *au pair*.

PART-TIME HELP

For part-time help, specific regulations regarding medical benefits, minimum wage, liability insurance while working and while traveling to-and-from your house and vacation days are matters to be checked. In addition to the above considerations and those listed for live-in help, also discuss at your interview:

- time expected for work and time work day finished
- duties and responsibilities
- who pays transportation to and from work
- meals, if any, to be furnished
- when work day falls on holiday

Instruct her to telephone you if she is ill or will be late for work.

LIVE-IN HELP

Although not usual in the U.S., live-in help is common in other countries. In certain countries it is taken for granted that expats will employ local people in their home. Where daily shopping is a necessity, it's truly helpful to have the assistance of someone who knows what, where and how to buy (maybe even bargain) for your food. They can deal with repairmen and vendors. There is the security of having someone in the house at all times.

Many factors are important as you seek to employ someone and these should be discussed at the interview. If at all possible, interview at your house or apartment -- this saves misunderstanding regarding size of home, quarters and furnishings. To communicate as completely as possible, speak slowly. Try to phrase some questions to elicit other than simple "yes" answers. Aspects to discuss are:

- Previous work experience and responsibilities
- References and reasons for changing employer

    Does she have letters of recommendation?

    Can you contact previous employers?

    Does she have a release paper, if required?

- What is her family situation -- single, married, children?
- What housing arrangements and privileges are expected?
- Salary

    What is expected and/or offered? Is base salary government-regulated? (Years of experience, responsibility for children and household, ability to understand and speak English and good recommendations can influence salary. It is best to stay in line with "the going rate" of what others are paying for comparable help.) A one or more month's salary is specified in some countries as an annual or semi-annual bonus.

- Is salary to be paid in cash or by check, monthly or weekly?
- Will you, as employer, pay or deduct any taxes or benefit fund contributions, pay for health care, give vacation pay?
- Health

    Require a medical examination by a doctor or medical clinic; this is especially important in developing countries. Stool test for parasites and bacterial organisms, chest x-ray and blood test always should be required when there are small children in the family.

    How will you deal with a maid's pregnancy?

    Will she be able to work six months or until the birth?

    Can she return to work for you after the birth?

    What happens in the case of illness -- hers or in her family, perhaps in another country?

- Ability to speak, read and write English

    Can she take telephone messages? read recipes?

- Food

    Check the usual procedure in your area. In some places the employer provides all food; some only rice; some give the staples of rice, tea, sugar, oil, flour, soap and toilet paper; some give a monthly monetary allowance.

- Uniforms

    If you want your help to wear uniforms, the employer pays for them.

- Weekly time off, holidays, vacation

    Local practices for working hours, days off and holidays should be followed when possible.

- Tell her what you expect from her -- having a clear understanding can prevent problems:

    - Personal characteristics: honesty, cleanliness
    - Give the example of a typical day and weekly time schedule.
    - Define your family lifestyle: respect for your privacy; you may like to cook sometimes; not expected or desirable to wait on the family hand-and-foot and if you expect her to travel with you to care for children.
    - Duties and responsibilities. Be as specific as you can at this initial meeting. Discuss what you expect when you are away on trips.
    - Your wishes regarding her telephone calls.
    - Your wishes regarding visitors on her day off, overnight visitors (family and otherwise!) and when you are out of town. Establish your own rules before the first visitors arrive. How will you handle dating?

- Trial period

    Always hire worker on a temporary trial basis. One week to one month is the usual time and sufficient to find out mutual compatibility. Agree on a trial-and-adjustment period so either can terminate. This termination can be without notice and severance pay is unnecessary.

Before you hire someone have the medical report, talk with references and see any required identification or registration document.

When someone lives in your house, a pleasant personality is essential. With children in the family, look for cheerful, smiling help. Be specific when you discuss the responsibilities you will assume and those of the maid for baby and child care. You want someone who will look after the children, not spoil, over-indulge or dominate them. Tell her the types of snacks you permit (carrots vs. candy) and stress your desire for children to wash hands with soap and water before eating. Giving medicine to children should be done only by or on the direction of a parent. Discipline might be jointly handled but punishment should be left to parents.

If you will have full-time help for the first time, remember that it is your home -- you, and the family, must feel at home. When the children want to make Koolaid or peanut butter sandwiches (within reason!), they should be allowed to. And shown how to clean up any mess! You may not always have full-time help!

What does a mother do when all the familiar duties in the house are done for her? Maids cannot, and should not, replace mothers. Having household help enables the mother to spend more time with children than was possible previously. It also permits a mother to pursue community service, language classes, work, university study and leisure pursuits. Careful thought and planning will be needed to set the right balance so you don't find you are allowing someone else to raise your children.

From the outset, any servant needs to understand what is expected of her. You may wish to give a written schedule to follow. At least, talk with her about a typical day's work and procedure -- and that you don't expect her to eat at the table with you or read the newspaper in the living room. Initial time spent with servants will establish their suitability and schedule.

Do start with a planned schedule then adjust it rather than start with none and have to make one; this could be construed as dissatisfaction. It is also better than frequently telling or correcting as this can be interpreted as criticism. Dissatisfaction with performance of a chore or duty should be mentioned matter-of-factly at the time it occurs. Undue criticsm may mean losing face. To correct and save face requires finesse. If there are some things you expect to do around the house regularly or occasionally (such as cook, care for plants or shine silver), tell the servant at the beginning. To suddenly begin tasks which she has done can indicate displeasure and cause loss of self-esteem (yes, face again).

A maid who will do your shopping is expected to give an itemization of purchases and cost. Give her a small notebook for the weekly vegetable, fish and other vendor purchases. Some food stores have charge accounts and you will have to decide if your maid can sign such accounts.

Patience is needed to teach a maid to cook your likes in food so be prepared to spend time with her. Picture cookbooks help. Be sure she knows that "1 cup" is a *measuring cup*, not just any cup on the shelf!

Emphasize food cleanliness. If you are in a country where food must be washed or treated before use, set the rule that everything that goes in the refrigerator must be washed -- from grapefruit and eggs to cans and bottles! In areas where there are known problems, a purchased preparation or a couple of drops of chlorine bleach can be used in the water. (Mix 1 tablespoon of chlorine bleach in 2 gallons of water and let vegetables stand in this 20-30 minutes.) Have one system for washing foods. It's complicated to explain differences or exceptions, such as wash tomatoes but not potatoes.

Be specific about what foods should be refrigerated. You may automatically refrigerate opened jars of mayonnaise, peanut butter and cans of coffee and wrap or cover other items, but this may be unknown to your new kitchen help.

Be sure your help knows to dispose of garbage regularly and in a way to avoid sanitation problems.

Don't assume that someone is familiar with all your cleaning preparations or ideas. In countries where people are accustomed to cold water only and dishwashing is done by hand, you may have to insist you want dishes washed with hot water and soap.

Try to make your maid's quarters attractive. A bedspread or curtains, a plant, fresh coat of paint on walls can do this. Tell her initially you expect her area to be kept clean and orderly. You should remember it is her living area and should be private to her. However, if things go beyond your likes, a talk is needed.

Take time to talk with your maid about personal cleanliness and appearance and perhaps give her a few toilet items, shampoo or deodorant, for example. Be sure she knows she has time each day for a shower.

If you live in an area, such as India or Indonesia, where you have a staff of help -- perhaps general maid or house boy, cook, laundry help, gardener and sweeper -- one member of the staff should be the "chief" or steward and you should give all instructions to the chief. That person will give directions (not supervision!) to the other staff. It's the responsibility of the head employee to have the household function smoothly. In the "macho" countries, such as in South America, you will need to be sensitive as to whether directions to men servants (the gardener or driver) will be more respected if given by the man of the household. Often you get more efficient service if a man telephones the plumber, even the local Sears Roebuck!

Since Christmas is a usual vacation time for many Western families, decide early what time off you will give for December holidays. It won't be a problem in Taipei with your Chinese amah (unless she is a Christian) or in Bombay with your Indian ayah. Before you leave on any trip, discuss the schedule and procedures you expect servants to follow.

Having live-in help will only work if you trust your servants and show that you trust them. Make them aware of this at the outset of their employment.

EMPLOYING A DRIVER

Driving may not be feasible for legal or other reasons. Prior to hiring someone:

- Ask for references *and check them*. Call or write to corroborate all information given you. You must feel confident this is the individual you want driving you, your spouse or children.
- Inspect applicant's driver's license. Is it valid? Can you check it with local authorities for driving offenses?
- Give all applicants a test drive in your car. Is he a safe driver? Does he drive defensively?

Some of the problems experienced with drivers have been poor driving ability, carelessness, talkativeness, tardiness and dishonesty. Knowing this, you can avoid them by discussing expectations, for example, safety, mileage records, receipts for gasoline and other expenses. Salary, hours, overtime and specific responsibilities for care of the car will need to be established.

Before hiring, make sure your insurance company will cover the driver.

MEETING MEDICAL NEEDS

Investigate Medical Facilities

Your new community is now your home. Just as you would if moving from Seattle to Spokane, it is important to get established with doctors. You'll want to find out quickly about all aspects of emergency and regular medical care. Be ready before a necessity arises.

Finding a **doctor** and needed specialists is first. Start to inquire soon after you arrive. This is especially important when there are children in the family. You never know when a fever, earache, severe diarrhea or an accute illness will develop. Ask business associates, new acquaintances and friends for recommendations. Americans will know of American doctors or ones trained in the U. S. if this is important to you. Often the U. S. embassy or consulate will have a list of English-speaking doctors.

Expect differences in doctor-patient procedures, language and relationships in your new location. In England when told to come to "surgery," it is the office. Doctors may not display academic diplomas as they do in the U.S. In some countries they do not like to be asked details of diagnosis or medications. You will want to find a doctor who understands Western expectations so you feel comfortable with one another. Ask him what to do in an emergency -- before you have one. You'll also want to know what to do when he is not available. Ask if he makes house calls. This is almost a thing of the past in the U.S. but not so in other countries. (In Hong Kong, veterinarians will make house calls!)

Locate the nearest **hospital** or clinic with facilities to treat round-the-clock emergencies. *And*, find out from your doctor which hospital he uses. Admission to emergency rooms (sometimes called casualty department) or hospitals is easier when you have a personal physician. It can be frightening to have even a small emergency and have to go to your first foreign clinic and doctor. Reassure yourself through preparation. If the route is complicated, practice driving to the emergency facility during slow traffic times, such as Sunday, so you know your way around flyovers and through one-way streets without the stress of a medical problem.

Ask questions about normal entrance procedures. Often hospitals require a deposit, sometimes substantial, before admission.

When you will travel and leave children at home with a friend, sitter, or household help give specific instructions for **emergency medical problems**. It may be necessary to execute a power of attorney enabling the person caring for your children to request emergency treatment by a doctor or in a hospital. Check with both to know that your children can be treated as you would wish. Also, notify the office of your children's school of your absence and the procedure to be followed in an emergency.

Date

To Whom It May Concern

We the undersigned,__(parents)__, being the parents of (child's name)__, do hereby authorize any physician licensed to practice medicine in__(city/country)__ to provide any medical or surgical treatment to our__(son/daughter)__ , __(child's name), during the period from/to __(dates of absence)__, upon the written authorization of any one of the following individuals: (list name, address and telephone numbers for more than one person -- such as friend, office associate, neighbor, maid or servant)

It is the intention of the undersigned that our __(son/daughter) be afforded all necessary medical and surgical treatment during our absence from__(city)__.

(Signature of father)
Name of Father

(Signature of mother)
Name of Mother

Ambulance service is sometimes provided by private hospitals. In an emergency, have your doctor request the needed ambulance for you. Police and public ambulances are also possible. Inquire about the services of all. What medical qualifications do attendants have? Is oxygen equipment available? Which hospitals do they take patients to? Be prepared -- ahead of time -- to call the service that meets your needs.

Prescriptions for medications must be issued by a local licensed doctor. You can show your new doctor the U.S. prescription but he will have to write a new one before you can get the medicine. Always ask that the name of a prescription drug be written on the container label. In a few countries it is necessary to present your passport to the pharmacist when getting a prescription drug. In some, doctors dispense their own prescriptions. Drugs requiring a prescription in the U.S. are sometimes available over-the-counter elsewhere.

Locate a **pharmacy** near you. Some cities have all-night pharmacies that, if you pay the taxi fare, will deliver a medicine to you. Inquire if this is possible in your city. You will want to have some first aid items at home so acquaint yourself with available aspirin, antiseptic solutions (hydrogen peroxide is good for rinsing wounds), creams or lotions for insect bites (bicarbonate of soda can be used in an emergency), antihistamines and other items you frequently need. When your children go on a school trip, include a few emergency items: antiseptic cream, bandaids, aspirin, Imodium AD or equivalent. Always check for an expiration date on medicine packages. U.S. limitations on the sale of medications are strict; this is not necessarily the case elsewhere.

Inquire if there is a local **blood bank** or transfusion service and the regulations and procedure for joining or using the service.

Some of the same U.S. **support agencies** you are familiar with also have international branches: Alcoholics Anonymous, Samaritans, Reach to Recovery and The Helping Hand. Classes for expectant mothers and fathers are found in many overseas locations.

Potential Medical Problems

The U.S. probably leads the world in preventive health measures. Our food and drug laws require inspection of meat, treatment of water, purification of milk and regulation of insecticides. Consumer groups are additional watchdogs for unnecessary air and water pollution and improper handling of consumables. There are strict drug dispensing laws and mandatory expiration information; sanitation standards are high. Living in Europe you will find many, but not all, similar protective measures. In other parts of the world, this will not be the case and the individual must assume his own preventive steps.

As a newcomer you may find you are susceptible to minor illnesses. This is not only true for you moving from Montana to Malaysia but also for the Venezuelan moving to Virginia -- or a Mexican to the U.S.! The stress and fatigue of moving, change of climate, food and water, and lack of immunity to "local bugs" can be contributing factors. Ask your doctor about special health considerations for your new locale. Respiratory problems? Insect bites? Is impetigo common? lice or worms? parasite infections? tuberculosis? If you know, you can take preventive measures.

Diarrhea, also known as Montezuma's revenge, the Thai tummy, Tokyo trot, Delhi belly and other tourist names, probably is the most common problem. Imodium AD, Pepto-Bismol and paregoric control diarrhea; however, they may not get rid of the bacteria causing the problem. If adult "traveler's diarrhea" lasts more than three days (for infants and young children, 24 hours), seek medical advice. Anyone affected with diarrhea needs to drink lots of "safe" fluids to avoid dehydration. A light diet of tea, toast, boiled rice and salty broth is recommended; avoid milk products.

In countries where monosodium glutamate (MSG) is regularly used in cooking, you may experience diarrhea attacks. This is very possible in Korea, Japan, China, Taiwan, Thailand and elsewhere. Too much MSG also can cause severe headaches and rapid pulse.

Don't confuse **dysentery** with diarrhea. Dysentery is a serious infection of the lower intestinal tract producing pain, fever and severe diarrhea often with blood. Water in rural communities that is contaminated by local sewage is the usual transmitter of dysentery. Eating unpeelable fruits and uncooked vegetables that have been fertilized with human feces ("night soil") is often the causative factor of the disease.

All **skin rashes**, cuts, scratches, wounds or insect bites should be given prompt attention.

If living in a **malaria** area, anti-malarial pills must be taken. Your doctor or pharmacist can advise you about them. In the U.S. it is necessary to see a doctor to obtain these, but in many areas where malaria is present, the preventive tablets can be purchased over-the-counter. Repellent creams also should be used. Some of the anti-mosquito coils contain toxic substances harmful to humans and should not be used indoors. Mosquito netting over beds may be advisable. A battery-operated mosquito repeller with a sound inaudible to people can be used near your bed. The best place to find these is in a gadget store.

Head lice are an easily contacted, contagious problem, particularly for children, and know no social barriers. Infestation seems to be more prevalent in warmer climates but the parasitic insects are everywhere. It is not necessarily a disease of poor sanitation. The nits and eggs attach themselves to the hair shaft and multiply rapidly. A special shampoo, such as Kwell or Derbac, is needed. Also, daily washing of pillow cases and bed sheets is required. It is usually necessary to pick the eggs from the hair -- hence the saying nit-picking!

It is not pleasant to talk -- or think! -- about **worms** but several types of such parasite infestations are prevalent worldwide. Medical treatment is required for all of these. Tapeworms come from meat, usually beef and pork, that is undercooked. Trichinosis infects pigs and men and is spread by eating infested and inadequately cooked pork or raw pork sausage meat

In countries where hygiene standards are not always high, other worm problems exist. **Roundworms**, although found worldwide, are most common in warmer climates. Infection comes from eating uncooked vegetables, especially raw salad items, which have been fertilized with "night soil," a common practice in tropical areas of Asia, India, Africa and South America. When there is a problem with roundworms, your doctor may prescribe treatment for all family members, household help and pets.

Hookworm infestation is also common in developing countries where sanitation is poor. Common symptoms include loss of appetite, irritability, weight loss, abdominal pains, diarrhea or constipation. It is primarily an intestinal tract problem and the eggs are passed in the feces and develop in the soil. The larva of the worms enter through tiny lesions or scratches on the soles of the feet. Prevention means don't walk around in bare feet. The larva also can be absorbed by drinking infected water or eating unwashed or uncooked fruits and vegetables. You'll recognize good or questionable sanitation standards when you get settled and will know to be careful about such a possible problem situation. Dogs frequently get hookworms.

In some world areas the anti-**tuberculosis** inoculation BCG is given automatically to infants and young children unless you request otherwise. Anticipate this and talk with your doctor about it. A child who has received this vaccine always will show a positive reaction regardless of whether or not he has had tuberculosis. The Tine test is not valid for someone who has had BCG. This means that x-rays are needed to test for tuberculosis and you may not want this as the alternative for lifetime testing.

Miscellaneous

Is **drinking water** from household faucets safe? You may be able to have bottled water delivered to your home. For tiny babies, check with your doctor to see if bottled water needs additional boiling. Recognize that if it is distilled water, it is also demineralized. Ask your dentist for his recommendation regarding fluoride treatment in your area.

When bottled or boiled water is recommended, be sure you use this to make ice cubes. In restaurants in developing countries you want to ask if the ice is made from bottled water (and not chipped off a block of ice on the pavement out back!). The most effective and safest method of water purification is by boiling. Bring water to a boil and maintain the boil for 15 minutes. Pour into adequately cleansed or sterilized containers and store in the refrigerator.

Filters on water taps can be used to remove suspended matter from water; however, they may not purify water, only clarify it. Charcoal filters require a change of charcoal every three to four weeks. All filters should be cleaned regularly, perhaps weekly depending on the status of your water.

Chemical disinfection is also effective. Most frequently this is by a chlorine-type purification tablet, such as Milton or Halazone. Baby bottles can be sterilized with these solutions. Two percent tincture of iodine USP should be used instead of the chlorine-type disinfectants in areas where amoebic dysentery is present. Add two drops to one liter of water and leave for half an hour. Iodine tablets and solutions especially made for water purification can be purchased. When traveling to areas where you are concerned about drinking water, take purifying tablets with you.

In areas where there are health concerns, insist that any **household help** have a physical examination before you employ them and annually thereafter. This should include chest x-ray and stool examination.

Set high **kitchen cleanliness standards** for any household help and check to see they are being maintained. In many areas all food to be refrigerated should be washed first. Depending on where you are, soaking or special treatment of raw fruits and vegetables may help reduce fertilizer contamination and destroy problem parasites. Some possibilities are:

- Soak in full strength vinegar or in a clorox-water solution (one tablespoon clorox to one gallon water) for 20 minutes. It won't affect the taste of your food!
- Use commercial solutions such as Globaline, Milton's, Hidrosteril, Potable-Aqua tablets or permanganate. Iodine solutions are considered superior to chlorine compositions.
- Instead of the soaking solution, dip foods in boiling water for 10 seconds.

If you're a house or hotel guest and concerned about food, eat the hot (cooked) dishes.

Iodized salt is not available everywhere. If it is not in your area, be sure to include fish and shellfish in your diet.

Know whether the **milk** you purchase is pasteurized. Many countries now have "sterilized" milk available in cartons. This does not require refrigeration until opened. Expiration date should be stamped on carton. *Buerre de cuisine* (cooking butter) is made from unpasteurized milk.

It is not advisable to eat **unknown foods** from street sellers or stalls, no matter how appealing the aroma, until you know any possible dangers from this. The safe way is: If you can't peel it, don't eat it -- without cooking. Bananas and oranges are safe, strawberries and lettuce are not. Eat, drink and be wary!

Sanitary standards and conditions vary greatly from the U.S. to South America, the Middle East, the Orient and elsewhere. Handwashing should be as routine as getting dressed and going to school or the office. Be firm in training your children to wash hands thoroughly and frequently, and always before eating anything. Contamination can be transmitted in such ordinary ways -- handling money, stamps, hand rails, door pulls, even elevator buttons. Instruct household help in the importance of washing hands, especially before handling food.

Your **regular medical examination** is most important when you are overseas as you may be exposed to more problems than at home. Don't put off a routine checkup, such as a pap smear or electrocardiogram, to have it done on home leave. You must accept that you need to take care of medical needs, especially preventive ones, where you live at the moment. Your semi-annual dental cleaning and checkup should be made as usual.

Doctor bills may be sent quarterly rather than the U.S. pay-on-the-spot or end-of-the-month procedure. It is proper in Iceland to discuss the charge with the doctor before you have the medical consultation.

On doctor's bills, prescriptions and other medical receipts, write the U.S. dollar equivalent for the day of payment. It may be six months or longer before you file an insurance claim and you should know the value of the dollar at the time payment was made. Keep a copy of all letters, bills and receipts for medical insurance claims.

In case of the **death** of a U.S. citizen while abroad, contact the nearest U.S. embassy or consulate immediately. They can advise on local rules and regulations and assist with completion of forms. Obtain a death certificate signed by a doctor and several *official* copies. (These will be required for insurance company, Social Security, shipping, etc.) Cremation may not be possible without a written statement to this effect by the deceased stating this wish.

Although not a major problem in the U.S., **rabies** is prevalent in other countries. It is spread mostly by unvaccinated animals, particularly dogs. Be sure your own dog or cat is vaccinated and kept restrained if you are in an area where rabies is known. Although most often transmitted from the bite of a rabid animal, it can also be transmitted by exposure of an open skin wound to infected saliva. Avoid all stray, unknown animals. If bitten by any animal, clean the wound and surrounding area thoroughly with soap and water and seek medical help. When possible, the animal should be confined for observation and testing.

TROPICAL AREAS, TYPHOONS AND TREMORS

TROPICAL AREAS

Living in a tropical area brings unique challenges. Food, furnishings and health are aspects for your attention. Also humidity -- it can challenge you physically and show its effect in other ways: from envelopes that seal themselves in your desk drawer to creeping mildew in your leather shoes.

Health

Tropical climates require the body to make adjustments to constant periods of hot weather and high humidity. Fatigue and exhaustion due to these energy-sapping conditions are not uncommon problems. Expect it to take a couple of months or more to adapt.

Dehydration is a concern in tropical areas. Everyone should drink lots of fluids daily to help replace water lost by perspiration. Cool fresh fruit drinks are particularly refreshing and especially good for children. Alcohol increases dehydration; tall mixed drinks are preferable to "neat" scotch. A little extra dash of salt on food can help your body maintain the proper water balance; rarely, salt tablets may be necessary.

Skin rashes of the prickly heat type are common in tropical climates. Baking soda added to bath water is helpful to relieve this. Free use of powder on the body after a bath or shower aids drying and can help alleviate a problem. Calamine or caladryl lotion is helpful for rashes.

Bacteria thrive in tropical climates and you want to be alert to impetigo, staph and fungus infections, cuts and insect bites. Any cut, wound or bite should be treated immediately. Keep your immunizations up to date.

Respiratory ailments, bronchial and sinus problems seem to occur frequently in tropical areas due to heat, air conditioning, humidity and long rainy periods. Get early medical help to avoid complications and prolonged problems.

In many areas swimming is a daily activity and a relief from the heat. Be alert for fungus and ear infections.

Plan your daily schedule so you are out of the sun and heat at midday -- which, in the tropics, can be from ten till three! Don't let a desired suntan become a sunburn. Frequent use of sun-blocking creams is necessary for everyone.

Insects

Tropical insects are unknown to most Americans. They are not all bad. It's important to know whether mosquitos in your area are disease carriers and to take all precautions, such as repellent creams or sprays and incense-type coils. When mosquito netting is used, the lower edges should be tucked under the mattress. Be sure it does not touch you. All holes should be mended. Most vital is the taking of recommended anti-malarial pills, such as Paludrine (taken daily) or Avlochlor, Nivaquine, Plaquenil, Resochine, Daraprim or Fansidar (taken weekly).

Small lizards that appear at night on ceilings and from behind pictures and curtains are frequent guests in tropical areas. In Greece they are called "gekkos" and in China "wall tigers!" They are non-poisonous and really are friends as they eat mosquitos and other insects (not clothing and furniture!) and are just as afraid of you as you may be of them.

To eliminate insects and odors in a problem garbage pail, tie a bag of moth balls to the handle and drop inside the pail. Keep tightly closed.

Scheduled fumigations may be necessary to combat a variety of household visitors and pests.

Worms

Worm infestations of several kinds are discussed in detail in the *Meeting Medical Needs* chapter. Though not restricted to tropical areas, roundworms and hookworms are frequent problems there. Both relate to sanitation. Food cleanliness is required. Depending on where you live, you may not want your children to go barefoot which can expose them to infection from contaminated soil.

Pets

Dogs and cats often are pest-infested in tropical climates. A regular schedule for de-worming may be advisable. A local veterinarian can tell you the problems of which to be aware.

Clothing

Summer in tropical countries is h-o-t. Some days even earrings can be too much to wear! Clothing should be loose, light in weight and permit absorption of perspiration. Cotton clothing is the coolest and most comfortable; cotton and polyester blends will keep a fresh look longer and are a useful compromise. Light colored clothing reduces heat absorption and is cooler than dark colors. Lots of changes of clothing are needed for small children. Men will like to have washable slacks. Non-elastic belts are more comfortable than elastic ones. Women will appreciate cotton lingerie, nightgowns and sundresses.

Clothes wear out faster when there are frequent changes and frequent laundering. Your whites may never have been brighter than in the tropical sun but your dark clothes may be dull. Turn colored clothes inside out on the clothesline and, if possible, hang them in the shade. Remove from the line as soon as dry. Pass this information along to your domestic help.

Musty odors and mildew are a nuisance, to say the least. Air conditioners and dehumidifiers are useful, probably indispensable, for keeping things dry in tropical areas. Electric heating rods or light bulbs in closets help avoid problems. The heating rods are placed about four inches from, and parallel to, the floor. A cage or screen protection should be over the rod to prevent burning yourself or objects, such as clothing or a plastic dry cleaner's bag that could fall directly on it. A 100-watt bulb gives off enough heat to be effective in most closets. Both rods or bulbs should be left on continuously. If these are not available or installable, leave closet doors open in air-conditioned rooms. When you will be away for a long period of time, leave the closet and wardrobe doors open and air conditioners running. If clothes cannot be stored in dry closets or air-conditioned rooms, air and sun them occasionally to prevent problems.

Use wooden, plastic or plastic-covered hangers to prevent rust on clothes.

Leather shoes, belts, purses and other items mildew easily in humid conditions. Keep such items in heated closets or expose them to the sun occasionally to be sure they are dry. Saddle soap is a useful preventative. Mothballs sprinkled in drawers or closets where such items are kept also will help prevent mildew and musty odors.

Food

Prompt refrigeration of food is essential.

Buy foods that might get buggy in small amounts, for example, cereals and flour. Store them in screw-top jars. Flour can be kept in the refrigerator or freezer to prevent infestation.

Never eat rancid food. To prevent coffee from becoming rancid, store it in the refrigerator. If it will not be consumed in a short period of time, freeze the contents of the opened can in a jar or plastic container.

A low-watt light bulb installed in a kitchen cabinet or small pantry does wonders for keeping spices, cereals, crackers, tea and the like, dry.

Good kitchen sanitation is important.

Furnishings

Locally purchased furnishings may be more suitable to the climate than things you might ship. For example, the rattan and wicker furniture of the Philippines is more suitable in a Manila house than the leather sofa and oak table from a Chicago condominium so you may want to consider purchasing at least some furniture in the new location. Normally, if rooms are air-conditioned a serious mildew problem is avoided, but don't be forgetful or depend on that. An upholstered sofa can be raised on small blocks of wood to allow air under it. Area rugs will be more appropriate than wall-to-wall carpeting.

Rattan, wicker, cane furniture and bamboo blinds can house insects and should be fumigated before delivery. Some countries require fumigation before they allow importation of articles made of these materials.

Frequent use of radios, tape recorders, television and hifi equipment will aid in keeping these mechanical items dry.

Humidity seems to speed tarnishing of brass and silver. Immediately after polishing brass, apply a light coat of a good paste wax to retard pitting as well as tarnishing. A small piece of camphor in your silver chest or drawer also prevents tarnishing.

Routinely check and wipe books. Try not to crowd bookcases. Sprinkle mothballs behind books to retard musty odors.

A light bulb in your piano will help keep it dry.

TYPHOONS

A typhoon is a tropical weather disturbance which passes through several increasingly intense phases, the last of which is extremely destructive. In the U.S. this type of storm is called a hurricane; elsewhere they are known as typhoons. The intensity of the expected winds determines the classification:

- tropical depressions have winds of less than 38 m.p.h.
- tropical storms have winds between 39 and 73 m.p.h.
- typhoons have winds of 74 m.p.h. or more

The accompanying rain, storm surge, strong wind gusts and flooding can be devastating.

Certain world areas are most prone to typhoons. Individual countries have their own signal alert system. If you are in a typhoon area, acquaint yourself with the warning signals and the recommended precautions to be taken. You should be concerned with family health as well as property safety.

Before the Typhoon

- Listen to a radio for latest weather conditions.
- Have a transistor radio with enough fresh batteries to last several days.

- Be sure your flashlights have good batteries and have an extra supply.
- Remove or secure loose objects outside the house, in a carport or car-park, on apartment balconies.
- Clear gutters and drains.
- Canvas awnings should be rolled up and lashed with sturdy rope.
- A television antenna may need to be taken down. Before you touch the antenna, unplug the television set from the electrical outlet inside your house.
- Install all available storm shutters.
- Be prepared to be without services, such as water or garbage collection.
- Have a two- or three-day supply of canned goods and non-perishable foods that do not need refrigeration or cooking. Purchase them in sizes that will supply enough for immediate consumption only.
- Have a supply of drinking water. Canned juices and soft drinks can be used in a water shortage emergency. Also fill large pans, buckets and the bathtub with water. You may never need it but it is better not to take a chance.
- Large windows should be taped with cloth-type (not masking) tape in lattice-work fashion. One big "X" of paper masking tape on a 4'x4' (or larger) window is not adequate.
- Fill the gasoline tank of your car. When there is no electricity, service station pumps will not work. Set brakes. Leave one window slightly ajar. If your car is not in a garage, place tape strips across the windshield.

During the Typhoon

- Stay indoors.
- Bolt doors and lock windows so they will not blow open.
- Close room doors to prevent drafts in case a window breaks. Be careful opening and closing doors when wind pressure is high. They can be slammed shut with extreme force and cause injury.

- Keep away from windows and doors. The family should be together in protected hallway or room. Even if water leakage occurs, keep away from windows. They can shatter inward and cause serious injury.
- Do not use elevators when there is danger electricity can be cut off.

In an emergency, sterilize water by adding three drops of household bleach to one quart of water or 1/4 teaspoon (10 drops) to one gallon of water. Shake or stir well. Wait 30 minutes before using. Diluted vinegar can be used as an emergency antiseptic.

TREMORS

Certain areas of the world are susceptible to earthquakes, for example, the Philippines, Japan, Turkey and Italy. Unlike typhoons, earthquakes give no advance warning. Contrary to quake scenes you have seen on television or in movies, the earth does not open, swallow up cities and then slam shut! Learn if your locale is prone to earth tremors and quakes and know what action you should take. Here are some general considerations:

Precautions

- Have a portable radio, flashlight with batteries, first aid kit, pipe and crescent wrenches together for an earth tremor emergency.
- Know where gas, electric and water main shutoff valves are. If in doubt ask the appropriate utility company.

During the Shaking

- If you are indoors, stay there. Open doors. When tremors occur a slight tilt can prevent opening a door and you do want to be able to get out when it is safe.
- Take cover under a table or desk or stand in a doorway. Stay as close to inside walls as possible but away from windows. The greatest danger is falling objects.

- Because electrical and gas lines can be jostled and broken, do not use matches or candles.
- If you are outside, move away from buildings and power lines. Do not rush indoors.
- If you are in a car, stop but stay in the vehicle. The car may jiggle a bit which helps absorb the earth movement.

After the Shaking

- Check for safety and fire hazards. Do not use candles or matches.
- Do not operate electrical switches or appliances. Earth movement may have broken water and gas lines and shorted electrical circuits.
- If you smell gas, open windows and shut off main valve. Leave the building.
- If electrical wiring is shorted out, shut off current at main meter box.
- If water pipes are damaged, shut off supply at main valve.
- Check sewage lines and emergency water supply. Don't waste water.
- Be prepared for after-shocks.
- Stay out of severely damaged buildings; after-shocks can cause further collapse.

Tidal waves frequently follow earthquakes. If you are near a coastline, go to the highest ground available.

TRAVELING ABROAD

Once settled in your new country, there will be opportunities to travel. For some, the best trip is the unstructured one. Nonetheless, some basic information helps. The hints in this chapter may be "old hat" to the well-seasoned traveler but helpful to those doing their first traveling and sightseeing abroad.

Traveling Necessities

Your **passport** is needed to get out of a country and into the next one. Some countries will not allow visitors to enter with passports that have less than six months validity.

A **visa** -- even if you are only changing flights or passing through on a train -- may be required. It may not be required for short stopovers *but* you need to know any time limitations. Ask your travel agent to handle necessary visa applications. Be prepared to supply photographs. *Do not take off without any required visas stamped in your passport.*

Know if any **inoculations** are required or immunizations recommended. Check the embassy or consulate of the countries you will visit for all latest information. Prescription drugs should be hand-carried and in their original containers. If of a narcotic type, carry a letter from your physician stating your need for the medication.

A copy of **your itinerary** should be left with family, friends or the office. Include airline and flight information, names, addresses, phone numbers and dates of hotels or homes where you can be reached.

Take **travelers checks** for the countries you will visit. (Personal checks can be difficult to cash when traveling. The receiver has no way to find out in a reasonable time period (it can take three weeks) if a check is good and probably will refuse it. The check record sheets should be separate from the checks themselves. (If left in the check holder, when you lose one, you lose both.) In such cases, you have the numbers and can report the loss. Some issuers of travelers checks will give immediate replacement checks.

A bit of the **local currency**, including coins, is needed immediately when you arrive in any country -- for a telephone, toilet or taxi. You'll get the best rate if you remember to get this from a bank before your depart. In addition, airport and other transportation exchange offices are not open round-the-clock.

Some countries have restrictions on the amount of currency, both local and foreign, you may bring in. There also may be restrictions on amounts permitted to be taken out. Check this information before you embark on your trip.

Read up on **local customs** in the areas you will visit so you don't offend -- by actions, words or dress.

Ignorance of **the law** is no excuse -- anywhere. It's obvious money should never be exchanged on the black market, but did you know:

- Taking antiquities from Turkey or religious objects from Thailand is a crime. Taking religious objects into the Arab countries is also a crime.
- Exceeding the limit on your credit card can land you in jail in Greece and elsewhere.
- Doing business when you enter a country with a tourist visa is forbidden in many places.
- In Mexico, South Korea and Spain, all parties involved in an automobile accident may be arrested until it is determined who is at fault.

Getting There

International trips are easiest to arrange when you use the services of a travel agent. They do not charge for their efforts and can help you get the most out of a trip. Ask them about:

- budget tickets and group rates
- all inclusive travel/hotel package offerings
- supplemental tickets or coupons for extra trips at no charge or for a small additional amount
- possible reduction in fare under advance booking and prepayment plans

Always ask about the limitations on changing scheduled flights. There may be no flexibility or alternate flights may be available only at substantial financial cost.

Remember holidays when making your travel plans. Each country has special ones which can mean difficulty in getting accommodations. Also, museums and other places of interest may be closed. If you arrive in Mexico City for a long weekend of shopping and sightseeing over Easter, you will find stores, businesses, banks and other places close at noon on Maundy Thursday and reopen Tuesday after Easter Monday! However, special events and celebrations over holidays can offer attractions and reasons to be there.

Always reconfirm flight reservations. Airlines request 72 hours notice. Make a note of day, time and name of agent taking the reconfirmation. Some airports/airlines have specific requirements regarding the time you must be at the airport ahead of your flight. Failure to be on time very likely will cause cancellation of your reservation and standbys given your place. If you are in an area or resort where flights are only a few days each week -- or weekly! -- you can have a real problem!

Know whether the flight at 8:05 is a.m. or p.m. The system where the hours after noon are counted from 13 to 24 is not universal. If you are traveling through several countries recheck schedules as you go and take extra care to get to the airport at the right time -- and, don't laugh, on the right day. Crossing the international dateline can cross you up! In most countries the date is written with the day first, followed by the month, then the year. Avoid confusion by always writing out the name of the month, but don't forget the more common number arrangement when you read ticket arrival and departure information.

Many international airports have "gone silent." Loudspeakers are no longer used to announce flights. You're responsible to check signboards for information.

Immigration/emigration? Embarkation/debarkation? These travel document terms often are confusing. You are immigrating as you enter a country, emigrating as you depart. The embarkation point is the place at which you board your flight (or ship), the debarkation point is the place where you get off.

Travel by Bus, Train and Car

Travel by bus, train and car can be most enjoyable. When traveling from one country to another, you will still have passport, visa and customs inspections at the border.

Buses in Europe and Japan are efficient and clean. In Southeast Asia, India and South America, however, you may be traveling with the pigs and chickens en route to the market and your suitcases or backpack given a place on the roof or on the running board!

Travel by train throughout Europe is a pleasant experience. Terminals are generally in convenient mid-city locations. The Trans European Express (TEE) trains are truly a comfortable, easy way to travel, the Orient Express luxurious. Train travel through Siberia and China may not be as accommodating or luxurious but certainly fascinating! Reservations are required on many trains. Most have smoking and non-smoking cars.

A driving trip can be the most enjoyable allowing you time to enjoy the countryside, stop to picnic in a shady spot or hike mountain paths. Everything can go smoothly with a good detailed map and adequate, readable road signs. When this is not the case, you can have an interesting challenge! Find out ahead of time about gasoline and service stations. In some countries a gas station is just that -- gas is sold and you can get air for the tires or a quart of oil for the engine, but a service station is needed to change oil, tires and other necessities. Know if stations close at midday and how late you can expect to find one open at night. In rural areas it's best to keep the gas tank full. You can run into areas with periods of no electricity which can mean no way to pump gas. An automobile association or rental car office should have an emergency telephone number for cars in trouble.

In some countries it is customary to tip gas station attendants. Also, it is "the system" in some areas to have a car watcher who expects some small coins as pay. This small amount given with a cheerful "I'd appreciate your watching my car" does a lot more than a brush-off. It certainly will be cheaper than a "missing" hubcap!

If you have a rental car ask the agent for any required permits to enter another country. Proof of insurance is usually an entry prerequisite to another country. Take out substantial liability and property damage insurance. Some countries have minimum and maximum age limits for rental car drivers (for example, minimum age of 25 in France and maximum age of 65 in the Philippines, U.K. and Sri Lanka).

Don't leave anything, especially valuables, in the car while you are sightseeing. Those warning signs seen in parking lots at scenic vistas (be it Hawaii or Sorrento) are telling you there have been repeated instances of theft. Stow everything possible in the car trunk -- *before* starting your day's journey. It is involved and frustrating to have theft incidents, especially when traveling in a foreign country.

Roadblocks are routine in Sweden, Switzerland and elsewhere to check on car fitness and to make driver alcohol tests.

Accommodations

Categories of hotels vary worldwide from deluxe to cheap. Your choice may be on the basis of location, cost or recommendations. Small European hotels, usually used by the locals, can be very nice and certainly less expensive than the center-city, international hotels. Bear in mind as you make reservations that classifications are relative to what is available. Although you may not need a deluxe room in Paris, you definitely may want it in Phuket or Bangalore. When making travel arrangements, obtain a written confirmation for your accommodations. It speeds up registration and, more importantly, can avoid a "full up" reception. Reservations are held, generally, until 6 p.m. If you will be arriving about or after that time, ask for a "guaranteed reservation." The hotel guarantees to hold the room; you guarantee to pay for it.

There are many possibilities for rooms other than hotels.

- In England and elsewhere the country inns are delightful, atmospheric places to stay.

- Many homes in Scotland offer "bed-and-breakfast." Not only are the prices less than hotels, you can enjoy the hospitality of a house and very welcoming hosts. Their breakfasts are fantastic, many-course experiences!

- *Zimmer* signs throughout Germany and parts of Switzerland mean a bedroom for the night.

- *Pensions* throughout Europe are less fancy and less expensive than hotels. Some offer meals.
- In Portugal the government-sponsored inns are *pousadas* and in Spain they are *paradors*. These are lovely, often luxurious, accommodations for reasonable prices. A very limited number of rooms are available so advance reservations are really a must. Even if they cannot accommodate you overnight, you can stop for a meal if convenient in your travel schedule.
- The Japanese *ryokans* (inns) will give you an authentic taste of a very different culture -- tatami mat floor coverings, futon "beds," soaking hot tubs and undoubtedly a television! It's a charming, but expensive, experience.

When registering at hotels, you may be asked to fill out a police information card listing your name, passport number, destination and reason for traveling. In some instances, you'll be asked to leave your passport at the reception desk overnight. This is a normal procedure required by local laws. Registration desks are the one place you can leave your passport without concern but if it makes you more comfortable, ask for a receipt.

Many hotels automatically add a service charge to their bill. This applies to rooms, restaurants, laundry and other services. When you register ask if this is the case so you can tip, or not tip, accordingly. An additional government accommodations tax is occasionally levied.

Hotels have safekeeping facilities. Use them. Not all will have the individual metal box with key. Some will have a small safe in your room. Some will issue a large paper envelope to enclose your items, identify it with a number, give you a receipt and disappear behind a door! The most common hotel thefts are passports, cash, flight tickets, credit cards, cameras and jewelry (in that order).

Most city hotels have same day laundry service. If there isn't a category for perma-press laundry on the ticket, call the housekeeping department and ask if it is possible to have a warm or cold water wash rather than the standard one of 90 degrees C. That's almost 200 degrees F! It's great for cleaning the kids' denim cutoffs but will permanently shrink their tube socks and T-shirts! Laundries (*dhobi*) in India are truly unusual and fascinating to see. You can hear them blocks away! They are large outdoor cement washing troughs with beating tables. You wonder how all your shirt buttons can be intact -- but they will be! "Dhobi itch" can occur anywhere. It is usually from clothes that have not been rinsed well enough and the soap left in them can be irritating, especially in underwear.

Just as you don't always drive on the right side of the road, hot water doesn't always come from the left spigot. Before you call the reception desk, try both spigots and see if the right-hand one provides the hot water you were expecting from the left one. When staying as a guest in friends' homes where there are full-time servants, ask if it is proper (or improper) to leave them a tip. If appropriate, your hostess should advise the amount.

Ways to Travel Economically

A group package is usually the most economical way to travel. These plans cover transportation, porter fees, transport to and from the airport, hotels, required government taxes, food, tips, intracity transport and sightseeing. Off- or low-season rates will save money. If this does not fit your plans and personality, there are other ways to economize.

As you work with your travel agent specify economy flights or special fares. Perhaps you can take advantage of flights on low-rate days or early morning hours. Consider train or bus travel. The Eurail pass offers discounted prices for train travel throughout Western Europe. Available for students and adults, it must be purchased in the U.S. Good for a month of travel, this begins when the ticket is first used. Other countries offer similar discount cards. Ask a tourist office where they can be purchased.

Sometimes it is possible to tour by renting drive-yourself live-in vehicles. These have cooking facilities which help cut food costs. A tourist or automobile association may be able to give you names of rental agencies for this type of motor home or "caravan."

When using rental cars, check before you go for special reduced rates. These may apply to a car returned to the same starting point or used a minimum number of days. You probably will have to book a week in advance and may have to pay up front but a savings of up to 30% is worth it. Discount coupon books in travel information packets may entitle you to reduced sightseeing admissions, free breakfasts and other benefits.

Travel guide books often give price information for hotels. Be sure you are not unpleasantly surprised by year-old information.

Write national tourist offices for suggestions and accommodation assistance.

- Stay outside major cities in small hotels. There may not be a newspaper kiosk or gift shop but lots of quaint charm.
- Make reservations as far ahead as possible so you get what you want. When writing hotels, specify economy or standard rooms. If no mention is made of the type of room wanted, you most likely will be assigned deluxe. Economy may mean a room on a lower floor with a view of the car park (instead of the park) and perhaps no television, but in Milan would you understand "Barney Miller" in Italian?
- A double bed is almost always cheaper than twin beds. Add a cot to accommodate a child. If children are below a certain age, sometimes up to 16, they may be free when sharing a room with parents.
- When you check in, or out, ask if there is a better price for paying with cash rather than a credit card.

Other possibilities for overnight rooms are the YMCA's and YWCA's. In countries where you can judge that accommodations are reliable, guest lodges, tourist homes (a *pension, zimmer* or bed-and-breakfast) and hostels are other possibilities. Youth hostels can be found in 50 countries at 4500 locations and offer inexpensive overnight accommodations. Family hostels are available in a few cities.

Hotel restaurants can be expensive, especially breakfasts when there is no snack bar and no *a la carte* choices -- but only the buffet breakfast at $14.00. Before you sit down and sip your morning cup of coffee, you may want to check the menu at the door for prices and any minimum charge. If you plan ahead, you can purchase fruit and other items to eat in your room or find a nearby bakery or coffee shop. With a family, it can make a big difference. Those hotel room packages of peanuts the children may tear into while you get your bags into the room cost double their supermarket price so carry your own snacks. When driving, picnic lunches can be enjoyable while giving children a chance to run and release energy. By taking canned soda, carton juice drinks or a bottle of wine you don't have to worry about finding safe water to drink.

Check tourist information sources to see if museums and other special attractions have reduced rates on weekends or holidays. Always ask if there is a student discount. These can apply for university years as well as the kindergarten through high school years.

Many good books are available with valuable information and insights to help you travel economically. Check out the Lonely Planet *On a Shoestring* series for many countries.

Packing

Travel as light as possible. Really ask yourself if all those clothes are needed. On most sightseeing vacation trips chances are you won't see many, if any, people who know you; therefore, only you will know whether it's the second or third time an outfit has been worn.

Most hotels have one-day laundry service; many have a stretch-line for hand laundry. Drip-dry clothes which you can launder save suitcase space by reducing the amount of clothes needed. Put the plastic bottle of liquid detergent in a plastic bag to protect against possible messy leakage. In an emergency, you can use shampoo for laundry.

If you like the convenience of a travel iron, purchase one with dual voltage (110 *and* 220). But when you travel to Australia and New Zealand, you can leave it at home. Hotels there have self-laundry facilities or the housekeeping department will bring an ironing board and iron to your room at no charge.

A travel clock is handy, especially when you will be staying in bed-and-breakfast type accommodations.

Many hotels do not provide washcloths so you may want to pack one or two -- thin ones that will dry quickly. Carry handkerchiefs and tissues when traveling. Eastern and Western toilets are different; hand towels and toilet paper often are absent in the former.

If your trip will take you into "back country" places in such countries as India, Malaysia, Kenya and China, take along some nuts, crackers, raisins or other snack items.

Be sure to leave some empty space in suitcases to put those souvenirs, planned and unplanned. There are lots of tempting items to buy whether you are in Florence, Baguio or Buenos Aires. If you are a "big" shopper or traveling with a list of unique objects you've seen in other people's homes and hope to duplicate, tuck some heavy string and sealing tape in your suitcase just in case you need a box to bring it (all) back!

Baggage

U.S. airlines currently permit two checked items with no weight limit. Weight of baggage, however, is still the criteria in other countries. The charge for excess pounds can be astronomical. Also, not all countries have the usual 20 kilo weight allowance, especially on domestic flights, for example, Taiwan. To avoid surprise payments and inconvenience, ask questions before you depart on your trip.

Airports sometimes set a flat fee for each piece of baggage carried by a porter. Look for signs telling you this.

Some airports are strict with regulations for carry-on luggage. The one piece allowed has size limitations and must fit under the seat or in the closed overhead compartment. The wheel-behind-you carrier for carry-on baggage is a great convenience. Although many airports have boarding directly into the airplane from the terminal, don't overload it so you can't carry it when faced with airport stairs, bus transfers to the plane and airplane steps.

Two small suitcases can be better than one gigantic, heavy one. Porters are scarce in many cities. In England, cabs have an automatic door-opening device controlled by a sit-in-place cabbie and you have to hoist your own luggage into the cab interior.

At the Airport

Customs requirements everywhere vary for non-residents, residents-to-be and re-entering residents. Know the regulations. As an example, although you could bring in 400 cigarettes when you moved to the country, as a resident you may be allowed to bring in only 200.

The security x-ray machines in airports are not always safe for photographic film. This is especially true for extra-sensitive, high-speed film. Repetitive x-ray exposure has a cumulative effect. Request camera cases and equipment be personally inspected.

You may be asked to register radios, watches, cameras and lenses when you enter a country. If this is the case, you can be asked to show them when you exit. This is a government measure to prevent selling or disposing of such articles.

Exchange money at banks or official changers in the airport or train terminal before you take a taxi or other transportation to your destination. You are ready to pay in local currency and it usually is a better rate than at hotels. To avoid double exchange rates, change money as you need it and only the amount you feel you need. When departing, before changing all your money to another currency, remember that most countries have an airport departure tax. Rarely is it included in the price of your ticket. It is common for international travel but in India, and perhaps other countries, there is also a domestic air tax.

Before you leave the airport ask the cost for taxis or other transportation to your destination. If taxis are non-metered, pre-arrange the price. This can avoid uneasiness and the unpleasant feeling of being "ripped off" which is not the way to start any trip, business or pleasure. Many airports have economical bus service to a center-city terminal or hotels. Look to see if there is transportation provided by hotels for their customers. Any charge for this can be put directly on your bill.

Health

The travel guide books you undoubtedly will read almost always have a section on health precautions for the country being visited so comments here are only to alert you to acquaint yourself with such information.

Changes in time and climate when traveling, and a go-go sightseeing schedule, can easily tire you. For summer travel or in hot weather areas, take it slow. Heat and humidity truly sap energy and cause fatigue.

Water purity varies all over the world and can cause problems. If you find carafes of water in your hotel room or bathroom, it should be used for drinking and for brushing teeth. To remind children to use the bottled water, take the paper or plastic wrapper that usually covers the drinking glasses, or the plastic shower cap generally provided, and put it over the cold water spigot. This will alert them that something is unusual.

The hotel restaurants used by most tourists provide bottled water for drinking. If in doubt, ask for it. In local restaurants, ask if bottled water is available or order packaged soft drinks. When really traveling off the beaten track, take water purification tablets with you.

Those hot or cold towels presented to you on airlines and in Asian restaurants are refreshing and convenient -- to wipe your hands. Since they are not sterilized or germ-free, avoid using them around your eyes and mouth. In certain countries you may wish to avoid foods that do not have to be skinned to eat, such as strawberries, tomatoes, lettuce and the like. You may think they are fine, but that may not be the case. Peelable fruits such as pineapple, oranges, watermelon and cooked vegetables generally do not cause problems. Also avoid eating greasy foods.

Recognizing that purity, pasteurization and refrigeration standards differ worldwide, in certain areas you may want to avoid dairy products (milk, coffee cream, butter, ice cream, whipped cream) as well as salads containing mayonnaise. If you have reservations about food being properly refrigerated, choose hot dishes rather than cold ones.

Digestive and intestinal upsets are common travel afflictions. You never know when or where such ailments will surprise you so it is wise to carry medications for such "attacks." "Traveler's diarrhea" is a problem that should last no more than three days. If it lasts longer, see a doctor. In addition to something you ate, diarrhea can be caused by excessive amounts of monosodium glutamate (MSG) in food preparation. Japan, Taiwan and Southeast Asian countries use a lot of this in their cooking. It also can cause palpitations and headaches so when problems arise, remember that MSG could be responsible.

Cholera and yellow fever inoculations are required for travel to specific tropical and sub-tropical countries. These countries also are the ones that most frequently have malaria. Even if you are only stopping or passing through, you may need preventive protection. See the *Meeting Medical Needs* chapter for detailed information on these diseases and others.

If your hotel bed has mosquito netting around it, you are being given a message. The netting should drape over the sides of the bed and be tucked under the mattress. It should not touch you. Use an insect repellent -- on your skin or sprayed in the room -- as well. Close sink and tub drains to keep out other creepy crawlers!

Items to be carried in an emergency first aid kit include: thermometer, aspirin (you can always use an adult aspirin for a child by cutting it into small dosage and dissolving in water), bandaids, antibacterial ointment, diarrhea medication, antibiotics, liquid or stick-form bug repellent, antihistamine medication or cream to relieve bites and allergic reactions to insects. Hotel staff can contact doctors for medical emergencies. The U.S. embassies and consulates usually have lists of English-speaking doctors and dentists in their area.

In some countries, such as New Zealand and Holland, if you suffer personal injury by accident, you are entitled to compensation under accident compensation schemes irrespective of fault. If you are injured while traveling, ask if this is the case in the country where the accident occurs.

Sightseeing

To get an overall picture of a new large city, an introductory guided bus tour is most helpful, after which you can explore special areas and places on foot. Tourist agencies have maps of the local places of interest, tours, hints on how to get around as well as other free information. Try one of these offices first for information.

Wear your most comfortable shoes, ones with cushioned soles and good traction. They will be much safer for walking on slippery wet stones, uneven steps, ramps, pebble paths and in dimly lit caves and tombs. In Asia, shoes are removed before entering a temple. Generally it is not respectful to sit on the raised floor or step of a temple to take off or put on shoes. Observe what others do. If you have a "Tour the Temples" day, wear shoes you can slip easily off and on! A few religions forbid leather in their places of worship -- this could be shoes, purses, belts and camera cases.

When using taxis for local transportation, your hotel doorman or someone else can tell you about fares. If taxis have meters, is the fare as it will be shown? One doesn't like to be surprised by a driver asking for double the amount saying, "Gas price higher." Whenever possible, set the price before you go. A tip is usual in most places. In a few, such as China, Japan and Yugoslavia, it is not customary, expected or even acceptable.

Signs on trams, in stores and elsewhere to beware of pickpockets let you know there is, or has been, a problem. Take preventative measures, mentally and otherwise. Professional pickpockets are slick and quick. Often working in pairs, most "work" in crowded, busy places: elevators, airports, subways and other public transportation, markets and festivals. To make it more difficult to slip from a pocket, men can use a wide rubber-band around their wallet. A suede wallet is difficult to remove. A wallet carried in a front pants pocket is less accessible than in a back one. The inside jacket pocket is safer than a back pants pocket but still accessible. Women can prevent a potential theft by carrying handbags tucked tightly under the arm and held by the strap. It is difficult to prevent purse stealing by the curb-riding motorcyclist snatchers or the fast-fingered fellows who reach in the open car window to remove a purse on the seat.

Shopping

If you have limited time in a city and are interested in folk crafts, ask about government handicraft stores. Also try the local museums where gift shops proudly display and sell artistic native items and good reproductions.

Always ask if there is a tax on items that will be leaving the country. In Europe several countries have a Value Added Tax (VAT). If you carry the item through customs (it can't be in a checked piece of luggage), they will refund the tax on presentation of the sales receipt and the article.

If a store accepts credit cards they may not give a discount. If you pay with cash or travelers checks it's a possibility. If a retailer asks you to pay the percentage charged him by the credit card company, he is probably violating his agreement with the card company.

Recognize at the outset of your trip that foreigners may be charged more for an item than a local person. This can be in everyday situations at the market as well as when you try to bargain in a shop.

Bargaining

Haggling is a way of life in some countries -- for an orange in a Caracas supermarket, a Big Mac in Morocco or a brass candlestick in Athens' Plaka. You have nothing to lose anywhere by asking for a better price. If you don't ask for it, it won't be offered! Nothing ventured, nothing gained. You should/must bargain in South America, Turkey and developing countries. You may/can bargain in Italy and Hong Kong. You should not bargain in Germany, Switzerland or England. Sometimes the seller immediately declares (whispers!) he will give you a discount. When he does, it's your invitation to seek an even greater price cut. Bargaining is sometimes discreet (the Grand Bazaar in Istanbul) and sometimes animated and very loud (Hong Kong's jade market). A large purchase can take considerable time while you contemplate, then discuss price, then feign losing interest and visit other shops or while you sip the offered cup of coffee.

There are no set rules for bargaining. Some travelers enjoy this "sport" and others detest it. When and if you bargain, participate in it with a sense of humor -- "It can't cost that much, I won't have taxi fare back to the hotel!" Don't try it unless you expect to buy something. Know what you will pay and recognize when it's time to give in. Many times you will find you are haggling over only 40 or 50 cents! Don't demean yourself or your fellow countrymen.

POTPOURRI

Alien Registration

Many countries require registration of foreign residents. You will need to know the time period in which you may be required to register with local authorities. When an identification card is issued, usually it must be carried with you at all times. The registration or i.d. card is sometimes a requirement before you can purchase a car, obtain a driver's license, open a bank account, rent premises or before household goods can be cleared through customs.

Banking

Currency in other countries will be a variety of different sizes and colors. (You'll miss these aspects when you return to the U.S.!) Likewise, banking procedures will differ.

Many U.S. banks operate internationally. Depending on local banking regulations, similar services to those provided in the U.S. will be available: checking accounts, savings accounts, security custody accounts, safe deposit boxes. Do not assume, however, that all procedures are the same. Ask about minimum balance requirements, the time it takes for deposited checks to clear, how quickly funds are accessible when you deposit a U.S. check and whether they have automatic debit service.

When opening an account in any bank, ask specific questions about checks and procedures and spare yourself surprises; for instance, bank statements may not enclose cancelled checks and may only give the account balance.

A joint bank account can require a special letter by the husband or he may have to appear at the bank with his spouse to complete the application. (That may be difficult for the American woman to understand, but few countries are as liberal as the U.S. regarding women's rights.)

Procedures for writing checks vary. The use of crossed checks is common in many countries: two parallel lines on a check indicate it is for deposit only. Unless the word "bearer" is drawn through on a check, anyone can cash it.

Banks may require 48 hours to clear any deposited local check, even if it is drawn on the same bank. Much more time is required for a foreign check.

Americans write dates with the month first: November 12, 1989 or 11/12/89. This system is not used universally; in fact, dates are more commonly written with the month as the middle figure -- November 12, 1989 then becomes 12/11/89. To avoid confusion you can always write the name of the month rather then use a number. However, you must understand the method used where you are; this is essential for documents with a time limitation such as driver's license, residence registration, permits and inoculations.

The use of the decimal and the comma in writing numbers in money figures is different in the U.S. and elsewhere. U.S. $234.56 may be written *Sf* 234,56 in Switzerland and U.S. $2,345.56 may be written *ff* 2.345,56 in France. In some countries the seven is crossed, 7, and the one is written to look like a seven, 1. Again, use the system where you are.

There always seems to be unexpected expenses when getting settled. Travelers checks can bridge a gap but do establish banking facilities as quickly as possible after your arrival. If you were not able to open an account with an international bank with an office in your new location, consider the bank where your company has an account. This can ease time restrictions on transfer of funds and establishing credit reliability.

Banks or official money exchanges should be used for changing money to the local currency as they give the best exchange rate. If you ask, better rates are achieved when exchanging large amounts of money.

Birth of a Child Abroad

The birth of a child abroad requires registration with local authorities *and* with the U.S. embassy or consulate. Do not assume anything will be taken care of at the hospital. It's your responsibility to find out how, to obtain the birth certificate and register the birth with the proper authorities.

A child born abroad to a U.S. citizen parent or parents generally acquires U.S. citizenship at birth. A *Report of Birth Abroad of a Citizen of the U.S.A.* (Form FS-240) must be completed at the embassy or consulate. The birth certificate, parents' passports and their marriage license are needed to do this. This certification of birth may be used as proof of citizenship and is acceptable evidence for obtaining a passport. If only one parent is a U.S. citizen, the U.S. parent must have met certain residency requirements.

Change of Address in Host Country

To move within a country may require official paperwork. Know the time limits you must observe regarding notification of address change -- it can be as little as three days. Those to be notified include driver licensing bureau, car registration office, tax office, alien registration agency, insurance companies and the post office, of course. Remember also to notify the U.S. embassy or consulate where you are registered.

Emergencies

Make a list of emergency telephone numbers. Household help and babysitters should be informed of those for fire, police, doctor and ambulance. Other numbers to include: electric, gas and water companies, electrician, plumber, taxi, husband's office, hospital, poison, drug and snake bite centers. In an emergency, you want to be able to reach necessary help without delay.

Exit Visas

A visa to exit from a country is required in a few places. It is issued for a restricted time and can take weeks to renew. *Where it is required, you must have a valid one at all times.* Be sure you allow sufficient time to get any required visas for children who will be visiting from the U.S. or other out-of-country schools.

Insurance

As anywhere, you will have certain insurance needs. Most countries require vehicle liability insurance, some for bicycles as well as cars and motorcycles. You also should consider collision, comprehensive and medical coverage.

Household insurance will be needed the day your shipment is brought into your new premises. Where thievery is common, ask about coverage for burglary. You may want a special theft endorsement to protect against loss where there is no evidence of breaking and entering.

If you are in a typhoon or flood area, know what your policy does and does not cover and whether special insurance protection is available and advisable.

Personal liability and medical insurance are others to consider. In a few countries you will be required to have pet insurance. Be sure to ask if school transportation services are insured or if you will need to obtain coverage for regular school buses and special trips. Workmen's compensation is advisable for any household help you employ.

Laundry and Dry Cleaning Symbols

Wearing apparel often has sewn-in labels with laundry and dry cleaning information. The most frequently seen symbols are:

DRY CLEANING	WASHING	DRYING	IRONING	BLEACHING
All processes (A)	Can be boiled (95)	Dry flat	Do not iron	Do not bleach
Standard process (P)	Water not over 60°C. (60)	Drip dry (III)	Cool	May use chlorine bleach (Cl)
Fluorocarbon process (F)	Water not over 30°C. (30) Not washable	Tumble dry low setting	Moderate	
			Hot	

When sending clothing to a laundry or dry cleaner, specify *each time* if it is to be washed or dry cleaned. To assume that a silk dress will be dry cleaned or a cotton shirt washed is a mistake.

Legal Status

U.S. citizens, children as well as adults, living or traveling abroad are subject to the laws of the country they are in. Before you go overseas become familiar with the laws of your destination country that affect foreigners. Ask your corporation about your legal rights. Visit the U.S. embassy or consulate in the new country to ask what legal problems foreigners encounter. You want to know what to do in case of a car accident, when you are robbed, etc.

Police often are intolerant of even the smallest deviation in behavior by foreigners. Laws regarding an arrested or detained person are different from those in the U.S. Many legal systems do not permit, nor are they required to, a telephone call to anyone. Many countries hold you as guilty until proven innocent, the reverse of American rights. You may have no right to be represented by a lawyer at first detention. Most countries do not accept bail. Few countries provide a jury trial. Officials may not speak English.

Drug law offenders face extremely serious consequences. Penalties for possession or trafficking are often the same. Pre-trial detention may last for months; prisons may lack even minimal comforts; diets often require supplements from relatives or friends. Sentences are long and also may include a stiff fine; death is demanded in some countries for drug offenses.

Manners

Americans are generally considered to be friendly, outgoing, self-confident (sometimes, too bold!) and outspoken. This often presents itself as being loud and rude. Speak in a soft voice. Listen to what others are saying without interrupting. Avoid speaking in a way that could be misconstrued as a demand or command. You will cause resentment if you do and also lose face in that person's estimation of you.

It is always best to begin conversations sharing opinions on general subjects such as weather, sports and the latest news. You can seek information about the city and things going on. Personal questions about family members, political concerns and business should be avoided, at least until you know it is all right to discuss such matters.

Be careful what you say in public places. Assume those around you understand English and do not make remarks that will cause embarrassment to you or them.

The publications of local American men and women's clubs as well as other English-speaking groups throughout the world are an indispensable source of specific "how to," "when not to" and "where" information. In addition to basic information on getting settled, among others, *Inside Information, Holland* will tell you about the protocol of serving drinks, making toasts and eating; the Malaysian *Selamat Datang* (Welcome) gives titles and forms of address which should be used; *Living in Geneva* gives hours when grass cutting is not permitted; and *Living in Japan* discusses woman's role in a man's society. Wherever you will be, books of these types will offer valuable inside information.

Be yourself -- but at the same time be sensitive to the way of your host country. In most places you will continue the Western mannerism of shaking hands. This is an expected greeting in most Latin and European countries. Shaking hands is done on entering and meeting people and again when departing, individually, with everyone -- men, women and children. Few countries outside the U.S. have our informal group greetings of "Hi, everybody" and "Bye, y'all."

As you know the customs of the country better and are together frequently with certain people, it may be appropriate to use their form of greeting. You will recognize when, and if, it is proper and comfortable to use a local mannerism.

Printed invitations to business and social occasions are common in many places. Sometimes an invitation is verbal and followed by a written "to remind" instead of the more usual "R.s.v.p." Often the dress for the occasion is indicated on the invitation and it will be interpreted differently in different places. "Casual" in the U.S. will mean sport clothes; in India a man will wear a shirt without a tie but an Indian woman undoubtedly will wear a sari and you may feel uncomfortable in your pink flowered culottes. A lounge suit is a business suit, usually dark, not a tuxedo or a safari-type outfit. When in doubt about what to wear, ask the host or hostess. This will be far less embarrassing than guessing.

It may be appropriate to take a gift on a first visit to someone's home. This might (or might not!) be flowers, wine or liquor, fruit or a fine tea. Find out from others what is appropriate. Also, does the man or woman present the gift to the host or hostess? In some countries a gift is opened immediately, in others it is opened after the guests depart. If it is usual to take flowers, as a hostess you may want to be prepared with several vases in the kitchen so the bouquet can be brought quickly to the entertaining area. As the one giving the flowers, be sure you are bringing an appropriate flower and color. If you order flowers for delivery, tell the florist the occasion, such as dinner, birthday or illness, so he can advise you. You want to know what is correct so you don't embarrass yourself or the person receiving the gift.

A handwritten note of appreciation after a party or special hospitality is a must in most countries. In Norway you would also telephone.

In many places it is not polite to telephone after 8:30 p.m. or before 9 a.m. except for an emergency. That can be a real adjustment for the American teenager! In Moslem countries, avoid telephoning a Moslem between 6:45 p.m. and 7:15 p.m., the hour of evening prayers.

It will take a while to know the manners and customs of your new country. In the meantime be observant and courteous and your intentions will be accepted as wanting to learn the ways of your hosts.

Receipts

Save receipts from purchases you make while overseas. Write the U.S. dollar equivalent on them at the time of purchase. If you've bought the item in Athens, Moscow, Peking, Madras or elsewhere where the alphabet is other than a,b,c,d,e, and you are not a linguistic whiz kid with a fantastic memory, you also should identify the item purchased. These receipts are not only for inventory purposes. When you move back to the U.S. certain items are dutiable and you need records of purchases. Antiques, classified as items over 100 years old, are not dutiable. The seller will need to write a note on his letterhead stationery describing the antique and its age.

The U.S. participates in a Generalized System of Preferences (GSP) agreement used to help developing nations improve their economic condition through export trade. This provides for duty-free importation of a wide range of products which would otherwise be subject to customs duty. The list of countries and products is updated annually. Consulates or the U.S. Customs Service,

Washington, D.C. 20229 or local branches, have a *GSP and the Traveler* booklet listing the beneficiary countries and items covered. This is important information to know anytime you travel in and out of the U.S., not just when repatriating.

Repairs

It is always wise to get an estimate for repair work in writing. This can avoid misunderstandings when the work is completed.

Shopping

When you see something you need or want, buy it then. Often it will be gone later. This is true especially for imported articles. You may not need the canned pumpkin in March but it may not be available in November.

Charge accounts are available in many places for daily deliveries, grocery and department stores. Be sure you understand the method of billing, finance charges, cancellation process, what to do if the charge card is lost and what your responsibilities are.

Know whether verbal agreements are binding. If you ask for something to be ordered are you committed to accept and pay for it? In Holland, you are.

As everywhere, stores close on holidays. Learn about the local holidays which may be new to you and do any necessary advance shopping. Chinese New Year, a lunar date, is a five-day holiday in many Asian countries and you could be surprised to find you have run out of milk on day three.

Save receipts. As in the U.S., merchandise cannot be returned without them. Some stores will not make refunds but will give you store credit. In at least one European country, stores have special hours for exchanges and returns.

Local thrift shops often are places to take your used, outgrown, unwanted items and perhaps discover a towel rack you haven't been able to find elsewhere, or a garden rake you did not bring or a scout uniform unavailable in a local store.

Telephones

Depending on your area, you may lease or purchase your telephone locally and then have to arrange with the telephone company for installation. International direct dialing is available in most countries, sometimes by special arrangement. Always ask about the waiting time for a telephone connection before you commit to your housing.

Read the front pages of your telephone book. They often are a source of information on postal zones, bus routes, typhoon signals and earthquake precautions. Commercial Yellow Pages are quite international, but they may be Blue!

Telephone bills sometimes are sent quarterly for basic charges and monthly for long distance calls. In some countries, the post office and telephone company are one and bills are paid at the post office.

Time

The 0810 (8:10 a.m.) and 2135 (9:35 p.m.) way of telling time is used by airlines worldwide and in many countries this same system is used in daily time-telling. This is one of those areas where you will need to conform to the system.

You also may have to learn certain time-telling terminology, for example, "half seven." Is it 6:30 or 7:30? In Scandinavia it is probably 6:30 and in Germany 7:30. You wouldn't want to be too early or embarrassingly late for a dinner invitation! Some places will not understand "quarter to ten" or "nine forty-five" but will know "15 before the hour of 10." Don't miss a rendezvous because you can't tell time!

Tipping

In a few countries tipping is unexpected even unacceptable. Where it is done, tipping should be appropriate to the country standards, not U.S. ones. You don't want to offend or make it uncomfortable for yourself and others.

Ask a person from the host country about tipping practices. They can tell you whom to tip and how much. Taxi drivers are not tipped in Taiwan but are in London; beauty shop attendants are tipped in Switzerland but shop owners who attend you are not. Americans, who more and more pump their own gas, are not accustomed to tipping gas station attendants as is done in the Philippines.

In most international locations, a service charge is added automatically to restaurant bills. None is expected; however, you may wish to leave the small coins left from paying the check.

U.S. Embassy or Consulate Services

Each United States embassy and consulate has a section to deal with the affairs of Americans residing and traveling abroad. Consular officers advise and help in many ways, especially if someone is in serious legal, medical, financial or other trouble. They cannot cash checks, find work for you or get residence or driving permits, nor act as travel agents or interpreters, search for missing luggage or settle disputes with hotel managers.

Consulates renew passports, add pages to an existing one and replace lost passports. A lost passport should be reported immediately to the nearest embassy or consulate as well as to local police authorities.

The birth of a child to a U.S. citizen should be reported to the embassy or consulate in order to establish the child's status as a U.S. citizen. (See *Birth of a Child Abroad* earlier in this chapter.) Adoptions and marriages should be reported also. It is in the U.S. embassy or consulate that you apply for a visa to bring an alien spouse or adopted child to the U.S. (All visas, in fact, for visitors or immigrants to the U.S. are issued abroad by consular officers.) Deaths should be reported immediately to them. While the next of kin is responsible for funeral arrangements, consular personnel can give assistance. Many consulates have notarial services.

Forms to apply for a social security number are available from U.S. embassies and consulates. Any dependent age 5 or over is required to have this number and it must be given on federal tax returns.

The embassies in London, Rome, Paris, Frankfurt, Bonn, Manila, Singapore, Tokyo, Sydney, Ottawa, Mexico City, Caracas, Sao Paulo, Jidda, Johannesburg and Nassau have a permanent staff member from the Internal Revenue Service (IRS) to assist with federal tax information and forms. Others are visited by an IRS person, usually in the spring, to help U.S. citizens with tax questions.

Americans living abroad were granted the right to vote in U.S. elections by the Voting Rights Act of December 1976. The laws state an American can vote by absentee ballot in a federal election only without fear the ballot can be cited as proof of liability for state and local taxes. If you have other ties with a state beside federal voting, you may have state or local tax obligations. Your legal residence is the state where you last resided before departing from the U.S., whether or not you own property there and whether or not you expect to return to that state. The U.S. embassy or consulate nearest you can give information on obtaining absentee ballots and will assist with any required notarization. Contact them for the *Voting Assistance Guide* and the Federal Post Card Application (FPCA). Start early -- at least two months ahead -- to be sure your vote is received in time.

Though not obligatory, visit and register with the nearest U.S. embassy or consulate. Registration enables the consulate to contact you in case of an emergency. One family member can register all family members. Take the passport for each person to be registered.

Consular offices often have a useful list of English-speaking doctors and dentists and other medical information.

If you find yourself in a dispute which could lead to legal or police action, consult a consular officer who can provide a list of local attorneys and can help you find adequate legal representation. The consulate will do whatever possible to protect your legitimate interests and ensure you are not discriminated against under local law. They cannot get you out of jail. If you are arrested, ask permission to notify the consular officer at the nearest U.S. embassy or consulate. If you are turned down, keep asking -- politely, but persistently.

Wallet Card

In your wallet or purse be sure you have a card or paper with your name and address. A driver's license, identification card, charge cards or bank checks may not have your address on them. In case of loss, there should be a way to contact you. Children also should carry identification.

It is a good idea also to carry an emergency telephone number list in your wallet at all times. You may not always be able to find a telephone directory. In addition to ones for family and employer, include the consulate, your doctor, pediatrician and automobile insurance company.

THE RETURN MOVE

Departure Details

Specific procedures must be followed when moving out of most countries permanently. An exit permit or certified disembarkation card, issued after tax assessments are paid and other necessary paper work completed, may be required. The release of your household goods can be delayed if all obligatory documents, properly certified, are incomplete.

Regulations may necessitate car license plates be returned rather than sold with your car. Get any refund due you for the unused portion. When selling your car, prorate registration fees and license plate costs (if not required to return them) with the new owner. Where applicable, check to see if there is a rebate for the unused portion of road taxes. Ask if there is a refund on your automobile insurance.

If you were required to pay an import duty or tax on goods brought into the country from elsewhere, you can be entitled to a refund when you depart the country permanently taking the items with you. The original entry receipt will have to be produced.

Don't forget to notify the post office and send change of address cards and letters. Use your original departure list as a guide to build a new one.

Packing and Moving

In most foreign countries a "moving out" sale, if permitted, is well attended by local people and expatriates. You may want to sell appliances, local light bulbs and fixtures, house plants, books and pantry items. Let your children participate in the housecleaning of their outgrown and unused toys and games. Use church and supermarket bulletin boards, daily newspaper and school newsletters to advertise sale items. In a few countries, Turkey is an example, all items brought into the country must be exported with you unless given to a local charity or the customs authorities.

Many of the questions and points raised in the *Packing and Moving* chapter will be appropriate again. Since you have moved at least once already, you might take a lot of steps with the packers and movers for granted. More than ever, you need to go over details, desires and special needs with the company moving you. If you are unimpressed with the mover's ability to communicate with you, an apparent lack of understanding or appreciation of your concern for various possessions, look for someone else.

Your jewelry and other valuables should be in a safe deposit box or under lock and key, not in a desk or chest of drawers where they are accessible for theft or can be inadvertently packed.

Packing techniques in Moscow will vary from those in Vienna. Know what to expect by asking questions. Insist that everything be packed *at your house* to avoid possible misunderstanding about broken or missing items. Discuss special crating, servicing of appliances and timing. Working hours vary and the 9-to-5 working day in Atlanta may be 10-11:30 a.m. and 3-7 p.m. in Athens.

If you are *really* fluent in the language, you may not need the supervisor present during all the packing hours but have his telephone number "just in case." It is important to have only two packers at a time so you can keep control of what is going on and how things are being packed. Many packers will not comprehend, let alone speak, English. Don't expect them to understand the value you give to certain of your belongings. When they don't understand how you think something should be done, there is a tendency to say it can't be done. Call that supervisor who speaks English! If something has been agreed upon between you and the moving company and the packers don't understand or are not prepared to do it the agreed way, such as crating old Imari dishes or a goldleaf mirror, stop them. Be insistent on what you want. You are the loser if things arrive damaged. The supervisor will want to right anything to avoid a future claim as well as protect his company's reputation.

When taking rattan or wicker furniture and other items into some countries, a fumigation certificate may be required. Ask ahead of time.

Receipts for things you have purchased since departing from the U.S. may be requested by U.S. customs. These must be carried with you. It can be one grand mess and expense to find them in a shipping container of household goods. Delays due to lack of proper papers can necessitate storage of the shipment; warehouse fees are never insignificant.

Read the documents you are asked to sign by the movers. If they are not in English, get a written translation before signing. You don't want unpleasant surprises because you don't know what you signed. Keep a copy along with the inventory and insurance papers, any weight certificates, inland, ocean or air bills of lading.

Know the name, address and telephone number of the destination agent who will receive your household shipment. Can the agent make any required customs entry for you? What papers does he need? Will a power of attorney be required? What is the estimate of his charges? Once you are in the U.S., telephone him to confirm your address and telephone contact number.

Importation of liquor requires specific licenses and there are federal, and maybe state, taxes to be paid. Any liquor should be sent separate from household goods. Houston, New Orleans, Norfolk, Boston, Savannah and Miami, as well as all West Coast ports, do not permit any wine or alcohol even with a bona fide declaration. If the wine or alcohol is declared, it simply will be confiscated and destroyed. If it is not declared, it will be seized, destroyed and the owner fined in addition to duties and taxes. If the fine is not paid, there is the risk the whole shipment will be seized and sold at auction after one year! In addition, certain states are "dry" and even if the harbor permits entry of alcohol with a declaration, customs will not authorize forwarding to a dry state. The U.S. Customs Service, Washington, D.C. 20229, publishes *State Laws on Importing Alcoholic Beverages*.

U.S. Customs Regulations

When you make the return move to resume U.S. residency, you are considered a returning resident by immigration authorities. At present, each returning resident is allowed to bring in personally, without paying duty, merchandise whose value is up to US$400 provided you have not already used this exemption within the preceding 30 days. The next $1000 worth of items brought back for personal use or gifts is subject to duty at a flat 10% rate. This applies to new purchases, not household items. They must be in your possession at the time of entry into the U.S. Articles in excess of the customs exemption will be subject to duty unless they are entitled to free entry, such as articles from countries under the Generalized System of Preferences (GSP). The *GSP and the Traveler* booklet lists participating countries and covered items.

A customs inspection of your household things may encompass all or none of your shipment. The destination agent, with your completed papers, should be able to handle this. Authentication of the age of antiques and bills of sale are helpful to establish duty-free entry. There are very specific U.S. customs regulations which you should know.

- Household furnishings may enter the U.S. duty-free if they have been in the possession of the owner for a period of at least one year and they are not imported for another person.
- Items shipped for later sale become a commercial shipment for which there are specific rules depending on type and quantity.
- Some items are prohibited: certain food items, plant cuttings and seeds, specific medicines and dangerous drugs, "piratical" books, obscene publications, lottery tickets, certain furs, reptile skins, etc.
- Certain restrictions are on ivory, tobacco, wine and liquor.
- Some articles require licenses or permits, such as firearms, ammunition and trademarked items.

These points bring out the necessity for you to know the current regulations and procedures. The following pamphlets can be obtained from U.S. embassies and consulates abroad, from local customs offices and from the U.S. Customs Service, P.O. Box 7118, Washington, D.C. 20044.

- *Know Before You Go - Customs Hints for Returning U.S. Residents*
- *Pets, Wildlife - Customs*
    Be sure you know state as well as federal regulations.
- *Trademark Information for Travelers*

Contact the nearest consulate if you need further information or clarification on duty status, duty rates and procedures involved.

If you expect to **import a car** into the U.S. specific federal import regulations are imposed. Before attempting to return with a car, ask at the embassy or consulate for their *Importing a Car* pamphlet. Other helpful information can be obtained from:

>U.S. Environmental Protection Agency
>Imports Section
>Manufacturers Operation Division (EN-340F)
>Washington, D.C. 20460
>
>U.S. Department of Transportation
>Office of Vehicle Safety Compliance, NEW-32
>National Highway Traffic Safety Administration
>400 Seventh St., S.W.
>Washington, D.C. 20590
>
>*Handbook for Vehicle Importations*
>Auto Importers Compliance Association
>12011 Lee Jackson Highway
>Fairfax, VA 22033

You and the Family

We've considered the many practical aspects of the return move. What about personal aspects? What about you?

The return move "home" brings thoughts of friends, family, football and a familiar culture. The anticipation of being close to loved ones again can be as exhilerating as your first glimpse of Egypy's pyramids or China's Great Wall. There is a natural, warm feeling about "going home." Along with these happy thoughts, you also must realize you are leaving a place that has become home. You have established a network of friends in your community. You have become involved in your foreign environment and your children have loyal school ties and swim team trophies. Moving always has emotional connections.

Many things have happened during the overseas sojourn. Most important is the fact that you have changed.

- You have accepted and adapted to the culture of a foreign country. Remember -- *you* have changed, you did not change the ways of the country.
- Your capacities to cope, be flexible and patient have increased immeasurably -- and you have endless tales to tell about

funny (and not so funny, at least originally!) incidents that happened (or didn't happen!). Anyone who has lived abroad can look back and laugh about many things, from inoperable telephones to slick toilet paper.

- You have become more tolerant and understanding in many ways.
- You have enjoyed opportunities to explore other countries and cultures. You are more worldly in knowledge and thinking.

Uprooting is physically and psychologically painful. Once again there will be the inconvenience of relocating. The family as a unit must discuss their expectations. A change in lifestyle is to be expected, as well as adjustments in the job assignment for the businessman and in peer relations for the teenagers. The wife, woman and mother will have adjustments in relationships, career and demands upon her. The interests of the family will have changed and expanded because of the opportunities you all have experienced and the people you have met.

Changes at "home" must be anticipated. What you left is not what you should expect to come back to. Your view of the U.S. during home leave visits is usually very insulated and some of the actual changes will be dramatic. Just as the family talked together about changes to look forward to and expect when you moved overseas, it is essential to talk about "going home" and what it means for each family member. There will be aspects each will miss and others to look forward to. Discussion about what is ahead will make adjustments easier.

After the moving preparations, a few days to unwind and relax are highly recommended -- a must, really. A vacation en route will enable you to put a physical and mental distance between the moving days, the life you are leaving and what is ahead.

For a period of time, you can expect to feel like a "foreigner" in your own country. After experiencing the service in hotels in Japan, Switzerland and other parts of the world, the non-service in many American hotels and restaurants will be appalling. You will never be prepared for the waitress who tells you, "Just a minute, hon," or the glare of the post office clerk when you ask the cost to send an airmail letter in the U.S. All too well you will be able to understand the adjustments a real "foreigner" makes when moving to the U.S!

Being realistic, everything won't be as it was or as you remember it. Even when moving to a familiar city, it will take time, and effort, to re-adjust. There will be differences in housing, school, interests, work situations and relationships with friends. You will find yourself comparing "home" to your international location! just as you compared it to "home" when you first moved overseas. *Re-entry stress is real.* Expect to experience many adjustments and emotional traumas, just as you did moving abroad.

Your mental energies in the U.S., however, won't be on speaking a foreign language but on the color and style of the telephone to have (and which of several companies to use) and which of the 27 varieties of bran cereal to choose. (Your previous "supermarket" offered only two!) Many trivial adjustments will be made: no one has winter clothes after four years in the Bangkok; the children don't know the current "lingo." You may have to unlearn habits: you no longer need to ask if the water is safe to drink; you do have to "bag" your own groceries; the car "boot" becomes the trunk again and the *autobahn* is I-95 with a speed limit of 55. Your metric knowledge will be reversed to inches and ounces and your shoe size from 39 to 8.

The return to the U.S. often means financial strain. The overseas allowances are gone. Buying a house is a very substantial investment. Refurbishing or remodeling a house rented while you were away will be expensive. Purchasing new appliances and cars may be necessary. Services are more costly than you remembered. Once again there may be state and city taxes. Advance planning is essential.

The businessman has a new job assignment. An overseas assignment usually means a greater job challenge, perhaps greater job status, more responsibility, more autonomy, more opportunity for creative work, more job satisfaction, more prestige, as well as travel and dealing with a variety of nationalities and cultural customs. In a return to the home office there are adjustments he or she needs to anticipate to be part of the group again, often in a monocultural environment and one that usually does not utilize the overseas experience.

The huge American high school can be very unwelcoming to a teenager. Social circles may be tighter than in the international school with its transient student body. Peer acceptance may come slowly. Younger school children and pre-schoolers will experience many of the same adjustments stateside as they did when moving overseas. If moving in the summer, plan ahead for a summer project for the children and/or family. Activities are family-oriented in many overseas locations and it can take time to find new interests and friends. Children have very sensitive feelings. A lot of listening and support by parents will help them through their difficult moments.

The wife and mother will find she needs to spend a great deal of time on family needs during the first months back. If she had full-time help who had responsibility for the children, the adjustment can be tremendous, from possessiveness to acceptance of babysitters. Returning to a do-it-yourself system will be a real shock in many ways. It is important to take time to renew personal friendships and get involved. Joining the hospital auxiliary, the tennis ladder at the club and other involvements are just as essential now as they were when you moved overseas.

Surprisingly, all the family should expect that few people sincerely will be interested in the experiences you have had.

- Your foreign assignment will still be "foreign" even to your family. They are glad to have you back home but expect you to be the same in thinking and actions as when you left. Expectations by your family from whom you've been away may be greater than you're ready for.

- For no logical reason, children frequently find they are ignored and chided by other children when it is discovered they have lived overseas.

- You may grow apart from your old friends -- even if you have been gone only two years. Although they may not ask what your life has been like, you will be "out of it" if you don't know the local college team is in the regional semifinals.

- People are interested -- to a very limited point! Then they are indifferent. You can expect your travelogue about the train ride through China to be interrupted with ball scores, problems of crabgrass and news of a local store sale.

- Many people will think you've been on a extended vacation!

Moving makes the family members more dependent on each other during the re-settling and easing back period. It can be a lonely time, a time of not being connected. Everyone has an established pattern and they have trouble remembering you're back and available -- for lunch, to visit a new museum showing or a foursome for bridge. Once again, you must make a new routine, and perhaps lifestyle, for yourself. Good communication and mutual understanding within the family will be a big help in all situations. Everyone's sense of belonging will be aided by pursuing personal interests but also getting involved with people and the community. As when you moved abroad, again, be a joiner.

Recognize, please, most of the changes and stresses mentioned occur also when you move within the U.S. Don't feel living overseas is causing all the problems. As long as you are aware of the adjustments to be made, you can prepare to meet the challenge of the re-entry from overseas living or in the domestic move.

With extemely few exceptions, the varied experiences and opportunities associated with living abroad will be some of the most rewarding times and fondest memories of your life.

APPENDIX

TEMPERATURES

ATMOSPHERIC

Celsius	Fahrenheit	Celsius	Fahrenheit
-17.8	0	25	77
-15	5	26	78.8
-10	14	27	80.6
-5	23	28	82.4
0	32	29	84.2
5	41	30	86
10	50	31	87.8
12	53.6	32	89.6
14	57.2	33	91.4
16	60.8	34	93.2
18	64.4	35	95
20	68	36	96.8
21	69.8	37	98.6
22	71.6	38	100.4
23	73.4	39	102.2
24	75.2	40	104

To change Fahrenheit to Celsius, subtract 32, multiply by 5/9.
To change Celsius to Fahrenheit, multiply by 9/5, add 32.

BODY

Celsius	Fahrenheit
37.0	98.6 - normal
37.5	99.5
37.8	100.0
38.0	100.4 - slight fever
38.5	101.3
38.8	101.8
39.0	102.2
39.5	103.1
39.8	103.6
40.0	104.0 - high fever
40.5	104.9
40.8	105.4
41.0	105.8

OVEN

	Celsius	Fahrenheit
	70	160
Very slow	105	220
(Cool)	110	230
	120	250
Slow	135	275
	150	300
	163	325
Moderate	180	350
	190	375
	200	400
Hot	220	425
	230	450
	260	500
Very Hot	275	525

Gas marks are not given because they vary from country to country.

An oven thermometer should be used to determine the actual temperature of each individual oven.

MEASUREMENTS

WEIGHT
    1 kilogram (kilo) = 1000 grams = 2.205 lbs.
    1 catty = 1 1/3 lbs.
    1 stone = 14 lbs. = 6.35 kg.
    1 pound (lb.) = 454 grams = .4536 kilograms
    1000 grams = 1 kilogram = 2 lb. 2 oz.
    100 grams = 3.5 ounces = scant 1/2 cup
    28.35 grams = 1 ounce = 2 Tablespoons (U.S.)

    1 metric long ton = 2,204.62 lbs.
    1 metric short ton = .984 long ton = 2,000 lbs.

CAPACITIES
    1 (U.S.) gallon = 3.79 liters = (U.K.) 128 oz. = (U.S.) 160 oz.
    1 liter = 4 (U.S.) cups + 3 1/2 Tablespoons = 1.06 quart (liquid)
        = 34 oz. = 2.1 pint = .26 gallon
    1 quart = .9463 liter = 9.5 deciliters = 4 (U.S.) cups = 33.8 fluid oz.
    1 cup = 1/4 liter = 2.4 deciliters = 8 ounces
    2/3 cup = 5 1/3 ounces = 1 1/2 deciliters
    1/2 cup = 8 Tablespoons = 4 ounces = 1 deciliter
    1/3 cup = 6 Tablespoons = 2 2/3 ounces = 3/4 deciliters
    1/4 cup = 4 Tablespoons = 2 ounces = 1/2 deciliter

    10 fluid ounces = 3 deciliters = 1/2 pint (U.K.) = 1 1/4 (U.S.) cups
    1 pint (U.S.) = 2 cups = 16 ounces = .47 liter
    1 pint (U.K.) = 2 1/2 cups = 20 fluid ounces = 6 deciliters
    32 ounces = 1 quart = 4 cups = .95 liter
    34 ounces = 4 1/4 cups = 1 liter
    1 milliliter = .03 fluid ounce

United Kingdom		United States		European
1 teaspoon	=	1 1/4 teaspoons	=	5 milliliters
1 Tablespoon	=	1 1/4 Tablespoons	=	15 milliliters
		1 teaspoon	=	1 coffee spoon
		2 teaspoons	=	1 dessert spoon
		3 teaspoons or 1 Tablespoon	=	1 soup spoon

DRY MEASURES

Ounces	Grams	Ounces	Grams
1	30	16 (1 lb.)	450
2	60	1-1/2 lbs.	680
3	85	2 lbs.	900
4	115	2-1/4 lbs.	1000 (1 kilogram)
5	140	2-1/2 lbs.	1125
6	170	3 lbs.	1350
7	200	3-1/2 lbs.	1500
8	225	4 lbs.	1800
		4-1/2 lbs.	2000 (2 kg.)

CONVERSION TABLE FOR METRIC-SIZE CONTAINERS

Metric	Nearest U.S. Equivalent
1.75 liter (59.2 oz.)	1/2 gallon (64 oz.)
1 liter (33.8 oz.)	1 quart (32 oz.)
750 milliliters (25.4 oz.)	4/5 quart (25.6 oz.)
500 milliliters (16.9 oz.)	1 pint (16 oz.)
200 milliliters (6.8 oz.)	1/2 pint (8 oz.)
50 milliliters (1.7 oz.)	Miniature (1.6 oz.)

LENGTH-DISTANCE

1 kilometer = 1000 meters = .62137 mile (approx. 5/8 mile)
1.6090 kilometers = 1 mile

1 hectare = 2.471 acre
1 acre = 0.4 hectare

1 square meter = 10.76 square feet
1 meter = 1.00936 yards = 3.3 feet = 39.37 inches
100 centimeters = 1 meter
91.44 centimeters = 1 yard
30.5 centimeters = 1 foot = .3048 meter
2.54 centimeters = 1 inch = 25.4 milliliters
1 centimeter = 1/100 meter = .3937 inch (approx. 3/8 inch)
1 milliliter = 1/1000 meter = .03937 inch = 4/100 inch

CONVERSION INFORMATION (alphabetical)

To change:

centimeters	to inches	multiply by	0.3937
feet	meters		0.3048
fluid ounces	milliliters		30.0
gallons	liters		4.546
grams	ounces		0.0353
inches	centimeters		2.54
kilograms	pounds		2.2046
kilometers	miles		0.6214
liters	pints		2.1134
liters	quarts		1.0567
meters	feet		3.2808
meters	yards		1.0936
miles	kilometers		1.6093
milliliters	inches		0.0394
ounces	grams		28.3495
pounds	grams		453.6
pounds	kilograms		0.4536
quarts	liters		0.9463
yards	meters		0.9144

YARD GOODS

90 centimeters = 36 inches (approx.)
100 centimeters = 39 inches
120 centimeters = 46 inches
140 centimeters = 55 inches
150 centimeters = 60 inches

BED SIZES

Divan	30 inches	x 75 inches
Studio	33 "	x 75 "
Single	36 "	x 75 "
U.S. twin	39 "	x 75 "
U.S. twin extra long	39 "	x 80 "
3/4 size	48 "	x 75 "
U.S. double	54 "	x 75 "
U.S. double extra long	54 "	x 80 "
U.S. queen	60 "	x 80 "
U.S. king	78 "	x 80 "

ELECTRIC APPLIANCE WATTAGE

The wattage figures given here are approximate. Appliances from individual manufacturers will differ in wattage so this list is general information only. Check actual wattage on each appliance manufacturer's plate.

APPLIANCE	WATTS
air conditioner	1000/1600
blanket	190
blender	250/350
broilers and grills	1350/1450
coffee maker	1200
fan - 12 inch	90/150
frying pan	1250
floor polisher	350/500
food freezer - 15 cu. ft.	340
frostless 15 cu. ft.	440
food mixer	200
food processor	500/800
hair dryer	1000/1400
heaters with fan	1500
iron	1100
microwave oven	600
power drill	500
projector w/1000 watt lamp	1100
radio and phonograph console	100/200
razor	7/15
refrigerator - 12-14 cu. ft.	550
frostless 12-14 cu. ft.	750
sewing machine	75/150
slide projector with fan	350/600
stereo	250
tape recorder	90/175
television	200
toaster (pop-up)	1200
vacuum cleaner	630/750
video cassette recorder (VCR)	150
waffle iron	800/1150
washing machine - automatic	515

To find watts when amperes are given, multiply number of amperes by voltage of appliance - for example, 5 amperes x 110 volts = 550 watts.

TRANSFORMER PRECAUTIONS

- Grounded sockets are safest for transformers. Any transformer over 1500 watts *must* be grounded.
- Do not handle a transformer when it is plugged into a socket. Disconnect before moving it.
- Transformers should be kept dry and well ventilated. Do not handle one when your feet or hands are wet.
- A transformer will feel warm when in use. If it is hot to your touch, something is wrong.
- Do not overload the wattage capacity of a transformer, i.e., total wattage rate must not exceed rating of the transformer.

BUSINESSMAN'S TRAVELING CHECKLIST

___ toilet kit
___ electric razor
___ hairbrush
___ hair dryer
___ medications
___ emergency medical kit
    (Imodium AD, antibiotic)

___ underwear
___ socks
___ belt
___ handkerchiefs
___ ties
___ shirts
___ shoes
___ suits
___ sweaters

___ ticket
___ passport
___ health card

___ travelers checks
___ regular checks
___ money (of country)
___ international credit cards

___ suitcase keys
___ business cards
___ expense account form
___ dictating machine
___ calculator
___ folding umbrella

___ reading material
    (books/magazines)

Vacation trips
___ casual clothes
___ tennis or golf gear
___ swim gear
___ sun glasses
___ camera/film
___ sun lotion
___ insect repellent
___ radio

Family trip
___ guide books
___ packaged towelettes
___ hand laundry detergent
___ tissues
___ manicure set
___ water purification tablets

You may photocopy this page.

BUSINESS LETTER OF RECOMMENDATION

(Letterhead of Organization)

Date_____

Consul General of_____
_____
_____

Gentlemen:

    Mr. _____ is one of our employees who is engaged as (a/an) _____.
    Mr. _____ plans to visit _____(country) _____ (on company business/for tourist purposes) and expects to remain there for approximately _____ (days/weeks/months).
    He is presenting herewith his Passport No._____.
We would appreciate your issuing him a (visa/tourist card) for his stay in your country.
    Thank you for your assistance.

                      Very truly yours,

                      _____
                      (Signature *and* title of signer)

POLICE CERTIFICATE OF GOOD STANDING

Place issued_____

Date_____

TO WHOM IT MAY CONCERN:

A search of the records of this office shows there is no warrant or criminal process outstanding in this _(city or country)_ against ___(full name of person to whom issued)_ , whose address is _____, nor has there been any during the past five years.

There is no criminal record on file of the said _(full name of person to whom issued)_ during the last five years, nor has this department any record of the said person's having been arrested for any antagonism against the form of government of _(name of country in which issuing authority is located)_ .

The said person is a citizen of _(name of country)_ , and he is the bearer of _(name of country by which issued)_ Passport No._____.

_____
(Signature *and* title of official)

Name in full of police or law
enforcement organization
with which the issuing
official is connected.

MEDICAL CERTIFICATE

<pre>
                    (Doctor's letterhead)

                               Date_____

   TO WHOM IT MAY CONCERN:

       This is to certify that (name of person to whom
   issued) of   (address)   has been examined by me and
   found to be in good physical and sound mental condition.
   He (or she) is not suffering from any contagious, chronic or
   incurable disease of a pernicious character.

                              _____
                               (Doctor's signature)
</pre>

This form will also suffice for pets, with certain logical variations.

TIME CONVERSIONS
at 12:00 Noon (EST) in Washington, D.C.

COUNTRY	TIME	COUNTRY	TIME
Algeria	5 p.m.	Malaysia	12:30 a.m. next day
Argentina	2 p.m.		
Australia (Canberra)	3 p.m. next day	Mexico (Mexico City)	11 a.m.
		Morocco	5 p.m.
Austria	6 p.m.	Nepal	10:30 p.m.
Bahrain	8 p.m.	Netherlands	6 p.m.
Belgium	6 p.m.	New Zealand	5 a.m. next day
Bolivia (La Paz)	1 p.m.		
Brazil (Brasilia)	2 p.m.	Nigeria	6 p.m.
Canada (Ottawa)	Noon	Norway	6 p.m.
Chile (Santiago)	1 p.m.	Oman	9 p.m.
China (Beijing)	1 a.m. next day	Panama	Noon
		Paraguay	1 p.m.
Columbia	Noon	Peru (Lima)	Noon
Costa Rica	11 a.m.	Philippines	1 a.m. next day
Czechoslovakia	6 p.m.		
Denmark	6 p.m.	Poland	6 p.m.
Djibouti	8 p.m.	Portugal	6 p.m.
Ecuador	Noon	Qatar	8 p.m.
Egypt (Cairo)	7 p.m.	Saudi Arabia	8 p.m.
Finland	7 p.m.	Singapore	12:30 a.m. next day
France (Paris)	6 p.m.		
Germany (Bonn)	6 p.m.	South Africa	7 p.m.
Germany (East Berlin)	6 p.m.	Spain	6 p.m.
Ghana	5 p.m.	Sri Lanka	10:30 p.m.
Greece	7 p.m.	Swaziland	7 p.m.
Hong Kong	1 a.m. next day	Sweden	6 p.m.
		Switzerland	6 p.m.
India (New Delhi)	10:30 p.m.	Taiwan	1 a.m. next day
Indonesia (Jakarta)	Midnight		
Ireland	5 p.m.	Thailand	Midnight
Israel	7 p.m.	Turkey	7 p.m.
Italy (Rome)	6 p.m.	United Arab Emirates	9 p.m.
Ivory Coast	5 p.m.	U.S.S.R. (Moscow)	8 p.m.
Japan (Tokyo)	2 a.m. next day	United Kingdom	5 p.m.
		Uruguay	2 p.m.
Kenya (Nairobi)	8 p.m.	Venezuela	1 p.m.
Korea (Seoul)	2 a.m next day	Yemen	8 p.m.
		Yugoslavia	6 p.m.
Kuwait	8 p.m.	Zambia	7 p.m.
Luxembourg	6 p.m.		

INTERNATIONAL TELEPHONE DIALING INFORMATION

*International dialing code for your country	Country code	Area code	Local number
Sample: 001	1	212	123-4567

COUNTRY CODE NUMBERS

Alaska	1
Algeria	213
Argentina	54
Australia	61
Austria	43
Bahrain	973
Belgium	32
Bolivia	591
Brazil	55
Brunei	673
Canada	1
Chile	56
Colombia	57
Costa Rica	506
Czechoslovakia	42
Denmark	45
Ecuador	593
Egypt	20
El Salvador	503
Finland	358
France	33
Germany (Dem. Rep.)	37
Germany (Fed. Rep.)	49
Greece	30
Guam	671
Guatemala	502
Hawaii	1
Hong Kong	852

COUNTRY CODE NUMBERS

Iceland	354
India	91
Indonesia	62
Ireland	353
Israel	972
Italy	39
Ivory Coast	25
Japan	81
Kenya	254
Korea (Rep. of)	82
Kuwait	965
Lichtenstein	41
Luxembourg	352
Malaysia	60
Mexico	52
Monaco	33
Morocco	212
Namibia	264
Netherlands	31
New Zealand	64
Norway	47
Oman	968
Panama	507
Paraguay	595
Philippines	63
Poland	48
Portugal	351

COUNTRY CODE NUMBERS

Qatar	974
Romania	40
San Marino	39
Saudi Arabia	966
Singapore	65
South Africa	27
Spain	34
Sri Lanka	94
Swaziland	268
Sweden	46
Switzerland	41
Taiwan	886
Thailand	66
Tunisia	216
Turkey	90
United Arab Emirates	971
United Kingdom	44
U.S.A.	1
U.S.S.R.	7
Uruguay	598
Venezuela	58
Yemen Arab Rep.	967
Yugoslavia	38
Zambia	260

* The international access dialing code differs for each country. Call your local operator from the country you are in if the information is not in the telephone directory.

For person-to-person calls, you must go through a telephone company operator. Credit card calls are possible from some countries.

USEFUL ADDRESSES

Chambers of Commerce

Chamber of Commerce of the United States
1615 H Street NW, Washington, DC 20062 (202) 659-6000

International Chamber of Commerce U.S. Council Inc.
1212 Ave. of the Americas, New York, NY 10036 (212) 354-4480

Regional office for Europe:
Council for American Chamber of Commerce in Europe
21 rue du Commerce
Brussels 4, Belgium

Other offices in specific countries of Asia and South America.

Legal Assistance

Contact Center, Inc.
P.O. Box 81826, Lincoln, NE 68501 (402) 464-0602
An international criminal justice and human services organization providing information and referral assistance to offenders, their families and correctional authorities.

International Legal Defense Council (ILDC)
1420 Walnut St., Philadelphia, PA 19102 (215) 977-9982
They provide legal and humanitarian aid to Americans arrested abroad.

Medical Services

Intermedic
777 Third Avenue, New York, NY 10017 (212) 486-8974
They have a worldwide directory of English-speaking doctors in 200 cities. They give information on immunizations in risk areas throughout the world.

International Association for Medical Assistance to Travellers (IAMAT)
475 Fifth Avenue, New York, NY 10017 (212) 279-6465
They have list of 3000 English-speaking doctors in 120 countries, most with post graduate degrees or training in the U.S or U.K. The list is free but they would appreciate a donation.

International Health Care Service
440 East 69th Street, New York, NY 10021   (212) 746-6305
Clinic provides information on local health conditions worldwide, administers required immunizations as well as its own recommended ones and evaluates traveler's health with regard to their itinerary. Has information on traveler's health insurance, finding English-speaking doctors and arranging emergency medical evacuations from foreign countries. Primarily intended to make travel in developing countries safer and easier.

Malaria Hotline at U.S. Center for Disease Control   (404) 639-1610

Medic Alert Foundation
1000 N. Palm Street, P.O. Box 1009, Turlock, CA 95380 (209) 632-2371
475 Fifth Ave., New York, NY 10017   (212) 213-4510
An individual with such ailments as epilepsy, diabetes, rare blood type, allergy to certain drugs can register with this group. They will issue a Medic Alert emblem to wear with warning of your medical problem. A wallet card gives specific information and instructions to call Medic Alert headquarters collect from anywhere in the world in case of accident.

S.O.S. International Assistance
Rt. 1 and Old Lincoln, Box 11568, Philadelphia, PA 19116
1-(800)- 523-8930 and (215) 244-1500
24-hour emergency hotlines. Can assist in many ways: emergency rescue, securing flight space, ambulances, hospital deposits, etc.

Travel Assistance International
1133 15th St., NW, Suite 400, Washington, DC 20005
1-(800)-821-2828 and (202) 347-2025

Pet Help

American Society for Prevention of Cruelty to Animals
441 East 92nd Street, New York, NY 10028   (212) 876-7700
They have pamphlet, *Traveling with Your Pet*. They maintain Animalport shelter for traveling animals at Air Cargo Center, Kennedy International Airport, Jamaica, NY 11430   (212) 656-6042

U.S. Customs publications for taking pets abroad and importing to U.S.:
    Pets: Foreign Quarantine Program,
                Center for Disease Control
                Atlanta, GA 30333
    Birds: Veterinary Services
                Animal and Plant Health Inspection Service, USDA
                Federal Center Building
                Hyattsville, MD 20782

School Information

Educational Advisory Services, Intl.,
Gwynedd Plaza 1, Spring House, PA 19477   (215) 542-7966
Consultants on schools and educational matters for U.S. and overseas schools.

European Council of International Schools, Inc.,
21B Lavant St., Petersfield, Hapshire GU 32 3EL, England.
Their annual publication, *Directory*, is an excellent resource on nearly all international schools throughout the world. Available by writing their Publications Section, $16.50 (1987).

School Match
c/o Wm. Bainbridge, Blendonview Office Park, 5027 Pine Creek Drive, Westerville, OH 43081.
A computerized data bank covering public and private schools of America.

Social Security Administration

U.S. Government Office, P.O. Box 1756, Baltimore, MD 21203
This office can give information on Social Security earnings and answer questions on your overseas status. International social security agreements eliminate dual coverage and prevent loss of benefit rights when someone has worked in a second country.

Student/Youth Services

College Entrance Examination Board
45 Columbus Avenue, New York, NY 10023-6992   (212) 713-8000
P.O. Box 592, Princeton, NJ 08540   (609) 921-9000

International Schools Service
126 Alexander Street, Princeton, NJ 08540   (609) 921-9110

American Youth Hostels, Inc.
75 Spring St., New York, NY 10012   (212) 431-7000
also in Delaplane, VA 22025   (703) 592-3271
They have a list of international hostels and services; issue multi-country hostel card.

Council on International Education Exchange (CIEE)
Student Travel Services
205 East 42nd Street, New York, NY 10017   (212) 661-1414
They issue international identification card for reduced admission prices, accommodations, train fares, tours; have discount guide, etc. Membership includes accident-sickness insurance while abroad.

U.S. Student Travel Service, Inc.
866 Second Avenue, New York, NY 10017 (212) 867-8770

United States Customs Offices Abroad

Bangkok, Thailand (Tel. 662 252-5040)
Bonn, Germany (Tel. 228-339-2207)
Brasilia, Brazil (Tel. 61 223-0120 ext. 459)
Brussells, Belgium (Tel. 2 513.44.50 ext. 2770)
Hong Kong (Tel. 5- 239-011))
London, England (Tel. 499-1212)
Karachi, India (Tel. 21-515081)
Mexico City, Mexico (Tel. 905 211-0042 ext. 3687)
Ottawa, Canada (Tel. 613 238-5335)
Panama City, Panama (Tel. 271-777)
Paris, France (Tel. 4296-1202, ext. 2392)
Rome, Italy (Tel. 4674-2475)
Rotterdam, Holland (Tel. 10-117560)
Tokyo, Japan (Tel. 583-7141, ext. 7205)
Vienna, Austria (Tel. 222 31-55-11)

United States Customs Service

for Customs clearance questions:
Office of Inspection and Control
1301 Constitution Ave. NW, Washington, DC 20229-0001
 (202) 566-2366
for Customs Service Leaflets:
Govt. Printing Office, Washington, DC 20401

United States Passport Agencies

Boston: John F. Kennedy Bldg., Room E123,
Boston, MA 02203-0123 (617) 565-3930
Chicago: Kluczynski Federal Bldg., Suite 380, 230 Dearborn St.,
Chicago, IL 60604-1564 (312) 353-7155
Honolulu: New Federal Bldg., Room C - 106, 300 Ala Moana Blvd.,
Honolulu, HA 96850-0185 (808) 541-1918
Houston: One Allen Center, 500 Dallas Street,
Houston, TX 77002-4874 (713) 229-3600
Los Angeles: 11000 Wilshire Boulevard, Room 13100,
Los Angeles, CA 90024-3614 (213) 209-7075
Miami: Federal Office Bldg., 16th Floor, 51 Southwest First Ave.,
Miami, FL 33130-1680 (305) 536-4681

New Orleans: Postal Services Bldg., Room T-12005, 701 Loyola Ave.,
    New Orleans, LA 70013-1931   (504) 589-6161
New York: Rockefeller Center, Room 270, 630 Fifth Avenue,
    New York, NY 10111-0031   (212) 541-7710
Philadelphia: Federal Bldg., Room 4426, 600 Arch St.,
    Philadelphia, PA 19106-1684   (215) 597-7480
San Francisco: 525 Market Street, Suite 200,
    San Francisco, CA 94105-2773   (415) 974-9941
Seattle: Federal Office Bldg., Room 992, 915 Second Avenue,
    Seattle, WA 98174-1091   (206) 442-7945
Stamford: One Landmark Square, Broad & Atlantic Streets,
    Stamford, CT 06901-2767   (203) 325-3538
Washington: 1425 K Street, NW, Washington, DC 20522-1705
    (202) 523-1355

INDEX

Absentee voting, 197
Accidents, 142
Accountant, 55
Addresses, 222
Adjustments
   businessman, 130
   children, 121
   cultural, 99, 104
   return move, 203
Adoptions, 197
Alien registration, 97, 188
American embassy/consulate,
   registration, 97,198
Amperes, 214
Appliance wattage information, 214
Appraisals
   furnishings, 47
   house, 13-14
   jewelry, 51
ASPCA, 59, 223
Atmospheric temperatures, 209
Attorneys, 56
   power of attorney, 56
   selling a house, 16, 20
   signing a lease, 114
Au pair, 151
Automobiles, see Cars

Banking, 49
   opening a foreign account, 96, 188
Bargaining, 187
BCG, 38, 162
Bed sizes, 213
Bicycles, 142
Bill of lading, 85
Birds, 202, 223
Birth abroad, 189
Birth certificates, 30, 34, 190
Blood banks, 53, 160
Body language, 129, 132
Body temperatures, 210
Books
   businessmen, 137
   children, 12
Businessman's travel checklist, 215
   book list, 137
Camera registration, 61
Cars
   importing to U.S., 203

   insurance, 141
   registration abroad, 140
   shipping abroad, 86
Chambers of Commerce, 222
Change of address, 42
   forwarding mail, 45
   in host country, 190
   stockholder companies, 43
   whom to tell, 45
Checklist, businessman's travel, 215
   papers to take with you, 88
   personal, 63
Children,
   adjustments, 7, 121
   immunization, 35-36
   manners and courtesies, 122
   medical power of attorney, 159
   Social security numbers for, 34, 197
Cholera, 35
Clorox-water solutions, 156, 164, 172
Closet rods, 168
Closing costs, 20
Clothes washer, 119
College entrance information, 55, 126
Conversion information, 209-213
Credit card accounts, 43, 45
"Culture shock", 100
Customs
   arrival inspection, 93
   clearance of furnishings, 116
   GSP, 194, 202
   inspections, 116
   registration of articles, 61
   U.S. Customs offices abroad, 225
   U.S. Customs services, 225
   VAT, 187

Damage/loss claims, 117
Death abroad, 165, 197
Dehydration, 92, 166
Destination agents, 71, 86, 201
Diarrhea, 161, 185
Domestic help, see Household Help
Drapes, 74
Driver, employing, 157
Driver's license, 57
   international, 57, 140
   obtaining abroad, 139
Dry cleaning symbols, 191

Duty, refund of, 199
Dysentery, 161, 163

Earthquakes, 172
Electric appliance wattage, 214
Emergency first aid items, 52, 185
    telephone numbers, 190
    water purification, 156, 164, 172
Employment permits, 148
Equivalents, see Measurements
Estimates
    house, 13
    moving, 67, 71
    repair, 120, 195
Exit permits, 199
    visas, 190
Exporting a car, 86

Federal income taxes, 24
First aid kit, 52, 185
Foreign country taxes, 28

General System of Preferences, 194, 202
Geysers, 111
Green card, 141

Health
    first aid kit, 52, 185
    immunizations, 36
    insurance, 38
Hepatitis, 36
Hifi, 77
High altitude cooking, 77
Hotel
    days, 94
    when traveling, 178
Household help, 148
    au pair, 151
    discharging, 151
    interview, 153
    live-in, 152
    part-time, 152
    permits, visas 148,
    registration of, 149
    salary record, 151
    training, 155
Household insurance, 50-51, 116
House-hunting, 110

Houses
    finding, 110
    selling or renting, 13
    tax concerns of selling, 24, 26-27

Identity card, 188
Importing into U.S., 201-202
Importing
    a car into U.S., 203
    liquor, 201
Immunizations, 36
Inoculations, 35
Insurance
    automobile, 50
    claims, 117
    general, 190
    household, 51, 117, 191
    life, 51
    medical, 50
    moving, 71
Internal Revenue Service (IRS), 24, 197
International
    certificate of vaccination, 35, 36
    driver's license, 57, 140
    road signs, 147
    time conversions, 219
Inventories
    household, 47
    mover's, 66, 83
    personal, 48, 62
    translations of, 66

Lamps, 77
Laundry symbols, 191
Lawyer, see Attorney
Lease, housing, 114
"Leave house", 114
Legal assistance, 222
    status and rights, 192
    U.S. residence, 197
Letters
    change of address, 42
    medical status, 218
    police, good standing, 217
    school power of attorney, 159
    recommendation, 216
    stockholder, 43-44
License, driver's, 139
    international, 57, 140
Liquor, importing, 201
Live-in help, 152

child care, 155
interview, 153
physical examination, 153
schedule and training, 155

Magazine subscriptions, 45
Mail forwarding, 45
Malaria, 37, 161, 167
Manners and courtesies, 192
Marriage
  certificate, 30, 34, 189
  registration abroad, 197
Measurements, 211
  bed sizes, 213
  capacities, 211
  conversions, 213
  length-distances, 212
  weight, 211
  yard goods, 213
Medical information, 51
  before you go, 51
  in tropical areas, 166
  inoculations, 35
  prescriptions, 52
  school emergencies, 124, 159
  services, 158, 222
Metric conversions, 212
Mildew, 168
Moving company
  bill of lading, 85
  cost estimate, 71
  insurance, 71
  packers, 84
  unpacking, 116
Moving expenses, 24, 26
MSG, 161, 185

Offer and counter-offer, 19
Orientation, 89
Oven temperatures, 210

Packing tips, 72
Paratyphoid, 38
Part-time help, 152
Passport
  applying for, 29
  loss of, 31, 197
  pictures, 30, 58
  renewal, 197
Permits, 33-34
  employment/work, 33
  residence, 34
Personal inventory, 48, 63
Pets, 58, 168, 223
Pictures
  household, 48
  passport, 30
PMI, 45
Polio, 37
Power of attorney, 49, 56
  children's medical, 159
Prescriptions, 52, 160
Priority of the right, 144
Prohibited items to ship, 68

Rabies, 37, 165
Realtors
  abroad, 109, 111
  listing a house with, 17
Receipts of purchase, 61, 194
Registration, alien, 97, 188
  at U.S. embassy, 198
  household help, 148
Renewal of passport, 198
Renting your house, 21
  tax concerns with, 27
Residence permits, 34
Return move, 199
  for U.S. customs, 201
Returning resident, 201
Road signs, 145, 147

School
  assistance groups, 224
  records, 54
Selling your house
  appraisal, 13
  closing and possession dates, 20
  earnest/deposit money, 20
  listing with realtor, 17
  offer and counter-offer, 19
  taxes, 24, 26
Servants, see Household Help
Skin rashes, 167
Smallpox, 35
Social Security (FICA)
  contributions, 20, 224
  numbers for children, 34, 197
State and local taxes, 28
Stockholder companies, 43
Storage of valuable items, 83
Student/youth services, 224

Subscriptions, 45, 46

Tax Guide for U.S. Citizens Abroad, 24
Tax records, 55
Taxes
  federal income, 24
  filing assistance overseas, 24-25, 197
  foreign country obligations, 28
  moving expenses, 24, 26
  renting a house, 27
  selling a house, 26
  state and local, 28
Teenagers, 10, 125
Telephone
  international dialing codes, 220
Television, shipping of, 82
Temperatures
  atmospheric, 209
  body, 210
  conversion formula, 209
  oven, 210
Tetanus, 37
Time conversions, 219
Tipping, 196
Transformer precautions, 214
Tropical areas, 166
Tuberculosis, 37, 162
Typewriter, electric, 77
Typhoid, 38
Typhoons, 170

U.S. Customs offices abroad, 225
U.S. embassy/consulate, 197-198
  adoptions, birth, marriage, death abroad, 197
  "returning resident", 201
  registration abroad, 198
  tax representatives, 197
U.S. Passport agencies, 225

Vaccinations, 35
VAT, 187
VCR's, 82
Visas, 31-32, 174
  exit, 32, 190
Voltage, 214
Voting abroad, 197

Wallet card, 198
Water
  heaters (geysers), 111
  purification of, 156, 164, 172
Wattage chart, 214
What to take, 80-82
Wills, 56
Work permits, 148
Workmen's compensation, 148
Worms, 162

Yard goods equivalents, 213
Yellow fever, 36

Virginia McKay has lived abroad over twelve years, in Switzerland, Germany and Hong Kong, and traveled extensively in many parts of the world. For over twenty years, she has been involved in various aspects of international living.

During her years in Geneva, Virginia was co-editor of the first edition of *Living in Geneva*, editor of two subsequent editions and *Communicating in Geneva*. In 1975, she established the *Geneva For Beginners* seminars which continue to be presented annually by the American Women's Club.

A founding partner, in 1979, of Hong Kong Orientations, the first internationally located service to assist corporations with their transferees and families, Virginia is now director of the company as well as of the Tokyo branch.